EMPOWERED
transformations

Real Stories of Hope

Empowered Transformations - Real Stories of Hope

Compiled by Jasmine E. Clarke

Copyright © 2023 FAITH-INSPIRED BOOKS. All Rights Reserved.
A Division of LWL PUBLISHING HOUSE.
A Division of Anita Sechesky – Living Without Limitations Inc.

ISBN 978-1-988867-85-4

Book Cover Design: LWL PUBLISHING HOUSE Multimedia Team
Inside Layout: LWL PUBLISHING HOUSE Editorial Team

No part of this publication may be reproduced, distributed, or transmitted in any form or by any means, including photocopying, recording, or other electronic or mechanical methods without prior written permission of the publisher, except in the case of brief quotations embodied in critical reviews and certain other non-commercial uses permitted by copyright law.

Publisher's Note: This book contains a collection of personal experiences written at the discretion of the authors. The word usage and sentence structure have remained unaltered as much as possible to retain the authenticity of the authors' voices. FAITH-INSPIRED BOOKS uses American English as its standard for its international platform.

Copyright Statement for Bible Scriptures identified as NIV: All Scripture quotations, unless otherwise indicated, are taken from the Holy Bible, New International Version®, NIV®. Copyright ©1973, 1978, 1984, 2011 by Biblica, Inc.™ Used by permission of Zondervan. All rights reserved worldwide. www.zondervan.comThe "NIV" and "New International Version" are trademarks registered in the United States Patent and Trademark Office by Biblica, Inc.™

Copyright Statement for Bible Scriptures identified as ESV: "Scripture quotations are from the ESV® Bible (The Holy Bible, English Standard Version®), copyright © 2001 by Crossway, a publishing ministry of Good News Publishers. Used by permission. All rights reserved. The

ESV text may not be quoted in any publication made available to the public by a Creative Commons license. The ESV may not be translated in whole or in part into any other language."

Copyright Statement for Bible Scriptures identified as NLT: Scripture quotations marked (NLT) are taken from the Holy Bible, New Living Translation, copyright ©1996, 2004, 2015 by Tyndale House Foundation. Used by permission of Tyndale House Publishers, Carol Stream, Illinois 60188. All rights reserved.

Copyright Statement for Bible Scriptures identified as KJV: Scripture quotations from The Authorized (King James) Version. Rights in the Authorized Version in the United Kingdom are vested in the Crown. Reproduced by permission of the Crown's patentee, Cambridge University Press

Copyright Statement for Bible Scriptures identified as The Voice: Scriptures marked THE VOICE are taken from THE VOICE (The Voice): Scripture taken from THE VOICETM. Copyright© 2008 by Ecclesia Bible Society. Used by permission. All rights reserved.

Copyright Statement for Bible Scriptures identified as GNB: Scriptures marked GNB are taken from the GOOD NEWS BIBLE (GNB): Scriptures taken from the Good News Bible © 1994 published by the Bible Societies/HarperCollins Publishers Ltd UK, Good News Bible© American Bible Society 1966, 1971, 1976, 1992. Used with permission.

Copyright Statement for Bible Scriptures identified as CEV: Scriptures marked CEV are taken from the CONTEMPORARY ENGLISH VERSION (CEV): Scripture taken from the CONTEMPORARY ENGLISH VERSION Copyright© 1995 by the American Bible Society. Used by permission.

Copyright Statement for Bible Scriptures identified as TM: Scriptures marked TM are taken from THE MESSAGE: THE BIBLE IN CONTEMPORARY ENGLISH (TM): Scripture taken from THE MESSAGE: THE BIBLE IN CONTEMPORARY ENGLISH, Copyright©1993, 1994, 1995, 1996, 2000, 2001, 2002. Used by permission of NavPress Publishing Group

Copyright Statement for Bible Scriptures identified as YLT: Unless otherwise noted, all scriptures are from the 1898 YOUNG'S LITERAL TRANSLATION OF THE HOLY BIBLE by J.N. Young, (Author of the Young's Analytical Concordance), public domain.

Copyright Statement for Bible Scriptures identified as AMP: Scriptures marked AMP are taken from the AMPLIFIED BIBLE (AMP): Scripture taken from the AMPLIFIED BIBLE, Copyright© 1954, 1958, 1962, 1964, 1965, 1987 by the Lockman Foundation Used by Permission.

LWL PUBLISHING HOUSE
Email: lwlclienthelp@gmail.com
Website: www.lwlpublishinghouse.com

Table of Contents

Legal Disclaimer ix

Foreword xi

Acknowledgments xiv

Dedication xv

Introduction 1

Chapter One - Clare McSween 7
    TRUSTING IN GOD'S PROCESS SO YOU
    CAN EXPERIENCE YOUR TRANSFORMATION

Chapter Two - Tara Lomonte 14
    FROM IMPRISONED TO EMPOWERED

Chapter Three - Evangelist Suzette Haylett-Radlein 23
    FORGIVENESS LEADS TO HEALING

Chapter Four - Charlene Wilson-Evans 31
    ACTIONS - SOME STEPS REQUIRE
    EXTRA STRENGTH

Chapter Five - Shelleanne Hardial 41
    TRANSFORMED FOR HIS GLORY

Chapter Six - Meg Knight 50
    ATTITUDE

Chapter Seven - Dr. Helga A. Clarke 59
    TAKE ACTION AGAINST PROCRASTINATION

Chapter Eight - Kerry Gordon 69
    OUTSIDE OF MYSELF

Chapter Nine - Sharon Walters 79
    SISTERLY LOVE

Chapter Ten - Lisa Patrick 87
    ...BUT GOD!

Chapter Eleven - Karen Mighty 95
    UNBOTHERED

Chapter Twelve - Koreen J. Bennett 102
    A BLOSSOMING CATERPILLAR

Chapter Thirteen - Rev. Carolyn J. Anderson 109
    EMPOWERED TO BE WHO YOU WERE
    CREATED TO BE

Chapter Fourteen - Alicia Grant 117
    HIS SPIRIT LIVES WITHIN ME

Chapter Fifteen - Jasmin Cher Monasterial-Baguio 125
    EMPTY NO MORE

Chapter Sixteen - Lisa Simpson 132
    I'M A SURVIVOR

Chapter Seventeen - Reverend Alice Blaylock 141
    HOW I WEATHERED THE STORM

Chapter Eighteen - Patria Robert Francis 148
    GOD'S AMAZING LOVE

Chapter Nineteen - Marcia Hall 155
    YOU CAN MAKE IT ON BROKEN PIECES

Chapter Twenty - Jasmine E. Clarke 163
    ONE STEP CLOSER TO SOAR

Chapter Twenty-One - Candace Lalor 171
    DISCERNING GREAT PERSPECTIVES:
    PEACE THAT PASSES ALL UNDERSTANDING

Chapter Twenty-Two - Lesa Rose Isaacs 179
    HE MEETS YOUR NEEDS

Chapter Twenty-Three - Joan Steward 186
    I'M MUCH STRONGER

Chapter Twenty-Four - Judy Brown 193
    EMPOWERED TO SHINE

Chapter Twenty-Five - Lisia Malcolm-Burnett 200
    IT WILL WORK OUT FOR YOUR GOOD

Chapter Twenty-Six - Rachel Colley 209
    GOD'S LOVE HEALED OUR FAMILY

Chapter Twenty-Seven - Maryanna Stevanovic 216
    NOW UNTO HIM

Chapter Twenty-Eight - Lesley C. Morgan 225
    DARKNESS TO DESTINY

Chapter Twenty-Nine - Denese Dihele 232
    BABIES COME FROM THE MAN UPSTAIRS

Chapter Thirty - Nerrissa Myers 239
    I'M AN OVERCOMER

Chapter Thirty-One - Marilin Reid-Henry 246
    TURNING LEMONS INTO LEMONADE

Chapter Thirty-Two - Dr. Rev. Inez R. Brown 254
    MY ENCOUNTER WITH THE MAN, JESUS
    – WHERE REAL LIFE BEGINS

Chapter Thirty-Three - Lisa Harewood 261
    EXPRESSIONS OF GOD'S LOVE AND FAITH

Chapter Thirty-Four - Janice Prescott 268
    NEVER ALONE

Chapter Thirty-Five - Sharon Riley 275
    A SECOND CHANCE

Chapter Thirty-Six - Jean Lawrence-Scotland 282
    RESTORATION

Chapter Thirty-Seven - Nasha Alexis 289
    TROUBLES WITH LOW SELF-ESTEEM

Chapter Thirty-Eight - Ruth Odia 296
    EQUIPPED TO SERVE

Chapter Thirty-Nine - Lisa Arthey 303
    MY NEW SEASON OF TRANSFORMATION

Chapter Forty - Karleen Juanita Poyser 310
    FAITH OVER FEAR

Conclusion 318

Sinner's Prayer 322

A Special Invitation 323

Legal Disclaimer

Empowered Transformations - Real Stories of Hope does not substitute any form of professional counsel such as a Psychologist, Physician, Life Coach, or Counselor. The contents and information provided do not constitute professional or legal advice in any way, shape, or form.

All chapters are written at the discretion of and with the full accountability of the Compiler, co-authors, FAITH-INSPIRED BOOKS, LWL PUBLISHING HOUSE, or Anita Sechesky – Living Without Limitations Inc. are not liable or responsible for any of the specific details, descriptions of people, places or things, personal interpretations, stories, and experiences contained within. The Publisher is not liable for any misrepresentations, false or unknown statements, actions, or judgments made by each author in this book, who are responsible for their own material and have shared their information in good faith to encourage others.

Any decisions you make, and the outcomes thereof are entirely your own doing. Under no circumstances can you hold the Compiler (Jasmine E. Clarke), the co-authors, the Publisher (Anita Sechesky), FAITH-INSPIRED BOOKS, LWL PUBLISHING HOUSE, or Anita Sechesky – Living Without Limitations Inc. liable for any actions that you take.

You agree not to hold the Compiler, the co-authors, the Publisher, FAITH-INSPIRED BOOKS, LWL PUBLISHING HOUSE, or Anita Sechesky – Living Without Limitations Inc. liable for any loss or expense incurred by you, as a result of materials, advice, coaching, or mentoring offered within.

The information offered in this book is intended to be general information with respect to general life issues. Information is offered in good faith; however, you are under no obligation to use this information.

Nothing contained in this book shall be considered legal, financial, or actuarial advice.

The authors and the Publisher assume no liability or responsibility for actual events or stories contained within.

The advice contained herein is not meant to replace the Professional role of a Certified Professional Coach, pastor, minister, physician, or any medical advice. Please consult with a doctor or family physician.

Foreword

Empowered Transformations – Real Stories of Hope, compiled by Jasmine E. Clarke, has been a journey of self-empowerment through her faith and determination to transform her life so that she can recover everything the enemy has stolen.

As Jasmine's Publisher, spiritual mentor, and Sister-in-Christ, I have been working closely with her over the last twenty-four months to guide her in praying effectively and learning how to break off strongholds that have attached themselves to her through negative life experiences and demonic patterns. Through her renewed mindset, Jasmine is passionately committed to encouraging other women who feel like they've lost so many good years because of the enemy's tactics to make them feel less than worthy of the blessings of God, weak or disempowered so they don't seek out their healing and deliverance.

You are invited into the lives of each author to glean from their testimonies, sharing what it took them to step into a place of healing, restoration, and power. Inside these pages, you'll find a variety of individuals' experiences from all walks of life, ages, and backgrounds. Jasmine has collaborated with some of the most authentic women who understand what it feels like to be rejected, abused, forgotten, or hopeless. They allowed the Holy Spirit to guide, heal, and empower them to live a life of blessings and hope.

I can say that this leadership experience for Jasmine has transformed her from the woman she once was over three years ago – a little more apprehensive but determined to follow the leading of the Lord in her life. To God be all the glory, honor, and praise for what He has done in her life and all the women in this beautiful book. I believe this anthology will bring the much-needed hope and encouragement so many are looking for.

From my perspective, I can honestly say that not everyone you meet will admit they have felt emotionally or spiritually weak. These are very private area in one's Christian walk and is often overlooked or neglected in our personal growth. It can also be the very thing that draws people closer together. Jasmine has carefully selected her co-authors based on their testimonies and levels of healing so their voices will convey the strength she was looking for to impact the readers. The chapters inside this book will inspire you to seek the *dunamis power* (see Mark 5:40-42) and the grace to recover the stagnant and dead areas in your life as you overcome trials and tribulations and walk with confidence and victory!

I recommend this book for anyone seeking solutions to coping with the stresses of daily living, diagnosed with a challenging illness, or contending with the confusion of where they fit into this huge and sometimes overwhelming world of lost trust and brokenness.

Congratulations to Jasmine and her team of co-authors! I am so proud of each one of you for sharing your stories to build others up and restore the human spirit into a place of perpetual growth and EMPOWERED TRANSFORMATIONS! It has been a pleasure to work with you on this anthology and to see your POWERFUL vision come to life.

Anita Sechesky

Registered Nurse, CEO, Founder, Owner & Best-Seller Publisher at FAITH-INSPIRED BOOKS, a division of LWL PUBLISHING HOUSE, ICF-Certified Professional Coach, Kingdom Life Strategist, #1 Best-Selling Author, Mentor, Holistic Book Writing Coach, Ghost-Writer, Keynote Speaker, Workshop Facilitator, Conference Host, INSPIRED TO WRITE Podcast Host, holds a Certificate in Religious Education (Deliverance Ministry & School of Theology, Principles of Spiritual Warfare) as a Freedom & Deliverance Minister, and the Founder & Moderator of FAITH INSPIRED LIVING Clubhouse Group

- Email: lwlclienthelp@gmail.com
- www.lwlpublishinghouse.com
- Facebook: LIVING WITHOUT LIMITATIONS in Print - LWL PUBLISHING HOUSE
- https://ca.linkedin.com/in/asechesky
- CLUBHOUSE: FAITH INSPIRED LIVING
- Instagram: lwl_publishing_house

Acknowledgments

I first must thank God, my Heavenly Father, for allowing me this opportunity to share the journey that He has brought me through.

I thank my parents, my family, and my extremely close friends for being so supportive and patient with me during this time.

I would like to acknowledge Anita Sechesky, my Publisher, for sharing her knowledge and inspiration which has motivated me to push myself to a position where I've never been before, which I truly appreciate.

I would like to thank the FAITH-INSPIRED BOOKS team at LWL PUBLISHING HOUSE for allowing me to share my vision in this book and for all their hard work behind the scenes.

Finally, I would like to thank these remarkable Women of God who decided to join me on this venture sharing their life stories of how God transformed them.

Dedication

This book is dedicated to all of our loved ones
and those special indivduals who faithfully encouraged
and supported us to write our stories.
We also acknowledge every person who has never given up
their hope and continues to be transformed
by the renewing of their minds.

Jasmine E. Clarke

&

"Empowered Transformation Anthology Team"

Introduction

It all began in the year 2020 when I called Pastor Pat Russell regarding an event I was inviting her to. Unfortunately, she was unable to take the call at that time and promised to return it the next day. The following evening, she called and asked the question, *"Jasmine, really, how are you doing?"* I sighed and said, *"I could just write a book!"* She chuckled and told me that she had an opportunity for me. I replied, *"What kind of opportunity?"* She stated that I could start by writing a chapter in her book. As Pastor Pat explained what I needed to do, I paused for a moment and then the Holy Spirit spoke to me. *"You wanted to write a book and now the opportunity has come to you. There's no need for you to go looking for a publisher because I've found one for you."* Wow! God really answered my prayers.

This is how my position as a leader was birthed: through the book Stronger Resilience, which was compiled by Pastor Russell. With her belief in me and her encouragement, I was able to complete the chapter for her anthology. Here was the challenge: I had to push myself to the point there was no turning back. I had to make up my mind just like Peter when he had to step out of the boat after Jesus had called him. I needed to encourage myself by quoting scriptures like:

"I can do all things through Christ who strengthens me." Philippians 4:13

There was a sigh of relief because it felt as if a ton of bricks rolled off my back. This has been one of the biggest accomplishments that I've ever made in my life.

In fact, being one of the co-authors in *Stronger Resilience* proved to me that I'm much stronger than I thought I was. In addition, I was invited to write as a co-author in *Soul Sister Letters* and *Rise Up*, both by Anita Sechesky, the Publisher of FAITH-INSPIRED BOOKS. By expressing my thoughts on paper, I have been able to share my experiences in life with others. Most importantly, God's directive guidance has made me realize there's been a transformation that has taken place in my life, and it was for me to continue to see where God wants to take me. I have become more confident and empowered as a Woman of God.

I have been so excited about this journey that I've been on. I have never done a project like this before. After the anthology with Pastor Pat was completed, God had put this idea within my Publisher's heart to pursue a proposal of doing my first anthology as a compiler. Did I ever feel overwhelmed and nervous? Oh yes! I would sit quietly at times and wonder if this was really happening. Where would I start? How would I begin to put this all together? I mean, there have been so many things that I have walked through in life. As these questions were jumping out at me, they became more possible because I am here today.

Being empowered has caused me to be more aware that many other individuals have never achieved that position. I do believe many people who have spoken over my life that I would never succeed, but God has proven them wrong. I must share this powerful vision because I clearly understand my assignment now. I am pursuing what God put in my spirit to do – to help others become empowered and be who God called them to be. There are numerous individuals stuck in life, not knowing where to go or what to do. They have tried to figure it out on their own and ended up against a proverbial brick wall.

As I sit here smiling and thinking about how far I've come, I know that I would not have gotten this far all by myself; it's because of God's grace. Even just looking at the book cover, I felt a shift take place and it has become a reality. God is so good, and I just want to give Him praise because I've reached another level. It's funny. I've always wanted to write a book but never thought that it would happen so soon. I've written journals to keep track of what God has done in my life and I always said that one day I would eventually write a book. I feel so blessed to be given this opportunity to be the leader of these outstanding women in this incredible venture; and to share with the whole world the lessons we have learned.

> *"The Spirit of the Lord GOD is upon me; because the LORD hath anointed me to preach good tidings unto the meek; he hath sent me to bind up the broken-hearted, to proclaim liberty to the captives, and the opening of the prison to them that are bound;"* Isaiah 61:1

This project is very important to me because there are so many people in this world who need to learn about the love of God. One thing is for sure. He's a God who cares for us so much that He'll make a way where there seems to be no way just to prove that He cherishes and loves us, even when we've gone through so many changes in our lives.

> *"For I know the plans I have for you, declares the Lord, plans to prosper you and not harm you, plans to give you hope and a future."*
> Jeremiah 29:11

I've realized that many of us have never experienced anything like the pandemic before. This really altered numerous lives around the world, leaving multitudes in despair, lonely, confused, discouraged, depressed, fearful, empty, and lost. You may wonder what can be done. Is there actually a God? Is He even concerned about us? Why did He allow this to happen? Well, I may not have answers to all these questions, but I do know that God really cares for us.

"For God hath not given us the spirit of fear; but of power, and of love, and of a sound mind." 2 Timothy 1:7

I decided to put this anthology of real stories together from 40 strong and powerful Women of God. Not everyone can travel around the world, but technology is so advanced that the Word of God can reach the four corners of the Earth.

When I got the vision for this book, I realized that there was more to life than what I saw through my own eyes. It made me think of how many more people around me are feeling the same way and not reaching their goals. There comes a time in our lives when we all need to do some kind of spiritual house cleaning with ourselves and let God and the Holy Spirit lead the way.

I trust that when you read each one of these chapters, you'll be able to relate to what these writers have walked. There is hope for you to become empowered and transformed by these stories. What these ladies share are real-life experiences they walked through and felt right within their spirits to share what God has done for them.

This anthology is meant to light a fire inside of you to create a burning desire to see what plans God has for your life. We all have so much potential to grow and blossom into that beautiful flower so that we can be seen in God's magnificent garden.

I believe that by the time you have finished reading this book, you will have a new mindset to move forward in a life that will allow God to stretch you into what He has called you to be. I pray that each of the lessons that they have learned will inspire and persuade you to thrive to be a more favorable you.

Jasmine E. Clarke is a Worship Leader and Author. She has a bachelor's degree in Worship Leadership and has held the position as a Choir Director. Jasmine has been a musician and vocalist of several musical ensembles. Her primary purpose is to glorify God by sharing her testimonies of what the Lord has done within her life and to proclaim the Gospel of Jesus Christ. Furthermore, Jasmine is empowered to help individuals develop their innate gifts that God has instilled within them, which will encourage others to believe that God can change their lives as well.

- youhavemanystoriestotell@gmail.com
- www.facebook.com/jasmine.clarke.5815
- LadyJay (specialinhiseyes)

Do not conform to the pattern of this world but be transformed by the renewing of your mind. Then you will be able to test and approve what God's will is — his good, pleasing and perfect will.

Romans 12:2

CHAPTER ONE - Clare Mcsween

Trusting in God's Process So You Can Experience Your Transformation

I am now living a life of peace, love, and abundance in the name of Jesus when compared to the life my children and I left behind. God has been our deliverer, supplier, and shepherd of our lives. John 10:10 says:

"I (Jesus) have come that they might have life and that they might have it more abundantly."

Thank God for opening that door for us because God's abundant life was not manifested in and through our lives back then. Life was made up of troubles, worries, and torments. There was no peace, no love, and no joy. It was an endless series of trying to survive and get along in life as best we could. This is my story. It is my hope that your eyes, hearts, and minds will be opened towards God's tender mercies as you read.

I was young, beautiful, and fell in love with someone whom I thought was handsome and would be the joy of my life. After a while, the babies started coming and the situation shifted, but not for the better. I discovered that this guy was addicted to drugs, and when he was under those influences, he was different. He worked himself into jealous rages that did not exist. He beat me with anything his hands could get, including a cutlass or a machete. I was thrust to the ground or dragged through the back door of the house into the muddy yard while being insulted, beaten, and accused of having other relationships. Sometimes when he arrived home, he frantically checked under the beds, looking for imaginative people he thought were there. Upon not finding anyone, the beatings would be more enraged, leaving me feeling soar and black and blue for days.

This was my life for over ten years – a series of beatings, accusations, and cursing. I would be fearful of his arrival at home at the end of each day because I knew I would be his punching bag. My friends and family stopped visiting our home because they were also accused of encouraging me to entertain other men when he was not home. The children also got their share of his anger because my son missed his death while trying to defend me during one of these rages. That man's addiction also caused us to be in continuous want and lack, both materially, financially, and emotionally. So, I opened a stall in the market, selling essential things to sustain our daily existence. However, he would be at a convenient distance, watching to see who was talking to me and how long we spoke. On my arrival home, the beatings and accusations would start again. I would cry from Monday to Friday because of his behavior and horrible treatment. I felt trapped and stuck in a relationship with no love and peace. Sometimes during the beatings, I would pretend to be unconscious. Then he would pick me up like a sack of potatoes and shower me at the pipe, preparing a meal for the family while apologizing and saying it would not occur again. I soon realized that all this was just a pretentious act by him because all of this was done so that he could be fulfilled with the acts of love accompanying a marital relationship. When he left for work on weekends, my children and I would be happy and comfort each other during this time, but on Mondays, we were back to being our sad selves again because he was back, and the cycle we were living would begin all over again.

One day, I was offered a job at a new company. The job and the pay were good. So now I was running my stall and doing the job. I introduced my friends and family to the company as vacancies became available, and they were accepted immediately for work into various positions. I was so glad for this opportunity where I could better provide for myself and the children. I also met other people working in the company and formed friendships which was beneficial to the plans my Heavenly Father had in store for me. Of course, at the time I was not aware of these plans. So, to prepare seven children and me for the next day, when we would be picked up at 7 a.m., I would do all my activities for daily living for the children at night. That was cooking and preparing their meals, grooming them, and so on to ensure that we all would be ready in the morning. This way, everyone will be on time – the children for school and myself for work. However, my partner would be there watching everything, making notes, and misinterpreting every movement. Hence, the beating would continue. Many days it was impossible for me to go to work because I would be so battered, bruised, and scarred that I would be ashamed to show my face in the community.

However, God is always in control of our lives if we invite Him to do so Without any suggestions from me, my boss asked if he could assist me in getting a visa so I could travel to the United States of America. I was shocked, surprised, and enthusiastic all at the same time at this suggestion, but I didn't have a passport and also was scarred at this unexpected turn of events because I knew that my partner would be very angry at such a thing. But I could see this was a light in my darkness. I remembered Philippians 4:13:

"I can do all things, through Christ who strengthens me."

So, I prayed and asked Him (God) to show me how to do this. A short while afterward, my sister came to visit. What a glorious day that was. I told her about the suggestion made by my boss, and she was very exuberant about it. She said, "Let's go and apply for the passport now." From a distance, it would appear as if I was accompanying her to get her passport. Oh, Glory to God, so I took my pictures while she filled out the form. God, you are so great. Picking up my passport, paying for my ticket, and booking my flight to Canada was all done by my sister. During this time, the abusive attitude and language continued, but I continued to ask for God's intervention each day. I did not know how, and I didn't know when my transformation and deliverance would take place, but I knew that He would not leave us nor forsake us (Hebrews 13:5). So I continued to pray. Sometimes, I would even question God and ask Him to hasten my time of deliverance because I was exhausted and disgusted with the way I was living.

My flight to Canada was booked for July 25th, 1993. I thank God for my day of **transformation and deliverance** because this is how I recognize that day. However, we had to work this through with guidance that can only be described as divine intervention.

On Saturday, July 24th, 1993, after working all day in the sun to get things sold, I bought groceries and sent my children home with the remainder of the money. They would tell their father that I was with my sister and would be returning home on Tuesday. I went to my sister's home because she lived about half an hour from the airport. During that night at my sister's residence, I could hardly sleep because I was praying for the safety and provision of my children while I was away. I was also praying about my safety as I had never traveled before. It was my time to let go of all my problems and let God take full charge of all that concerned me. I was going through my metamorphosis, and I was going through it with Him but, at the time I was not aware of the impact this experience would have on our lives. So, the next day, after saying goodbye to my sister and thanking her for all the hospitality shown to me, I entered the plane to begin my journey to Canada. I chose Canada because my niece was already living and working there. She would be a better person to guide and direct me on how to get things done.

It was a long trip, with many things to see and adventures where God manifested himself by providing for me when I was hungry and putting people into my life in a miraculous way. These people would later in my journey provide shelter and protection. What a merciful God and Father we serve. During my journey, I was able to live and relive the verses of Psalms 23 repeatedly because whenever a need presented itself, the hand of God was immediately outstretched to bless and make sure I was comforted, most times even before I could pray about it. Because the plane was delayed in Barbados, it was very late arriving in Canada. Cell phones were not as popular in those days as they are now. So, there was no way for me to communicate this to my niece who was picking me up at Pearson Airport in Toronto. Upon arrival, there was no one to pick me up, so I had nowhere to stay until she could return to do so. But with God's divine intervention, a woman who befriended and sat with me during my journey offered for me to stay at her home until my niece arrived the following day. It was a place where I was safe and protected and all my needs for the short visit were met. His goodness and mercy were always shown each step of the way, even providing a job for me in Canada within a short time of my arrival. This was indeed an immediate transformation through an instant network by God's angels of destiny. After years of weeping before God, He turned my mourning into dancing (Psalms 30:3-6, 11-12).

Friends, as you read my story, give your hearts and minds to Christ Jesus. Confess your shortcomings to Him because He is able and just to forgive us of all our unrighteousness and bring us into everlasting life (1 John 1:19). He is a promise keeper and will never leave us nor forsake us (Deuteronomy 31:8). In this way, you will grow to trust Him in everything so that when you call on Him in prayer, He will hear, and your prayers will be answered. If you are in an abusive relationship, tell Him about it. Ask Him to take control of all that is oppressing and offending you. Talk to Him about every fear, every low self-esteem, every frustration and anxiety that is holding you back so that you cannot go forward. Now, we may not know when He will answer because He works at his time, but after experiencing Him, we will be assured that His answer is on the way and our deliverance is sure.

Let us pray

Heavenly Father, I bring my friends who are reading my story before you. Please let each one receive an encounter with you so that they will realize that you are real; that you are able to save and are strong to deliver. There is nothing that is too hard for you. Thank you for your healing power that can strengthen every soul in their weakest moment and for you to cleanse us from all unrighteousness. In Jesus' most holy name I pray. Amen.

Clare McSween is an author and a Mary Kay beauty consultant. She holds the positions of early childhood teacher and hostess at her church. Clare's primary purpose is to share God's love through her testimonies of what the Lord has done within her life and to declare the Gospel of Jesus Christ. She is liberated to help individuals develop the indwelling skills that God has imprinted within them which will stir up their souls to trust that God can and will transform their lives too.

CHAPTER TWO - Tara Lomonte

From Imprisoned to Empowered

Many times in life, most of us try to achieve or overcome everything we need to on our own through our flesh, our limited capabilities, and our current understanding at the time they are occurring out of worrying and fear. This is not how our Father meant for us to live. He wants to be the ruler in our lives and look to Him and surrender our fears to Him; to show Himself the one true God. The scripture Matthew 6:27 (NLT) says *"Can all your worries add a single moment to your life?"* I hope my story will allow your faith in God to grow in your life so He may take you from a personal prison to divine empowerment.

Having lived through so many forms of pain in my life, I accepted it as normal, either through physical, sexual, or mental abuse traumas, family loss, car accidents, and repetitive strain injuries from work – to name a few. Pain can come in many forms: physical, emotional, or spiritual, and we don't get through this life without experiencing some form of it. I'm sure you can identify with this either personally or with close family and friends if you look at your immediate environment.

Sometimes we develop habits that seem innocent enough until we wake up one day and realize that we've allowed them to master us, affecting all other aspects of our lives for years to come. Drugs, alcoholism, abusive relationships, bad habits, lack of motivation about one's future, or not allowing ourselves to believe there is more to life causes destruction through the years. The mind starts believing that this is all there is and focuses on negative scenarios, which in turn draws us into exactly what we don't want. What we feed our brains indicates how mentally healthy we are in life. Just like our bodies need good food for nourishment, what we read, watch, and listen to and who we surround ourselves with have a great impact on our mindset. Nothing happens overnight and some things are so subtle that when we arrive at this destination, we ask ourselves, *"How did I even get here?!"*

Our bodies often respond to the traumas and hurt that we have experienced once or repeatedly over the years subconsciously and eventually cause us to look at our lives and choices if we want to improve our situation. Money doesn't seem so important once we lose our health. We will do just about anything to gain our strength and youthful mobility back to what it was before our takedown. I fully experienced this in my late twenties, at the prime of my life and it almost crushed me and devastated my life forever.

I lost myself in a deep depression for many years in my teens, twenties, and thirties even though God was right there with me every time. I only called on Him once there was an issue and needed a rescuer. Sometimes, we are our own worst enemies when we resist guidance from others, show ignorance, and have a lack of understanding of the Word of God.

Who would have ever thought that I, the most free-spirited, music-loving, dancing queen, social butterfly, who lived for love and serving others, would have been committed to a full stop in body and life at the young and precious age of twenty-nine?

Before this imprisonment in my body, I was living the so-called good life on my own at the age of twenty-seven. I had finally found a career that I loved, which was in aesthetics, at a high-end spa in downtown Toronto. I was living in the center of the city, in the eye of the activity and entertainment sector, away from the small town that I felt I had escaped from and dreamed of leaving since I was a teenager. I got myself to a place where I could be carefree and attend to my heart's desires. Never being one for the spotlight or making friends easily, I was now surrounded by so-called friends and always out on the scene in the big city, taking care of me, working hard, and playing even harder, and was now beginning to see the fruits of my labor. I had independence, love, friends, freedom, and the social life that I adored.

After a year and a half of working long hours and many days with no rest, my physical restrictions began in the form of bursitis, starting in my left shoulder. I tried so hard to overcome and persevere for three months while working, waiting for it to just subside. I would do anything not to give in to the inflammation or admit that I was unable to continue my work. Having a high pain threshold, I endured the excruciation, even though it was unbearable. I fought tooth and nail to get past it and hold on to my career. I also needed to keep the new apartment that I just got settled into when the walls came crumbling down around me. It seemed no one in any management role cared to do something to help me and my coworkers were unable to assist me even if they wanted to.

I finally gave in, switched careers, and wound up back in a corporation providing customer service. My headset was like an umbilical cord that connected me to the dialer and computer, and I sat in a cubicle all day other than timed breaks and lunch, punching in and punching out, and having no social interaction with my customers. This was not my idea of a dream job. After a year of adjusting and working just to pay the bills, I was promoted to a new department where I made new friends with my colleagues. I was finally settling in again and was finding success in my position, showing all my sacrifices were going to pay off. Then, one day, a young coworker and close friend passed away unexpectedly, hardships in my dating realm were overwhelming, and some departmental changes all transpired simultaneously. I fell into bed one night as my youthful, free-spirited self, and hours later, I awoke into a body that imprisoned me. I had no movement from the neck down; I was locked in physical bondage. I had no answers as to what was happening and was in shock and devastation. There wasn't any outward appearance of physical bruising or pain, so I had to justify and explain myself as if I was just looking for attention or any easy way to get paid time off of work. All I had ever done was try to overcome any obstacles that came my way, commit to my responsibilities, and go over and above my call of duty to perform in any way I could. I was always there for people, to serve and nurture to the best of my abilities and now I was left to decay and suffer alone in unbearable pain and confusion in my apartment with only God and my mom to show I was loved and that my life mattered. My day turned to night and my light was once again veiled in darkness on all levels.

Going to bed as one person and waking up as another is like stumbling into a dimension of time and life that I didn't search for or desire. It felt like I was being punished to suffer or that I was born just to be living the consequences of hardship, loneliness, and pain on my own for crimes I didn't even know I had been committing. There was no future to look forward to, just perseverance through each day, one minute at a time, and seemingly no way out. Doctors and management at work either didn't believe me or had no answers on how to help. I was the sacrificial lamb and I wanted to just sleep and never get up. Experiencing anxiety which I had never suffered from, along with pain all over my body fully prevented me from any movement and isolated me from the world I knew and wanted to get back to. My body was in full muscle contraction from head to toe daily. This is fibromyalgia, although no one knew what it was at that time, and no one cared to believe it.

There didn't seem to be an end to the tunnel, let alone a light at the end of it. My existence now offered only depression, weight gain, chronic full-body pain, and having to justify myself to everyone; like I had to prove why I had the right to exist, breathe, or ask for help. There were no answers…and no help. I was lost, scared, alone, and confused – locked in a physical and mental prison. It felt like a life sentence. Have you ever been there, where your life, as you know it, just spins out of control and you find yourself in an abyss of time and space?

After three, long, brutal years at the age of thirty-two, I was conclusively diagnosed through multiple tests on every level. Finally, I had the justification and knowledge as to why I was experiencing this brutal nightmare. Once again, I had to accept moving back home with my mom, leaving my career behind, and trying to figure out what my body wanted and how to heal over time. I attended a pain clinic weekly for two and a half years, getting forty-two injections of nerve-blocking at each visit just so I could go two days a week without intolerable pain and have some mobility while learning how to cope the other days until it became manageable. When I turned thirty-six, I had overcome most of my fibromyalgia and physical issues. It had been a long and winding road over seven years of trial and error and perseverance. I got another chance at life again; I was newly resurrected in my body, and I am so grateful!

A few years after this, at the ripe age of thirty-nine, I started to work out and train my body with a fitness instructor whom I went to diligently and trained hardcore, which molded my body to a level I have never been to before in my life. I was now at the height of my fitness level and strength training, and I was lifting weights that were more than I weighed. Renewed in life, mind, and emotions, I got certified as a fitness trainer and then began to enable and instruct others on their journey of change and self-empowerment. What a transformation!

Here I am today, looking back on it all, twenty years older in age from the beginning of that long journey but now feeling much younger physically, spiritually, and emotionally – new in peace and hope each day. Oh, how the Potter can mold a new vessel with His hands through prayers, willingness, obedience, and faith.

My story is to empower and encourage even one person to never give up. If what is happening in your life feels beyond your control, you are never alone. You are valuable and are here for a reason. There is always hope and possibility.

"Ask, and it shall be given you; seek, and ye shall find; knock, and it shall be opened unto you: For every one that asketh receiveth; and he that seeketh findeth, and to him that knocketh it shall be opened."
Matthew 7:7-8 (KJV)

I am in such a wonderful place of spiritual peace and love that now what affected me can no longer affect me that deeply again, no matter the storms. I wish I had found this love and understanding all those years ago, but the journey is part of the process which is the most important on our road to awareness, self-love, and healing.

Whether we try to go it alone and allow it to overwhelmingly devastate our lives, or invite Him to help us, heal us, and provide our strength, peace, and hope amid the journey is our choice. God created us and is the greatest waymaker there is. And what seems like a miracle to us is nothing to Him who created us all. Jeremiah 32:27 (KJV) says *"Behold, I am the LORD, the God of all flesh: is there anything too hard for me?"* What seems like punishment at times is also protection from God or a redirection in life to get us back on track with who He created us to be. He gives us free will but also is our redeemer from our own mistakes. What the enemy means for harm, God turns it for good eventually.

I am so willful and determined in my flesh and own mind; a strength and gift He provided when He created me. However, our strengths sometimes can also become our weaknesses, if not applied correctly. Hindsight and experience allow us to look back in time and reflect. Through this reflection, I can say that not only did I have no other choice than to surrender but I can also attest that overcoming allows us to be a living testimony for others; to empower, and to be the beacon of hope needed. He is now using me as His vessel. While I was in the midst of the despair, I could not have seen so far ahead in the future and would never have believed what He would achieve through me if someone told me at that time.

"The Lord is near to the brokenhearted and saves the crushed in spirit." Psalm 34:18 (NLT)

"Get along well with God and be at peace; from this something good will come to you. Receive instruction from his mouth; put his words in your mind." Job 22:21-22 (CEV)

We also tend to value our lives; especially how precious they are when facing painful situations. It helps us to appreciate our lives and our loved ones even more, not taking anything for granted. Once we have overcome, it also teaches us that we are survivors, and it builds our endurance and strength.

God does not want you to try harder. He wants you to trust in Him deeper. Stop trying. Start trusting. This will change everything in you. Never give up. One day, you can become the story that heals and empowers others. I can truly attest to this time and time again. *"Our most beautiful dreams are born from our most unpleasant nightmares."* Matshona Dhliwayo

God comforts us so we can comfort others.

"Blessed be the God and Father of our Lord Jesus Christ, the Father of mercies, and God of all comfort, who comforts us in all our tribulation, that we may be able to comfort those who are in any trouble, with the comfort with which we ourselves are comforted by God."
2 Corinthians 1:3-4 (KJV)

Take comfort in God. He will not forsake you.

Tara Lomonte is an entrepreneur by heart. She is an experienced professional medical aesthetician operating her own small mobile business, HuemanShades. In recent years she was also a certified Fitness Instructor. Tara created and continues to develop her own overseas and online jewelry business, AXA Signature Jewellery, in which she is a self-taught designer. Tara's primary purpose and motivation  is to inspire and encourage others to hold on to hope and faith through powerful testimonies of her transformational life experiences of overcoming trials and tribulations through God's love and saving grace.

- www.linkedin.com/in/misscanguilla
- AXA Signature Jewellery
- Tara Lomonte
- AXA Signature Jewellery
- HuemanShades

CHAPTER THREE - Evangelist Suzette Haylett-Radlein

Forgiveness Leads to Healing

Let me start by saying God is always in control of our lives even when we are hurting. We can all agree that hurting others usually results in more hurt. 50% of the time, those who are hurt are also the ones who have caused harm to others throughout their lives, whether it be to their husband, children, or even to themselves. At this point, sharing your struggles with others is an excellent approach to relieve the stress and grief you are carrying around. Although it may not change the issue, doing so will make you feel better. Most of the time, we don't get the chance to speak about how we are feeling or what we are going through because of people stereotyping us. As a result, we lock ourselves in a closet and scream before returning to the front with a smile on our faces while inside, we are dying. When we talk about our problems and others hear what we have been through, it can help them to understand that they are not alone, and it can also bring healing to you as a person. I will be sharing my story with you because I know that my redeemer lives.

At a young age, I was sent to live with a family member. I was assured that I would go to school and they would assist me with everything I needed. I was thrilled to be going to school and starting a better life, but after living with them for the first two months, things started to go south. I came to the realization that they didn't truly love me since they would give me all the household laundry to wash while I also had to make breakfast for everyone and clean the eight-bedroom house. I also had to iron the clothes. A promise was made that I would be sent to school, but I never attended one. I was more of a helper than a relative; I was abused emotionally, physically, and mentally and treated like an outcast.

One day, I was given some clothes to wash. As I began to wash the clothes, my relative came to the back of the house and inquired about their spouse. When I replied that I didn't know, they began to yell at me before leaving. When they returned, I was stabbed twice in the back with rusty scissors. I fled to the side of the road and collapsed. A neighboring woman arrived at the back door just in time, picked me up after I fell, and asked me what had happened, but when she noticed that blood was dripping down my back, she dialed 911. When the police arrived, my relative pretended to be mentally ill. I was taken to the woman's home. When I returned to my relative's home, they asked me to prepare dinner for the family. Their spouse was always working late and would only come home at night. On that evening when I got stabbed, they came home earlier than expected and asked for me. The lady next door sent her son to call my relative's spouse and they came to her house. When they saw me, they became so upset, stormed out of the lady's house, and started to argue with my relative, telling them that they needed to stop abusing me and send me back to my home. The spouse couldn't do much because my relative would tell them to mind their own business. The spouse was a loving person, but they had to stay away from me because of my relative.

On a daily basis, even when it was not my fault, my relative would beat me. They would curse me and tell me to get up and go to bed no matter how early it was. Whenever I would sit down to watch television, they would say that it was I was attempting to seduce their spouse. Even in the wee hours of the morning, my relative would come to my room, slap me, and ask me why I was still in bed. This treatment continued for a few months until one day I was asked to prepare callaloo and saltfish with green bananas for breakfast. When I finished cooking, my relative came and sat down at the table. After tasting the food, they spit it out and threw hot tea on me, saying that the saltfish was too salty and that I was trying to seriously hurt them. The spouse yelled at my relative and questioned why they would do that. My relative then reached for the knife and asked the spouse if they wanted to hit my relative for me. The spouse then got up from the table and went to work while I went to clean up myself and then the floor.

My relative would go to the store and buy groceries, but if I asked them to buy me deodorant and lotion, they would refuse. Instead, the spouse would buy them, and I would tell my relative that the neighbor gave them to me. If I needed clothes, the spouse would also take me to the store to buy the clothes and would tell me to choose the items that I liked. The same day, the spouse took me to the store and also took me to the hairdresser to perm my hair because my relative would not comb it. My relative was already home when we returned from the store. They met us at the gate and immediately started to fight the spouse. Afterward, my relative turned to me and gave me a proper beating and also called me all kinds of derogatory names. I went to bed that night in excruciating pain. This was too much for me, so the following morning when my relative left for work, I packed my bags and gave the children their porridge in bottles which I had boiled and left. I didn't know the area very well, so I asked around and took the bus according to the directions I had received to the best of my recollection. I ended up getting off at the wrong stop, and as I was waiting at the bus stop in the pitch-black with the sun setting, I was crying because I was so scared. A young man approached me and asked why I was crying. When I explained, he said, "Come with me; I'm taking you to my grandmother." I followed him, and when I got to his house, his grandmother asked him what he was doing with the young girl. He replied and told her what I had told him, and she pulled me into her arms and sobbed, saying, "I'm so sorry for everything that's happened to you." We talked for the majority of the evening while watching television, and she also gave me a bed to sleep in. She also gave me meals and dressed the two wounds in my back because they were infected. She provided me breakfast and fare to home the following morning.

    My granddad was surprised to see me when I arrived back home. He asked me what I was doing there, and as I explained everything to him, I saw tears welling up in his eyes. That day, my grandad had been torturing himself for sending me to my relative's place. My granddad saved me when my relative tried to attack me again at his house two days after I returned home. My relative was about to hit me with a cutlass when he stepped in front and grabbed their hands. He then ran my relative out of his yard and locked the gate. My relative was standing at the gate cursing and swearing that they were going to hurt me very badly.

I was just eleven years old when my relative abused me and accused me of something I hadn't done. All these things happened to me at this young age. When I was a child, it took me months to venture out on my own. I was too afraid to go to the store or even walk alone. At night, when I went to sleep, I would dream that my relative was going to beat me. In the morning, I would wake up terrified, expecting my relative to slap me while I was still in my sleep. Years passed, and as I got older, it became increasingly difficult for me to act normally like other kids because I was constantly thinking about what they had done to me. I didn't talk to my relative again after that day until I was invited to a family reunion in 2014. When we met in the US, I asked my relative why they attacked me, and they began to explain why they did it. I responded that it was untrue and then explained what had happened. When they realized what they had done, they sobbed and apologized to me. I accepted the apology and told them that the harm had already been done. After pleading with me for several weeks, my relative finally realized the truth, and I decided to forgive her.

Most of the time, when people accuse you and hurt you, it's not what they think; however, when they learn the truth, they apologize and begin to heal. I was harboring a great deal of resentment toward my family. I was just bitter and blamed everyone for everything in my life until one day God called me. I started to do a self-examination and realized that I had so much unforgiveness in my heart that was walking around with me. I had to pray and ask God to help me forgive my family so that I could apologize to them all. What role does God play in everything that happened to me and my relative? I believe that God let these things happen to me to prove to me that He is in control of my life, as it is said in Job 1:8: *"Have you considered my servant job?"* For years I believe Jesus said the same thing to me, *"Have you considered my servant Suzette."* And so, I had to go through all this at a young age.

Jesus will always put things in place to protect his people. There are times when we get hurt so often that we ask the question, *"Why? Why did those persons do this to me?"* The past is something that should be forgotten, but unfortunately, a lot of people let it define them. They become miserable, cunning, selfish, greedy, and blame it on the past or people in their past, saying, *"I am this way because of how that person mistreated me."* Or what so and so did to them. God wants us to know that the past has no power over us and that we can let go of it because we have been renewed by his love and redeeming grace. So, rather than changing negatively because of our unfair past, we should only show God's works in us by saying, *"I am nice, smart, forgiving, sweet (etc.) because of Christ's love and forgiveness in my life. It is no longer I who live, but Christ lives in me. So, I live in this earthly body by trusting in the Son of God who loved me and gave himself for me."* God wants us to experience continual restarts, rebirths, redefinitions, and to literally rebrand our lives. He never meant for this full life to be boring but intended for us to experience the excitement and inspiration of perpetual transformation.

This is a life of faith where we achieve and fail, rise and fall, suffer and recover, experience loss and gain, and then after having pursued and endured, fulfill our destiny. This transformative experience is what it means to walk with God. We cannot change until we move on and move forward until we get emotionally unstuck from yesterday's thinking and living. Only then can we pursue God's dream of who we are meant to be.

"The Lord is near to the brokenhearted and saves the crushed in spirit." Psalm 34:18 (ESV)

I speak about my past because I know it will help others. When these things happen to someone, it is good to find out why they did those things because when they start to let you know, you will be able to correct what they are saying, and they will know that they are accusing you of things you didn't do. It is evident that the world is full of suffering. Physical, emotional, and spiritual pain has been and will be an intrinsic part of the human experience. The archetypal example of our suffering was Jesus Christ, who was persecuted and crucified by the Roman officials. Suffering will indeed come, but God can give us grace and power to overcome every trial and fulfill our purpose and mission in His kingdom. The Bible gives counsel on the meaning of suffering and how we can best endure it.

"He heals the brokenhearted and binds up their wounds." Psalm 147:3 (ESV)

God wants us, his people, to forgive those who hurt us. So many people ridiculed and hurt Jesus, but He forgave them. God says:

"Do not fear, for I am with you; do not be dismayed, for I am your God. I will strengthen you and help you; I will uphold you with my righteous right hand." Isaiah 41:10 (NIV)

Don't strike back against someone who hurts you. The apostle Paul says in Romans 12:

"Bless those who persecute you; bless and do not curse. Do not repay anyone evil for evil. Let us be strong and courageous do not be afraid or terrified of them, for the Lord your God goes with you; He will never leave you nor forsake you." (NIV)

The good news is to keep going, no matter what other people say. Your one true companion throughout life is God and He will never abandon you.

Evangelist Suzette Haylett-Radlein was born in May Pen, Clarendon on the beautiful island of Jamaica. She is wife to Mr. Illya Radlein and mother to three boys and one girl. Suzette is a certified Sunday School teacher, an ordained evangelist and pastor, a counselor, a chaplain, and a UN Peace Ambassador. When not busy with church ministry, she finds solace in dancing, swimming, traveling, and watching adventure movies. This is Suzette's first book as co-author and wants to tell her story about rising up where she reminds us that God is an on-time God even when it doesn't seem that way.

CHAPTER FOUR - Charlene Wilson-Evans

Actions – Some Steps Require Extra Strength

Strength is the quality of physical, psychological, and emotional power. Strength is the capacity of one's desire, optimism, and motivation. It is a virtue of one's belief.

Imagine climbing the steps to an ancient Chinese temple as an assignment for a world religion final paper. And the innumerable steps that are confronting each student's journey seem impossible without placing one's foot on the first step, which is seemingly tedious. This assumable venture can propel fear of losing marks, discouragement is given access to permeate the mind, giving up hope and throwing in the towel on a beloved subject because the final steps are too demanding, and the vision becomes an overnight fleeting thought. In this situation, who will these students hold responsible for the sacrificial tuitions that were invested? Is the professor of the course to be blamed or should the student take the journey one step at a time?

The cycle of life tends to throw all kinds of shaped balls within a circle and the one that rolls in an individual's direction can either break them or strengthen them. Sometimes, they will search and wonder where they will get the strength to be locomotive. How do they retrieve it?

Will it make them feel better? Will strength be the only motivating factor in discovering their purpose that changes or ruffles one's comfort zone?

Climacophobia (the fear of staircases or of falling down stairs) may set in when reaching for those steps of the Chinese temple, and it could be attributed to a medical condition. And the enthusiasm that favored the ambition obtained in the initial commencement of the course study depletes gradually.

Over the years I have seen, counseled, and listened to various ethnic people struggling with the hurdles, or factors, that create dominance with male power in employment, religion, and relationships. The pulpit dominance within the church ranks has been condescending to the potential and God-given calling from God being manifested in women of multicultural ethnicity has plummeted through "glass ceilings." Biological, gender inequality, and social biases continue to exert improper exegesis of the Holy Scriptures which has violated an unknown percentage of women in the churches. These determined women of God, although they have been stereotyped, spot on, damaged but standing up, battered but squaring their shoulders, limping but holding placards, letting their voices be heard, have trail-blazed the journey, leaving us that are broken requiring extra strength, drawing on the bums, holding on to the satin sheet that slides and tumbles over oneself, wiping the tear-flooding eyes and the runny nostrils to push, hold on until we can muster the steps and the strength to stand.

> *"But we have this treasure in earthen vessels, that the excellency of the power may be of God, and not of us. We are troubled on every side, yet not distressed; we are perplexed, but not in despair; persecuted, but not forsaken; cast down, but not destroyed;"* 2 Corinthians 4:7-9

Allow someone to hold the weak hands if falling. Do not die from internal clogging of the heart valves. The violation of the physical persona of the woman forcing indelible damage to her emotional and psychological health is horrendous while losing loved ones, immigration instability, homelessness, and societal rejection. The pivotal attempting focus tends to showcase the unfulfillment of one's void and harboring the unmet dreams, feeling sorry for oneself, waiting to experience resilience that leads to confidence, initiating the building blocks to positive self-esteem, self-endurance, gaining control, and so much more. But, still wonder why they cannot feel fulfilled. That's because there is a different approach in every situation.

A strength-based model will not be applicable for each victim because Strength Renewal does not flourish overnight. There were many days and nights I put myself on the table. I performed my own self-examinations and emotional surgeries especially during the COVID-19 lockdown periods because I needed to unclog my internal bleedings. Suppression season for some embedded stuff had to be filtered.

Denial is a deceptive factor that encourages façade and suppression. Expression of one's true emotions is expected to be concealed. *Help is needed to hold* our hands, or we need a listening ear, not advice on how to move on. *Just listen and don't speak.* Some of us have poured into the jars of people most of our lives, giving of our substance without reservation. Circumstances will arise that can suddenly deflate our diaphragms, and the people that we poured into forsake us when intolerable issues arise making our lives as an omission.

Traumatic experiences have forced me to walk out of my mind which is the first stage of locomotion before putting my feet on the floor every morning. If the journey doesn't start in my mind asking the Holy Spirit to push me out of the state of repression, defeat will command my day. I'm a pastor who struggles with post-traumatic stress disorder and anxiety due to a motor vehicle accident and other encounters. I self-medicate with constant prayers, internal and external praises, and the repeating of scripture verses. I'm my number one cheerleader, the mirror in my washroom is the second phase of my locomotion, and the renewal of my strength – my reflection in that mirror is my audience. I herald self-praises before I apply face cream, etc. Yes ma'am, yes sir, I assure myself that I'm beautiful and that I love myself the best out of all my mother's children…and I'm God's heritage. *Negative words from people can be very detrimental to a person's character.* I've had my share of gainsayers in different seasons of my life, and I employed them as stepping stones – motivational platforms that became the creative patterns in my pathway. Negative sayings can incarcerate an individual so that he or she can become suffocated by internalizing their emotions – caged, needing resuscitation. Pain and rejection are known to steal support systems that can be beneficial to our resuscitation. Pain and blinded eyes have shaded many journeys; the will to live. Locomotion becomes limited. Don't let the lungs in the body determine your breathing status. Disannul the weakness in your emotions and **SCREAM! STOP SHUTTING DOWN AND LIVE!**

There is not a vaccine or an immunity from troubles and unforeseen events. I challenge us to become someone's backbone after weathering the storms, providing a cushion of support to climb the stairs to the Chinese Temple. Tell your story to save a life if needed. Produce a non-judgmental atmosphere, a ray of comfort that will incorporate the shedding of weaknesses and insecurities. Life throws again some burdens that can be handled on its own, and there are days we reap stuff in the garden we did not sow. Reaping what is sown is the law of nature. The seeds that are sown now in people's lives where strength can be regained will enlighten the walk, keeping the eyes off every throng and remain focused on the destiny. Let's recognize that the principle of sowing and reaping strength will propose our attitudes for growth and the discouragement. The anxiety that travailed in the chest of the students attempting to climb the steps to the Chinese temple has stopped blaming the professor and is now appreciative for the lessons learned, the experiences gained as each step whispered or highlighted a virtue they didn't know they had.

Many times because of the necessity that is laid on us although broken, shattered in many pieces, we cannot retreat; or deny the strengthening power of God-Jehovah. Jesus Christ knows the worst about us, and He believes the best about us without reservation. Women of God, when we have been through our stuff, taunted by our past, our abusers that still eat at us as we reflect on the pain they have wrenched in our insides, we have to maintain our purpose and allow God to validate us. Many of us ladies who wear our self-esteem in our shoes and wait around for men to validate us, dying on the inside hiding our black eyes under thick layers of powder and make-up; restraining our giftings and privileges, necessity is laid on us.

Climbing the China wall, we must start where we are! The position taken at times seems humanly senseless. That's why we have to attribute our efforts to God without reservation. Our steps need an extra push and **IT HAD TO BE GOD!**

The climber could be a prospective minister's wife who is all excited about living in faith, eager to do exploits for God, and complimenting her husband. Being called the "1st Lady" is a mold that some women superficially fit because they chose not to be themselves but what the congregation and their husbands force them to be. You, 1st Lady, need to launch your own self-evaluation, self-knowledge, your own modest fashion wardrobe because you will be constantly changing. 1st Lady, you will need to have *YOUR MIND* to stand on your own premise and merits, to look inside you, to determine your value, and to be willing to work with others although you might not see eye to eye. Balance and management of church, home, kids, and being the Ladies' president will be on your shoulders. Are you still asking, 1st Lady, if you will need some extra strength for the journey?

The struggle will be real, especially in the scrutiny of the gainsayers and nit-pickers in the assembly who think they should traditionally align your dress code, your hairstyle, and if head covering is a requirement. Remember, that will be a door kept ajar for the clothing police with a 1st Lady Job Description Manual. 1st Lady, surround yourself with community support networks; don't be entrapped with exclusivism. In every aspect as related in previous paragraphs, *BALANCE IS VERY PIVOTAL.* Gain strength from weaknesses; don't become overly frustrated, aggressive, or feeling discouraged if your husband is overtaken with church matters and people's issues.

Mrs. 1st Lady, climb up in your daddy Jesus Christ's arms.

- Outpour yourself all over Him.
- Grab your napkins; allow the bawling to gush out.
- He, God, will not call you a drama queen as you lay at His feet.
- He, God, will not condescendingly say, "Can't you see I'm busy? You are too needy."
- Don't be afraid to break; but yes, just tell Him.
- Renew your strength.
- Give Him your suppressed emotions and repeated rejections.

Did you ever think that your pastor husband is drawing on your strength – being a pastor and leader of a flock? His male ego will not subject him to establish his fears. You, 1st Lady, are the neck of it all. Compose yourself. Become that intercessor. Embrace yourself in God's strength. Balance yourself in the Word of God. In all your adjustments for ministry, 1st Lady, **DO NOT LOSE YOURSELF.**

Some steps require extra strength which can lead to impatience very quickly. If we do not achieve our desires in an acquired time frame, prayer can become hard work not extending our time to listen for an answer. I have discovered in the years of my relationship with Christ Jesus, that troubles produce patience in the soil of adversity which tests the anchor of my faith in God. There are people who are instrumental in our growth, who were designed to erode our roots and fragment our stabilities, but their intentions have led to our maturity. We can pray, get the response we need, and forget to pinpoint the answer when it comes. In our prayers, we request Strength from God and instead, we are plummeted in a season of distress and trials, but supernaturally we gain **Strength**.

Every perspective of life, even "right versus wrong opinions," can leave an indelible scale on one's life in every dimension of life being pursued. Do I need to be right all the time or can I allow somebody's opinion to bear some weight around me – that's strength. Other people's conflicts or biases in their viewpoints can strike us publicly or privately which can take us off guard. Will we easily embarrass ourselves vocally or will our behavior be controlled by our God-given spirits in the midst of adversity? Let us flush old grievances, stop rehearsing them, and don't let us be stereotyped "women cannot let anything go." If we are going to disagree to agree, let us do so without being barbaric, but gather *STRENGTH* and remain gentle. Be an encourager, a teacher, a good listener, and be delayed in speech to gain wisdom.

Courage and Strength are two virtues that shine in the crown of a queen. Every mountain that we have climbed, Queen, the bridges we have crossed steers us to our promised lands. There were different sizes and color giants on our journey, but thanks be to our Almighty God we are here to tell the story. We had to face these giants and are still facing them with the supernatural power of God. This should bring us into a praise break. **H-A-L-L-E-L-U-J-A-H! TRULY GOD-JEHOVAH IS** worthy of all praises. Strength is found when courage refuses to be dominated by *FEAR*. Strength becomes fueled by courage – the tenacity to want to maintain a firm grip when life dictates defeat. Your hands are trembling with the rushed adrenalin in your face and the racing thoughts and heartbeat become a symphony sending life's summary of all your failures on the movie screen as you are about to escape this world. But here comes *STRENGTH*, whispering in that still small voice, "Let me hold your hand. Give me your hand. Let me carry you."

Did you say you have lost everything? So, who gave you courage, the confidence to live, to prove God's WORD, to muscle the strength to be a role model to others at this stage of your life? It was you and God, Queen. Yes ma'am. Aren't you grateful you stuck it out; developing the convictions, proving "them" wrong? Queen, self-discipline has mainstreamed you. Strength gained has not only cushioned you, but your admirers are still in shock at how you made it. You battled through people-pleasing. You remained focused, although you had to trade your happiness for sorrow, and loneliness for a set time factor to burst through the cocoon. Look at the colors of your wings. You are not any butterfly, but a rare species that magnetizes nations to you.

The spotlight is now on you, Queen.

- Let humility, your submission to God's will enfold you.
- Showcase Mercy and Truth.
- Remind yourself of the best practices to engage the Kingdom of God.
- Revise the kingdom principles and adopt the values; delight in God's statutes and seek for Godly women.
- Every Queen needs another queen. Learn vicariously.
- Don't reject mentorship.

- Have an open mind, but don't be gullible.
- Ask God for a Spirit of Discernment.
- Do not avoid pressure. If you do, you will not be able to recognize what fabric you are made of.

Rest, walk in the Strength of God, and you will sit in the presence of kings and queens.

Rev. Charlene Wilson-Evans shares a God-centered, personal relationship with her savior and mentor, Jesus Christ. Acts 17:28 is her daily motivation: "For in him we live, and move, and have our being." Pastor Charlene holds a bachelor's degree in theology, is an ordained evangelist and pastor, serves as Chaplain for prison ministries, is a Certified Social Worker, and is an author. She ministers nationally and internationally in conferences, retreats, and convocations. Pastor Charlene is married to Pastor Audley Evans bearing two miracle daughters.

- @pastorcharlenewilson-evans
- Pastor Charlene Wilson-Evans
- godsassemblyworshipcentreinc/messenger

CHAPTER FIVE - Shelleanne Hardial

Transformed for His Glory

Distraught by the news, I quickly found the bathroom to isolate myself from the world. With tears streaming down my cheeks as I knelt on the floor, I turned my face to the wall like Hezekiah (see Isaiah 38:2) and prayed, *"Lord Jesus, forgive me of my sins. I am truly sorry for what I have been doing. You now have my undivided attention; so, do with me as you please. I surrender my life completely into your hands, and I will serve you unconditionally for the rest of my life. Thy vows are upon me oh Lord until death."* Beloved readers, that prayer transformed my life at age seventeen!

Oftentimes I would tell my children that there is a significant reason each person was not born as an adult; rather, we grow and mature into adulthood. Guidance, particularly spiritual guidance from the Holy Spirit, is vital to the lives of believers in that we circumvent many costly mistakes. However, that is not to say that we will not make unsound decisions at times. I know I have made some terrible mistakes (as hinted in the above prayer), but I am forever thankful to God who teaches me through His Word how to overcome my errors.

During my pre-teen years, I had surrendered (or so I thought) my heart to Jesus Christ. I was excited to start my spiritual journey with the Lord. As such, I was actively involved in ministry through my consistent attendance and participation in church services, vocational bible school, youth retreats, Bible studies, teen's choir, and prayer meetings. When I began high school in Jamaica, I got distracted by the wrong students to the extent that I desired their company more than seeking the presence of the Almighty God. Though I was not participating in a promiscuous lifestyle (at that time) like some of my classmates, I was intrigued with the idea of having a boyfriend. Instead of finding friends that were like-minded in terms of God-fearing and God-serving, I was *"...drawn away of [my] own lust, and enticed"* (James 1:14, KJV). Further to this, in Grade Nine, I entertained the conversation of one particular male who was interested in starting a relationship with me. Despite the warnings from my parents, particularly my Christian mother, and the Holy Spirit, I plunged straight into a relationship with the said male.

At fifteen years old, I allowed the enemy to trick me into employing a nonchalant attitude towards making reckless decisions such as following my boyfriend home repeatedly after school. For two years, I believed the father of lies – Satan (see John 8:44) to make my own mistakes despite the pain and repercussions, rather than learning from other people's mistakes. To that end, I became secretly rebellious toward my mother who recognized that I was living contrary to God's will while those around me were oblivious to my behavior. Although I had backslidden in my heart, the Holy Spirit was always there tugging on my heart to repent and yield to His plan. Jeremiah 29:11 declares:

"For I know the thoughts that I think toward you, saith the LORD, thoughts of peace, and not of evil, to give you an expected end." (KJV)

Many times, we forfeit the plan of God for the deceitful and harmful devices of the devil. In particular, knowing that I had an extremely strict mother (which I am now thankful for), I foolishly agreed with my teenage boyfriend that he could accompany me home. Unbeknownst to me, my mother had left work earlier than expected to travel home with a colleague. While my friend and I were talking in the living room, I heard my mother opening our gate. Petrified to the extent of doing the unthinkable, I told my male friend to hide in our guest room while I went to my bedroom to pretend as if I had just gotten home, and was putting away my school uniform.

Shortly after her arrival, my mother called me to inquire about my day. To my dismay, my mother's colleague – a close family friend – went into the guest room and immediately came back out with an expression that alerted my mother that someone else was in the room. Stricken with disappointment, my mother assumed that I was in an intimate relationship. Even though I tried telling her that it was not so, my disheveled appearance of pretending – that is, my half-removed uniform, sent a negative message. As a result of my mother's broken trust, she transferred me to a different high school in an attempt to sever my relationship with this particular male friend. At that point in my life, the enemy bombarded my mind with thoughts that it was okay to engage in a promiscuous lifestyle since I was accused of living as such when I was not. Unfortunately, I succumbed to the enemy's deceit.

This experience sensitized me to the power of words, and the dangers of accusation in that, out of anger, my mother accused me of something that I was not guilty of which the devil used as a gateway to lead me to embrace a secretive sinful lifestyle. In the midst of carrying out my unwise decisions, my loving Heavenly Father would caution me through my parents, the Bible, and His servants. Most importantly, I am grateful that it does not matter how far you and I may have wandered from the Lord, *"If we confess our sins, [H]e is faithful and just and will forgive us our sins and purify us from all unrighteousness."* 1 John 1:9 (NIV)

The finale of my escapades with males came to an end when my mother told me about the death of my church peer whom I had a relationship with. Overcome with grief, and a recognition that God was speaking directly to me through the death of my peer, I locked myself in the bathroom to pray for forgiveness. Upon leaving that bathroom as a seventeen-year-old girl, I experienced a phenomenal spiritual renewal that grounded me in Jesus Christ for life! God removed all the guilt, shame, and anguish from my past. That is, whenever the enemy reminded me of my faults and the past, the Holy Spirit would give me a sense of inner peace to know that God had already forgiven me of my sins, and had started a new chapter in my life – a covenant-keeping season. Therefore, we must believe the Word of God irrespective of our past in order to rebuke the devil whenever he attempts to throw our messed-up experiences in our faces. In fact, *"…where the Spirit of the Lord is, there is liberty"* (2 Corinthians 3:17, KJV). Hence we have freedom from the shackles of our past and a renewed mind!

In all of our experiences, we should choose to see the hand of God working things out for our benefit and for His glory; notwithstanding the fact that some of what you and I may encounter and experience are consequences of our actions. To that end, it behooves us to seek the Lord for wisdom as to how we must respond to our circumstances. For instance, Joseph was deeply hurt by his brothers in that they not only contemplated killing him but also sold him into slavery (see Genesis 37:18-28). When Joseph saw his brothers two decades later, he had the authority to punish them for what they had done to him. However, through God's compassion, rather than chastising his brothers, he forgave them and provided for their needs. As a result of Joseph's relationship with the Almighty God, he knew how to employ an attitude of forgiveness, love, and care despite the horrific experience between him and his brothers.

Joseph declared, *"You intended to harm me, but God intended it all for good. He brought me to this position so I could save the lives of many people"* (Genesis 50:20, NLT). This scripture reveals that God orchestrates our lives to impact the lives of others. In other words, this chapter – my personal story exemplifies that even though it seemed as if the devil had destroyed my life through a promiscuous lifestyle – of me walking a path of self-destruction, the Lord was more than able to save, sanctify, and empower myself to share the blessed hope of a transformed life, worthy of living in Jesus Christ.

I have had the firsthand experience of God healing me from every physical, spiritual, and mental debris that I had entangled myself with through having multiple partners. The Word of God is powerful to change and maintain us when we commit all our ways to Him. Essentially, you and I ought to obey the leading of the Holy Spirit and meditate on the Word of God in order to live out our transformed lives to please Him and witness to those around us. Significantly, no matter how troubled your life may have been or currently is, Jesus Christ will make a way for you to have a purposeful future in terms of making you an overcomer.

As a result, He will equip and empower you through the Holy Spirit and His Word to bless those you encounter.

It is imperative to share our stories and be transparent so that people can understand how God has delivered us from the enemy; where we now live fulfilled lives despite the ungodly paths that we had taken. Many times, the devil tries to hold us hostage in our minds with feelings of disgrace to the extent of muting us through fear so that we do not tell our experiences of how God has pulled us out of some mucky situations. As such, I want to challenge you today to remove those spiritual lip seals and (in your own way) declare the faithfulness of the Almighty God in your life. That is, identify some turbulent seasons that God has saved you from, and encourage someone. And, this is also a moment to encourage yourself to reflect on your actions to measure if you are living that transformational life.

During my rocky relationship with my mother, who I am indebted to for not turning her back on me, she kept praying and discerning how best to manage my erratic behavior. As a result of her consistent prayers, as well as my conviction (triggered by the death of my male Christian friend) to stop living a double life, God created an opportunity for my mother and me to travel overseas for her annual vacation. Preoccupied with thoughts of how I would tolerate her in the same room for six weeks, my frame of mind was not prepared for what the Lord was about to do. Beloved readers, those six weeks turned out to be the beginning of the greatest relationship a mother and daughter could ever have.

A couple of days after our arrival in Canada, a special young man – a family member of the household where we were staying – came by to introduce himself and welcome us. At first, I had no interest in him, but over the period of six weeks, we spent time at prayer meetings, family dinners, and causal outings. Throughout our meetings, to my surprise, my mother was unbothered by my growing friendship with this particular male. Further to this, the Holy Spirit revealed to me that he would become my husband. A week remaining before my return to Jamaica, the said male proposed to me. He assured me that he would wait until I completed teacher's college before getting married.

My answer was a resounding yes in that "*…[I knew] that God cause[d] everything to work together for [our] good…*" (Romans 8:28, NLT). Importantly, at the time of the engagement, I was two months away from celebrating my eighteen birthday; whereas he was about to celebrate his twenty-first birthday within a month. Additionally, this male friend openly shared his intention of marriage with my mother. As a result, my mother and I spent time praying together for the will of God to prevail in my life pertaining to a life partner.

Who would have thought that my broken relationship with my mother earlier in the year would have blossomed into a beautiful mother-daughter friendship to the extent that I refer to my mother as my heartbeat? God supernaturally transformed our relationship in that a renowned minister prophesied to us (after we returned to Jamaica) about our newly formed mother-daughter bond that God had ordained. My mother and I were in awe of God because this minister could not have known about the mending of our relationship beforehand except by the Holy Spirit.

Based on my experience, I know that God will mend every broken relationship in our lives that we give to Him. Most importantly, He will help us to make sense of our daunting and unpleasant experiences so that He can minister to others through us of His saving grace. However, you must believe that God will transform your life regardless of what your natural eyes see. We have to put our faith to work by spending time studying God's Word and living accordingly.

In order to cast our anxieties on the Lord who deeply cares for us (1 Peter 5:7), we need to *"...live by faith, not by sight"* (2 Corinthians 5:7, NIV). Thus God has already set the plans He has for us in motion since the day we were born. So, you and I should build our relationships with Him on a daily basis to discern the right actions and decisions to make.

For those dark years of my teenage life – making the wrong choices – I felt empty, unhappy, broken, and constantly worried as a result of not only entertaining the lies of the devil but also acting them out. As such, I have made a commitment to encourage the hearts of God's people, especially young people, to steer away from the enemy's trap, and focus on God who will guide them on the right path. And, exemplify the wisdom of the Lord by not only learning from their mistakes but also from those around them to avoid actions that can cost them their health and even their lives.

In closing, transparency (in our testimonies) is of critical importance to create an impact for the glory of God. I am confident that the God who gave me a spiritual makeover will do even more for you. Ask Him!

It is noteworthy that my fiancé and I had an intimate-free engagement for three years until we got married. To date, we have been married for sixteen years with three beautiful children.

Significantly, do not give up on yourself. Even when people may have condemned you for your actions, know that God will forgive you and bless you with a fulfilled future.

 Shelleanne Hardial, PhD is the registrar and administrator at the Covenant International University and Seminary Canada campus and is a trained elementary teacher with a PhD in Education. She is a born-again black Jamaican Canadian Christian, a wife, and a mother of three beautiful children. Shelleanne believes in God's transformational power that is exemplified through individual and collective stories for His glory. She is passionate about spiritual and educational empowerment in the lives of God's people, especially young people. Shelleanne has volunteered in various roles such as a youth coordinator for over ten years at Covenant of Promise Ministries

- shelleannehardialbooks.ca
- kingofglory844820206.wordpress.com
- shelleanne.hardial
- shelleannehardial
- SistaShelleanne

CHAPTER SIX - Meg Knight

Attitude

"Your Attitude determines your Altitude." This is a phrase that is commonly used, but how many know that your attitude will take you where your character cannot take you?

It is so important to have a positive attitude during your Transformation stage. Never react to the debris that's coming at you. The tempest will rage, and the water will come above your head at times, but do you know if you swim against the waves, or even try to fight and react, you use up unnecessary energy? And you will get tired, and frustrated, and then begin to speak negative words – even wanting to curse God.

Let's take a look at the example of Job, a man who loved God so much. He was a faithful and just man who knew no sin. However, after the approach of Satan to test Job, we know the story of how he remained calm. The bad news kept coming, the words of defeat were coming, and he heard the voices of men telling him that he was foolish and that he should curse God and die. Job wasn't going to bow down to the voice of men. He proclaimed, "Though he slay me, yet will I trust in him."

The problem with us is that we panic during our storm. If you and I didn't have purpose, if we were not a threat to the devil, there is no way he would be tormenting your spirit. There is no way all hell would have been broken loose in your life.

At a very tender age, the Lord placed a special anointing upon my life. Not understanding who I was, whose I was, and what it was that I had, the enemy decided to play with my mind. After losing my mother at a very young age – she was my strength, my strong tower, the one who would show me the way to live when she went unto God – I became exposed to the hands of the devil. The Bible tells us that the devil is like a roaring lion, walking about seeking those that he can devour.

I became so exposed to the world and the sins of the world that I found myself in situations and circumstances I could not remember getting into. I was always in the wrong places with the wrong people.

There was a season in my life when I gave room to the devil. I allowed the devil to access my personal files. I slowly started to see my world tumbling down; things were falling apart in my life.

I lost friends – the ones who I stood by, the ones who I grew up with, the ones who I gave to and in trouble for. And when the tables were turned, I was abandoned and called names that I wouldn't dare put in this book.

I was going through a stage of depression, anxiety, and panic attacks. I was taking medication just to stay high so that I wouldn't feel the pain of separation, loneliness, abandonment, lack of self-worth, insecurities, not being good enough, and the fear of the unknown. I tried so hard to be accepted in a world that was filled with rage, lies, and deceptions.

I had the opportunity to see things unfold before my eyes; things that I never thought a woman of God like me would experience in life.

There was a point in my marriage when I couldn't find myself. I was drowning deep into a world that wasn't my own. I became a stranger to myself; you can become a danger to your own life. It doesn't matter what I did. I could just pick myself up.

What I did not understand was that God had a special seal upon my life, but somehow, I couldn't identify what that was. And even though I was not able to understand the calling of God upon my life, I wouldn't accept my desired assignment. I was trying so hard to change my family dynamics and save my marriage.

I almost missed my Transformation season due to my attitude.

I gave room for the devil to come into my life through many different channels. First of all, the devil used my marriage as an access door. My relationship became a distraction full of unfaithfulness, infidelity, arguments, and fights – just a big mess. Of course, as humans, the goal is to fix what is broken. Nothing else mattered except to see happiness. So, when I didn't see God doing his job – coming through and fixing this problem for me, I got more frustrated and irritated. I would get angry when people came, encouraged me, and mentioned the name of Jesus. I was ready to walk away from that conversation.

I just didn't want to hear anything about the name of Jesus, or purpose, or gifting, or anointing, so I turned to drinking. Wow! This was where I would block out the world by drinking and feeling amazing. My body would be numb to the things of the world. I was in a zone of my own…until that feeling disappeared.

This particular struggle has been my biggest downfall. It crippled my life and also took me out of my state of depression.

During my marital issues, with all that was taking place, I truly had no clue what to do. I believed I had tried everything humanly possible to fix what was broken. However, I never once went to God and asked him for help. So I was even drifting further away from God. I remember working at a particular store, and while working there, many old relationships with friends and family members were established because, of course, they wanted discounts or link-ups. Due to the state of mind that I was in, I didn't care as long as I had people who would make me feel good and I could do something good for them at any cost. I was happy.

This was due to the carelessness of my attitude and the resentment I had toward myself. I was looking for something which I thought they could give to me. I was lost and had no self-worth. Most of my days I spent crying because everything in my life was broken. I just couldn't rise up – it didn't matter how I tried.

I was a walking mess, almost like the walking dead. I looked alive on the outside, but on the inside, I was a danger to myself – toxic, just a hot mess.

I allowed myself to fall into a trap that only God alone could have rescued me from. I started giving away the merchandise where I was working. The truth was I couldn't help myself. It's almost like I found an inner joy by giving away these things to people. I hardly took anything for myself because I was just looking out for others and listened to many of their stories.

One day when I was home, I heard a small voice say, *"Do not go back to the job. Just quit."* I thought it was my mind playing tricks on me. Then another day when I was scheduled to work, I heard the same voice say, *"Do not go to work."* I ignored the voice again because my relationship with God was unstable. I had disobeyed him and taken matters into my own hands. I came out from under the covering of my father, yet He was still looking out for me.

So, I remember going to work that particular day, and somehow, I felt a heaviness in my spirit. I just couldn't tune in because the eyes of men are blinded by their sins. I was never looking at God. I was always looking at my sins, my issues, and feeling sorry for myself.

During my shift, I was called to the office and I was asked if everything was okay. I wasn't acting like myself. Then I broke down in tears. During my entire dilemma, no one ever asked me how I was doing. Everyone wanted to tell me about Jesus and the calling on my life, but not once had they asked what I was feeling. No one knew that this was all a setup for my failure and my deliverance.

When I broke down, I told the manager that I felt like giving up. I just wanted to end my life because the problems were too much – the lack, the broken marriage. I just could not find myself. I had no feelings in my body, soul, or spirit.

Not knowing that those words cannot be used lightly coming up in a conversation, immediately the police were contacted. Here came more trouble. The people that I had allowed to come into the store to take merchandise, or that I gave to, they were watching me. This was a setup from the Father himself. No, the devil didn't do this. You see, God really does have a purpose for my life, and this particular assignment, nobody else can do…except me.

I was escorted out of the store by two police officers. To spare me the shame and embarrassment, they did me the honor and waited until they reached the police car outside to handcuff me and place me under arrest. With tears running down my eyes, I was speechless. I am not one to ever lie, so that is not something that I could have done. I chose to remain silent.

Yes, each of us will give a personal account to God (Romans 14:12).

At this point in my life, it was no longer me that was in control. I was afraid because I didn't want to lose my children. The company wanted me to pay back over six thousand dollars. So this is the funny part of the story: some of the people that I gave to and allowed to come and take things for their children and family members during that Christmas season, when I told a few of them what had happened, a few helped with the cost in a positive way. Yet, the ones that were considered my friends stabbed me in the back. They turned against me, called me a liar, and said that I just wanted their money. The names they called me were absolutely shameless…and they abandoned me.

So here I was, alone again to face this affliction, this tribulation. I couldn't say anything to my family because I was so ashamed.

This sort of predicament was uncomfortable. I became humbled and I was silent because there were no friends to turn to. I had a few options at this moment. The lawyer himself couldn't help me because I didn't even have money to pay him. At this point, the company wanted me charged and sentenced to six months in jail. The truth is that I didn't run to God immediately and beg his hands. I was still in shock from the fact that so-called friends who I jeopardized my job and sanity for walked away and left me to suffer and die. I felt like I was locked away in a solitary prison and it was me against the four walls with no one to talk to. I turned to a few people for help. Let me tell you that when you are in a sticky situation, you will know exactly who is for you and who is against you.

It is important for me to move quickly away from the memories that destroy me. I can say that God came through for me. When this was taken to court, I had a few setbacks because I could not keep up with the lawyer's fees, so an attorney that I went to church with took on my case. Because I did not have the money to retain him, and he was a busy man, he told me to plead guilty to just get it over with. I know that God is the lifter of Meg because the prison gates did not want me. When justice demanded me to die, His grace and mercies showed up. I spent many days and nights crying – if only my pillow could talk. All the tears. God has a plan for my life, and even in my darkest hour, He showed up.

The Word of God declares, *"That weeping May endure for a night, but Joy comes in the morning."*

When the judge gave his rulings, I was placed under house arrest with the following instructions, *"You seem like a smart young lady. If I were you, I would get rid of those friends."* Those were my conditions.

I was only allowed to go to four places for three months: dropping my daughter at school, buying groceries, checking with my parole officer, and this is the funniest part, the judge told me that church was one of the conditions. I had to go to church.

When you try to abort the assignment, God will permit you to go through some painful experiences to correct you, and to bring you closer to Him. The calling of God is without repentance. Jonah is a perfect example. He rebelled against God's instructions to *"Arise, go to Nineveh, to preach the Word of God."*

Don't think God will ignore acts of defiance. Discipline comes. Reaction comes. God had called me for such a time and commanded me to lay hands upon the sick, to preach the Gospel. How can I use my anointed hands to steal, and heal?

God had put fire in my hands back in 1999 at a youth retreat, and he commissioned me to heal the sick, so can good and evil be associated with the same hands?

This is out of the character of the Father. He wasn't going to have it, so He had to humble me.

God, you love me too much that not only did you send your only son, Jesus, to die for me, but in my affliction, when I was in the darkest part of my life, in the gutter, when I was naked and ashamed, you still loved me. When friends walked away from me, you became my friend. You wiped away all of my tears. You told the devil, "Not this one." You closed the prison doors. Who could it be but you, Almighty God, life-giver, judge in the courtroom, my defender, my shield. You hide me under the shadow of your wings.

When the bible tells us that we have an advocate, indeed we have one. But remember, Job in his affliction remained faithful. He kept his composure and did not react to the voices that he heard in the background. He kept his eyes on Jesus. He may have lost a lot in the beginning, but the end is when the reapers will reap. So, the process was painful; it was embarrassing, I may have lost some people, and God will allow you to walk in the shadows of death, but be sure that He will never leave you or forsake you.

I stand upon the Word of God in Jeremiah 29:11:

"For I know the Plans I have for you," says the Lord. "They are plans for good and not to hurt you, but to give you and a future and hope."

In the end, God will get the ultimate glory. His name will be known among men, through my voice and Your deliverance. Thank you, Almighty God, for loving us.

In a time when it seems the prophets of God no longer exist, Meg Knight uses the rich prophetic anointing as evidenced in her life through her preaching, teaching, healing, and intercessor praying ministry. An ordained minister, she attended Tyndale Seminary. Meg is an itinerant minister and the founder of Broken but not Destroyed Ministries, empowering women to understand that although they may have encountered some of life's most difficult traumas, they can and do overcome by the Blood of the Lamb and by the word of their testimonies. She is also a prolific speaker, author, and Co-host of *Your Next Move Up*.

CHAPTER SEVEN - Dr. Helga A. Clarke

Take Action Against Procrastination

"Procrastination is the grave in which opportunity is buried."
Alyce Cornyn-Selby

Procrastination is our ability to postpone or delay doing something. It is an unpopular topic, but an age-old problem. Statistically speaking, 20% of adults are chronic procrastinators while approximately 80% - 95% of college students are enmeshed in some degree of procrastination. Some time ago, I began a deep introspective look at procrastination and its effect on my life. I penned this enigma detailing procrastination's versatility and power to disrupt, delay, and destroy the lives of those who buy into it.

I AM PROCRASTINATION

I am Procrastination! I am not your friend!

But I got you to believe me and even buy into my deceptions.

I'm extremely wealthy, I have robbed millions because foolishly they followed my directions.

My path is non-productive leading into futility,

but you ignored your bright future, by shunning your responsibilities.

I am Procrastination! I own you! I track you daily!

I put ideas in your mind of all the things you cannot do today,

and convince you that tomorrow is the better way.

I will never tell you the things you were capable of doing but too fearful to try…

It was much easier for you to believe me and let your destiny go by,

another day, another week, another month…

I am Procrastination! I am the thief of time! But you don't know that

because I keep you in the dark.

I give you energy for unnecessary things that keep you from getting a start.

I engineered games, social media, telephone, friends, and even sleep…

all good things to be used wisely, but I use it liberally because I play for keeps.

To keep you addicted…distracted…disillusioned…is my plan.

I am Procrastination! I do not speak the truth!

I take pleasure in lying to all those who choose to listen.

I am very convincing; I discern those who are apt to go down my paths

and lead them into a web of doubts, fears, chaos, my prison!
I let you spend your time occupied in temporary pleasure,
then later watched you shed a tear when finally, you are risen.

Choose not to listen to my fable, this nullifies my effect on your future,
you begin by not putting off for tomorrow the plans you have for today,
for when discipline is present, I cannot step in your way.
But you must make sure that anxiety and doubt are not tolerated,
because nothing can hinder your success when fear is obliterated,

I Am Procrastination!

As described in this enigma, I realized that procrastination had left a horrible trail of bad habits and greatly affected my life. You see, I am a visionary at heart and can share my vision and ideas with ease. I can passionately and strategically facilitate, participate, and watch those ideas become a project that can benefit others. But on the other hand, when given an unfamiliar or challenging task, I would put it on the back burner until the very last minute. Although I hate the stress and time constraints of the rush, I realized that it was almost normal for me to procrastinate when given a task outside of my comfort zone. I continued this pattern for a while until I had a come-to-Jesus moment that forced me to take inventory of my habits.

One year while pursuing my nursing degree, I proactively preregistered for my fall semester courses. Those courses were crucial as they were only offered in the fall. Failure to register for the fall courses or failing them would have resulted in a year's delay in my degree completion. Thus, I was very happy that I registered for all my required fall classes in advance. My only remaining task was to pay for the courses by the assigned date and my space in the class would be solidified. I could have made the payments prior to the assigned due date, but I became lackadaisical and placed the task on the "tomorrow" list.

On the "presumed" course payment deadline, I went to the registrar's office and stood in line for what seemed like an eternity. I finally made it to the window to pay my fees, only to be told that my scheduled payment date had passed, and all the courses that I had so meticulously chosen, were removed from my schedule. To add insult to injury, the other students who were on the waitlist to register for fall nursing courses had done so and the classes were completely full! I was devastated! I had to wait for the following fall semester when those classes were offered again! I was distressed and angry. But, at whom? It wasn't anyone's fault but mine. I procrastinated on something of importance to my future.

When procrastination is at play, work assignments, projects, examinations, everyday tasks, or even decisions are avoided until the very last minute. In hopes of completing the task, we throw ourselves into overdrive productivity, overwork our adrenaline, and cause our stress levels to skyrocket. Yes, the task will most likely get done, but the unnecessary pressure could have been avoided if the tasks were completed in small, timely bites.

I realize that it is not enough to know procrastination statistics or that it is *"the thief of time,"* but we must also recognize the subtleties at work behind the scenes of procrastination and how we can act against it. Awareness can produce positive changes. This methodology works in every area of our lives where negativity exists, including procrastination. In the next few pages, I want to identify some factors that may cause procrastination, how to recognize them, and steps to overcome them.

Procrastination: The Fear Factors

Fear is real! In some cases, fear can be easily identified. For instance, there was a time in my life when I was deathly afraid of certain critters. At the sight of them, I would be paralyzed with fear. Although I was mocked and laughed at, the fear of critters was my reality! And it took me many years to gradually overcome it. But in other cases, fear can be subtle or lay dormant in our lives. Although this fear is not readily seen, it is evident in its ability to delay, stall, or postpone our lives. The unseen fear is sometimes revealed in our actions or inactions and is a driving force behind procrastination.

So, how exactly does fear function as procrastination?

Fear of Being Criticized

Fear works in the underdeveloped areas of our lives. It can reveal itself through our emotions, low self-esteem, lack of confidence in ourselves, or even doubting our God-given abilities. For instance, let's consider criticism. Although constructive criticism is a tool to help us learn and grow, it is hard for some to receive it. Individuals who are unable to accept criticism tend not to commit or complete tasks out of fear of being criticized. They push tasks further and further away until forced to face them. They don't usually put forth their best as there is a fear that others may not like their work and will judge their efforts. The usual response of someone afraid of being criticized is, *"No one will like it anyway so what's the use?"*

Fear of Failure

When there is a fear of failure, we tend to freeze up and do nothing. But in freezing up and doing nothing, procrastination is given the right to stifle our productivity and bury opportunities.

Sometimes we look at the success of others and tell ourselves that it could not be us. We even add the term *"bad luck"* to describe our endeavors. As the American novelist Robert Mosley said, *"If it wasn't for bad luck, I'd have no luck at all."* But what a bleak and faulty way to view your life!

The reality is that life or your ability to complete a task has nothing to do with luck. But it has everything to do with us and the realization of who God has created us to be. We must act against this faulty thinking of "bad luck" and fear of failure as this will destroy our destiny. As a believer in Jesus Christ, the enemy will never show you the awesome person that you are. The enemy never wants God's children to know the glorious privilege given us to accomplish great things. He will never show you the glorious future that lies ahead. Instead, he chooses to reveal the areas of our lives that are still under construction. He magnifies our weakness to cause us to believe that we are incapable of accomplishing anything. He does that masterfully by using procrastination and fear factors against us.

Honestly, fear will always be with us, but it does not have to stop us. If you are a believer in Christ, know that fear is not from God. Thus, procrastinating is not of God. I believe it is Joyce Myers who said, *"Do it Afraid."* The Scripture admonishes us in 2 Timothy 1:7 (NIV) *"For the Spirit God gave us does not make us timid, but gives us power, love and self-discipline."* Therefore, anything that produces fear in us is of the devil and must be annihilated! Procrastination is a thief that robs you of your time, resources, opportunities, and causes much regret.

When the fear of failure becomes our bed partner, then we self-sabotage. We kill our triumphs before we even begin. We repudiate the Word of God and the truth of His promises over the shouts of the devil's lies. We were created to be successful. Our Father God has equipped us with all the tools necessary to accomplish our assignments, and there is no failure in God. Philippians 4:13 states *"I can do all things through Christ who strengthens me."* With that truth on the inside of us, we can reject the lie of the evil one and lean upon God for help. God has graced us with power and wisdom to prepare and execute every task with excellence! He is willing and able to help us.

Procrastination: The Lack Factor

Procrastination also reveals itself in our "lack." One may focus on their lack of education, lack of confidence, lack of resources, or lack of self-esteem. These lack factors talk us out of starting or completing assignments. "Lack" causes us to focus more on what we "think" we don't have than the assignments that need to be completed. But we must know that lack in one area of our lives does not determine lack in all areas. Not having a formal education doesn't mean you are not smart or cannot undertake what you are assigned to do.

I, too, once struggled with the "lack" factor. Prior to completing my formal education, I was asked to speak on a platform where other speakers had more letters behind their names than could be counted. And, of course, the enemy showed me my "lack" and made me feel disqualified for the assignment of speaking God's word. I almost fell for it! As each speaker spoke, the more nervous I became. I felt as if I didn't belong. Although I had studied and prepared, I began to doubt my qualifications. I even wondered to myself, *"What am I doing here?"*

But despite the enemy's loud roars of lack, the confidence of God rose inside of me. I reminded myself that *"greater is He that is within me…"* and that God was my reason for being there on that platform. Whatever your lack, I just want to remind you today that God is greater. Whatever seems to be above your capabilities, God can give you confidence, strength, and strategy. He never disappoints!

Overcoming Procrastination

So how do we overcome procrastination?

First, let's identify who you are. *Are you a chronic procrastinator who puts everything off until the last minute? Or a situational procrastinator who shies away from a task that seems greater than your ability? Are you easily distracted? Do you have low self-confidence or always focus on what you lack? Is fear a factor?*

Why is this important? It is significant because if you can identify the tendency that causes procrastination then chances are, you can act against it.

For me, I noticed that I would hit the delay button on tasks that seemed overwhelming. So, now I focus on one or two things at a time. I research all aspects needed to complete the tasks and talk about the project with someone. In doing so, I receive feedback from others and realize that I'm far more knowledgeable and capable of completing the task than I thought. My confidence in my ability to complete the task ultimately grows.

Secondly, practice breaking your task or assignment into small bites and begin as soon as you can. For example, I am currently taking a Masterclass course that is teaching me how to tell my life story authentically and engagingly. Each week, we are given the assignment to practice our story. As a word of advice, my Masterclass Coach recommended that I rehearse my stories twice per day. Honestly, at first, I had a problem with it. Why? Because my previous tendency would be to wait until the last minute and rehearse before the class begins. But after rehearsing my life story twice a day, "no more, no less" as per my Coach, I realize I am more confident and less stressed.

Think of it this way. Imagine being a college student and studying for an exam the night before. You might pass the exam, but how much information was retained? What if you would have read a chapter and studied key points daily? It is more likely that you would have retained more of the information and quite possibly become skilled in the subject matter.

Finally, it would be helpful to keep a daily to-do list. This helps me greatly! Whatever was not finished on one day, rewrite it on the top of the following day's agenda. In this manner, it will always be fresh on your mind. If you cannot get it all done, work on what you can. The key is to just begin!

Conclusively, I must confess that it took me a while to really understand the depth of procrastination, its effects, and how it can cause us to miss great opportunities. If we recognize and deal with the factors that cause procrastination, it does not have to be the grave in which opportunity is buried. Procrastination causes regrets and is not of God! He desires for us to live our best life in every way possible. God wants us to be strategic, diligent, and disciplined. It is not His desire to see His children under the great stress and strain of procrastination. We have been given the greatest gift from God to be able to change our situation and by His grace, we can!

Dr. Helga A. Clarke is a passionate pastor-teacher, robust intercessor, and strategic motivator. She is the founder of Daughters of Destiny International and Beyond Limitations Coaching Group, where she equips women to reach their full potential both socially and spiritually. Dr. Clarke is a nurse by profession, holds degrees in Ministry, and has accumulated various other certifications. Dr. Helga's heart for missions has led her worldwide sharing the Gospel. She is the author of *"Forgiveness Is Not an Option,"* a testament of forgiveness and love. She is a wife and mother of four adult children, ten grandchildren, and two great-grandchildren.

CHAPTER EIGHT - Kerry Gordon

Outside of Myself

"Come, let us reason together says the Lord." (Isaiah 1:18)

God has invited His people on many occasions to "come." His call is to invite an action on our part and to bring us into His presence. Moses was invited by God on many occasions to "Come." He called him to *"Come up to the Lord, you and Aaron, Nadab, and Abihu, and seventy of the elders of Israel, and worship you afar off"* (Exodus 24:1a).

Is God calling us today to Him? Yes, He is. He wants to show us the path to life and He cares enough to call our attention to areas in our lives that need to be corrected. God's people had sinned continuously, but God continued to call them out of their disobedience into obedience with Him.

He wanted them to have a conversation concerning their sins and He would in His mercy remove every trace of their sins. Their sins *"though they be like scarlet, would be as white as snow; though they be red like crimson, would be as wool"* (Isaiah 1:18). God is still calling us today, to "come" and have a little talk with Him.

Dear Readers,

I can still remember one particular day when I had one of those "Come, let's have a talk" day with our Heavenly Father. I cannot say that it started off as one of those pleasant conversations that gave me that special gracious feeling.

Quite to the contrary.

His Words, *"Come, let me show you,"* revealed a side of me that took me quite aback. The picture of "me" left me feeling chagrined in that I allowed the "little things" to distract my focus. I had to repent speedily before my Heavenly Father for the attitude that was displayed.

I am not sure if you have ever had one of those days where you were so focused on the little things, being just a little out of place, that you found that you were "outside of yourself." That is being outside of your normal self that you "think" you know. I have had one of those days and perhaps more of those days than I wish to remember where God had to give me an attitude check.

My focus had often shifted from gratitude to that of not a very grateful attitude. I have often felt as though things just never seem to be how I wish them to be; life with its ebbs and flows seems to have me whirling at a swifter speed than I can keep pace. However, I must stop to engage you with my experience of being "outside of myself."

The day began with the usual family routine. The buzzing of the alarm clock shook my husband from his deep sleep with a jolt. It seemed to scream, *"Time to rise and prepare to leave for work!"* Still blurry-eyed, he quietly tip-toed across the room in an effort to not disturb me.

However, his kind gesture was thwarted as he accidentally bumped into the night table. I woke with a start as he apologized and disappeared into our ensuite.

He emerged later to say his usual goodbyes and I mentally followed him outside of our room. I was accustomed to his usual. I know he would stop to peek through the window-covered blinds overlooking the front of our house. I smiled as I recall him taking a leaning stance as he tried to peer into the darkness of the pre-dawn. I changed position as I heard the one stair creak softly as he crept down the stairs. I heard the opening – and closing – of the garage door, catching sight of the headlights of our vehicle rounding the corner.

I snuggled deep beneath my covers as I tried to fall back asleep, frowning as I remembered that most of my night had been spent rather restlessly.

I was unable to quiet my thoughts of the previous day for some unknown reason. The ruffled sheets and the pain thundering through my weary limbs were a constant reminder of that.

Thankfully, I was off for the day and my fatigued body had anticipated this morning of rest.

However, this was not to be as I heard my daughter entering the hallway to get ready for her morning commute to school.

I heard as she quickly descended the stairs, escaping the one creaking stair. Unfortunately, the noise that ascended from the kitchen was still enough to erase the thoughts of sleeping.

I soon heard the front door open and close with a firm bang as she left the house. Propping myself on my elbows, I peered through my bedroom window. I observed her huddled form, dressed in winter garbs as she quickly crossed the street, almost engulfed in the scant daylight. I watched as she went past the last house to enter the main street.

I fell back with a thud, plumping and rearranging the pillows, hoping that this motion would summon sleep. Just as I thought that we had just about reached a compromise, I heard a loud "Bang!"

My head shot up off the pillows, dazed and confused. I listened intently as I heard my son as if he was falling off his bed. He bounced into my room with a note to be signed for his teacher. I thought, *"Now?"* I grunted as I propped myself up on my elbow. *"Not last night, but now?"*

He switched on the lamp at my mumbled instruction as he handed me the paper. I blinked as my tired eyes struggled to focus on what was written there. After a quick read, I signed the note and handed it back to my son. He bounded out of my room to descend to the familiar place, you guessed it, the kitchen.

The clanging and banging of the pots and pans sounded like an orchestra in total disharmony. The loud singing of the kettle seemed to scream its impatience to be done with its duty of providing hot water. I listened to the clamor until I heard the garage door creak open as the chain jumped in place and jangled shut behind my son. I saw him bounding with winged feet in a race against the clock and his own sprinting record. I shook my head in disbelief, but could not stop the endearing smile from cambering my lips. I observed the boundless energy of youth that seemed to devour each step in an agile, blistering manner.

I yawned, stretched, and listened to the silence that engulfed me. Ah, sweet rest. I remained in a motionless position, daring not to "scare" the sleep away. I felt my body relaxing as I drifted on Sleepy Isle. I was lulled farther away as if floating on the ocean, feeling peaceful at last. I am not sure how long my journey lasted, but when I awoke, I felt rejuvenated, ready to take on the tolls of the task at hand. I planned that my tasks should not take me too long as I had eliminated a few tasks last night, post-dinner. I had left an impeccable kitchen and was so sure that it would just be a matter of light cleaning. I soon discovered that my expectations would change in a moment.

The descent to the kitchen took me down the same route as my family; down the staircase, stepping over the one creaking stair. My first observation in my descent was shoe prints, yes, shoe prints on the clean wooden floors! I calmly reassured myself that it would just take a few seconds of mopping to remove and restore the floor to its shine again.

However, I was not prepared for what greeted me from the kitchen. I froze on entering as I viewed the stacks of dirty dishes, pots, pans, and utensils.

Half-eaten toasts and unfinished beverages told the tale of lateness. Teens who were too late to clean up their mess. I strolled over to the kettle to prepare water to make a hot cup of Earl Grey tea.

I plugged the kettle in, but there was no humming sound or any indicator light. The kettle had been quite temperamental these days; perhaps in protest of being overworked. I did the usual jangling of the cord, maneuverings of the switch, plugging and unplugging of the cord.

Finally – either in defeat or acquiesce – I heard the kettle roaring, and later, the shrill whistle that indicated that the water was ready. I chose a large cup, made the tea, and retreated to the Family room to decide on my next course of action.

I hugged the warm cup with curled fingers and delightedly sipped the steaming liquid, smiling as its warmth branched through my body. My stomach appreciated the warmth and comfort, but it was not enough to erase the sight of the mess that was piled in the kitchen.

I stared into the gas fireplace and watched as the sparks leaped off the logs. This seemed symbolic of what I was feeling, as the anger-like flames leaped from the pit of my stomach, burning in my chest.

I wearily padded off to survey the disorder and contemplated a strategic plan. The stove seemed like a good place to begin, so I set about the task of scrubbing furiously at the stubborn grease that was left on its surface. I felt a tinge of accomplishment... until I stopped to look back at the sink and all the other areas.

The sight of the mess stirred something akin to fury within me as I remembered the earlier orchestral sounds. I was vigorous in the clanging and banging of the pots, pans, wooden utensils, and metal utensils. *"Why am I the only one who is left to perform this task?"* I muttered heatedly to myself.

As I went on, I felt a Martha-like spirit take hold of me, feeling as though I had been abandoned by Mary. I scrubbed furiously in a vain effort to restore order. I was thoroughly displeased as I continued to mutter, with the disorderly mess that I was surrounded by, doing very little to quell my mounting frustration.

Suddenly, I heard the distinct voice of the Holy Spirit. My hands froze as I heard the words, "*Kerry, come up here and let me show you what you look like when you are behaving in this way.*"

I felt myself being transported upwards toward the kitchen cupboard. I felt as if I was standing on a chair looking down on me, standing and arguing and looking oh so angry! I could not believe that was me! My only response was, "*Not good.*" The Spirit responded, "*Not good.*" I felt my deflated self descending to the ground. I was humbled and found excerpts of Solomon's writings flooding my senses.

The first of the text was from Proverbs 21:19: *"It is better to dwell in the wilderness, than with a contentious and an angry woman."*

I thought to myself that I would never want to be referred to as a "contentious woman." I reflected on my attitude and repented.

I was now transformed from Martha, who was concerned with serving and having everything perfect, to Mary who was willing to sit at Jesus' feet and learn of Him.

Martha was the perfect hostess, who probably loved to have a welcoming, fresh, and clean house for her guests, but omitted the most important part. Her heart!

She needed to seek to learn from the Great Teacher and to have a shift in her attitude. Martha asked the Lord if He did not care that her sister Mary was not helping her. She wanted the Master to send her sister *"to give [her] a helping hand"* (Luke 10:38-42).

Our Master was not concerned about the temporal but rather the spiritual. He knew that He did not have a lot of time left to spend on earth and He was more concerned with preparing others for His work.

Mary was eager to learn of Him and so, had the right attitude. I, on the other hand, was like Martha, occupied with the temporal things and having things in perfect order. The Spirit taught me a new lesson on being mindful of the spiritual things instead of being absorbed with the temporal. I realized how easy it was for our gaze to shift from God.

My attitude changed as I now went about my tasks with thoughtfulness, calmly scrubbing the etched particles from the pots and pans. My previous attitude had been that of being unthankful and not honoring God in all things. I was reminded of Paul's writing. *"Whether therefore you eat, or drink, or whatsoever you do, do all to the Glory of God."* 1 Corinthians 10:31.

This came across in a tangent way as I had never really given thought that scrubbing pots, and pans, and cleaning a home was a way to honor God. My thoughts were more on the side of having a clean and organized home.

We should not forget that our service to God also comes in how we treat our family and our friends. My trip outside of myself elevated me to a higher plane that showed me not to be bothered with the "little things" of life. I should maintain an attitude of gratitude, being thankful to God for a supportive and loving family, food, and a place to call home. Some folks would have been thankful for these pleasures of life. I sighed as somehow I was reminded of a saying from my grandmum. She was adept at finding appropriate words for every situation. She often quoted this poem, which was written by Mary Arlis Stuber:

Thank God for dirty dishes,
They have a tale to tell.
While others may be hungry,
We're eating very well.
With home, health, and happiness,
I shouldn't want to fuss.
By the stack of evidence,
God's been very good to us.

I realized that a view of me outside of myself was not a very comforting sight, but God had to show me so that He could lead me into the paths that I should go. Has God had to take me on a few trips? Oh yes! I am learning to view myself as God sees me and to ask Him to work on my attitude in various situations. So, my dear readers, as you have journeyed with me, I just wish to remind us that we never know what things will trigger certain attitudes in us.

Sometimes it's the "little things" that get us. Will we allow that to thwart our progress in God? No. I am thankful that He cares enough to correct my attitude and lead me back on the right path.

God needs me to be "outside of myself" and trust Him when I feel afraid and unsure of a task or a path to take. He needs me to not look at the situation surrounding me, but instead to look up to Him.

Kerry Gordon has been a Registered Practical Nurse (RPN) for over 25 years. Her interest in caring for those who have health challenges was born at an early age with the desire to help the sick and suffering. Kerry acquired an education in nursing despite many setbacks and firmly believes in "nursing from the heart." She accepted the Lord at a young age and used her singing talent in ministering as a worship leader  and group leader. Kerry's goal is to continue ministering in whatever capacity that the Lord chooses and to share her experiences with others through writing.

CHAPTER NINE - Sharon Walters

Sisterly Love

"And be not conformed to this world but be transformed by the renewing of your mind, that he may prove what is that good and acceptable and perfect will of God." Romans 12:2

Growing up during the 50s through the 70s was very difficult. It was a revolutionary time due to many organizations, clubs, and demonstrations that called for political and civil changes. These marches, strikes, or demonstrations resulted in demonstrators being beaten, imprisoned, or killed for the cause of community and eventually worldwide changes to bring about world peace. Unfortunately, many did not live to see the implementation of the changes they demonstrated for.

In my country, Guyana, racism and colorism were rampant. Once a person was of fair complexion, the general approach was they could do no wrong. Furthermore, these individuals were often afforded preferential treatment to the extent of being placed in levels of authority, often without the necessary qualifications. This bias was seen in every aspect of life through communities, social gatherings, schools, and churches.

    This was reflected in my home, as the preferential treatment of one child demonstrated colorism compared to the darker children. My parents made eight children, of which I am the oldest. During my early childhood, I lived with my aunt and uncle, who had no children of their own but were wonderful parents to me. They owned a bakery with a storefront and would provide the community with delicious cakes and pastries, which people enjoyed. It was not uncommon to see a line of customers waiting in the early evening for freshly baked bread or cakes. I loved my aunt and uncle very much because they taught me how to be self-sufficient and productive. Their home was filled with love and laughter. However, one day when I returned home from school, my aunt introduced me to a visitor who was dressed formally. During the introduction, I was informed that he was my stepfather, and I was to leave my aunt's home immediately to live with my mother and him. My aunt and I were devastated by this turn of events, and we reluctantly packed my things.

    The journey to my new home was long and adventurous. I enjoyed seeing the unique sceneries and places and listening to the descriptions and explanations given to me by this new father. During the ride, this newfound stranger instructed me that I was to call him Daddy or Father, moving forward. When we arrived, my mom was ecstatic to see me and at first, things seemed to be very promising. I was attending a new school in the city and made new friends. The school was about to close for the long summer holidays, so one day, I asked my mom if I could visit my aunt during the holidays. Her reply was, *"No, and you are never to ask that again."* I tried to ask further questions but was told that I was being ungrateful to her and my stepfather because they did so much for me. I could not understand this and I cried for many days, which upset my parents and caused me to be grounded. With this punishment came my realization that life for me was about to change.

Soon, I learned to cook, do laundry by hand, and clean the house as they both had to go to work. Then the babies started arriving, I had to skip school to assist at home while my mom was hospitalized, and looking after the babies was added to my house chores. Even when they woke up at night, it was expected that I would get up and attend to their needs until they returned to sleep. If these chores were not completed in a timely and proper manner, my mom would get the whip and I was beaten severely with no place on my body exempt from this torment. Sometimes, she would complain to my stepfather, and he would beat me on my hand or the soles of my feet, which was always so painful.

I must say I love my family, and despite all this, there were happy moments. For example, everyone's birthday was celebrated at home. My mother baked a cake, some delicious food was cooked, and a birthday celebration would be done. They would take us on picnics and visit history and educational buildings and sites. When my father was transferred to other areas of the country, the whole family would go with him. In this way, we traveled quite a lot and saw many interesting and scenic places, which was pleasing; however, it was difficult to maintain friendships because transfers in those days were sudden and unexpected. The one constant thing was the ability to attend church no matter where we were. My parents ensured after settling down in the new home, we all got dressed and attended church – mostly an Anglican Church but occasionally a Pentecostal Church. At the age of nine, I had my First Communion and Confirmation in the Anglican Church.

However, I loved the Pentecostal Church because the scriptures were broken down so I could understand. At that time as well, every child who attended the Pentecostal Sunday School was given a pamphlet or booklet to take home. These circulations explained scripture most realistically and simply, enhancing my interpretation and understanding. I loved reading these in my spare time. I learned about praying, learning bible verses, and the way God expected us to live from day to day. So, one Sunday while attending the Pentecostal Church, I decided to dedicate my life to the Lord. When I did this, I felt so light and happy in my spirit until I told my parents. They were offended and we were not allowed to attend that Church for quite a while. It was a devastating moment for me, however, the ray of sunshine for me was my ability to keep the leaflets and booklets that I received from Sunday School which I continued reading.

Eventually, the constant whipping and daily chores made me feel unwanted and unloved in the home. I started praying to God for deliverance in any form. Running away was not an option because my community would have been alerted and on watch due to my stepfather's status. The only option was to stay and endure the negative words and actions displayed to me daily. Some of those statements included, *"You are so stupid," "Your sister is nicer than you,"* and so on. These words for me felt as though someone was rubbing salt in an open and fresh wound. They stung, they hurt, and they were degrading. As a result, I became wary of people, shunning them and avoiding building connections at any cost. And being afraid of my parents, I was hesitant to describe these feelings or the impact their words and actions were having on my daily life.

One day I was given a copy of the New Testament. I started reading the book of Romans and Chapter 12, Verse 2 kept repeating in my mind:

"...and be ye transformed by the renewing of your mind."

The more I thought about it, the more I tried to live it daily. I prayed about my resentment toward my parents and I prayed for a new place to live where I could be happy. I had a friend whose daughter was in my class, for by this time I was a student in the teachers' college. I introduced this dear friend to my parents and she introduced her mother to them. Well, on her wedding night, she and her husband died. After the funeral service, my deceased friend's mother asked me if I would consider living with her family and assisting her with her granddaughter who had just lost her mother, my friend. I told her I would let her know later. God was in control, but I did not know that at the time.

My mother went to visit my friend's mother unbeknownst to me about a week after the funeral. During their conversation, it was agreed that I would stay with my friend's mother and take care of her granddaughter. On my arrival home, when my mother told me the news, I had to control myself from showing my enthusiasm. My mother said, *"You may leave in two weeks."*

I was so happy and eager to leave because at home I was sharing a bedroom with my sister, and where I was going, I would have a bedroom for myself. This would be a place to call home, where the preparation of my meals was not my sole responsibility but the shared responsibilities of a caring adult; a place where I would no longer have to do laundry for a household of ten or attend to babies. What a Mighty God we serve.

I was fifteen years old when I moved to my friend's mother's house. It was a happy moment for me. I hugged my parents and bid them goodbye when they dropped me off. Upon entering my new residence, everything was prepared for me and I discovered that I even had a bathroom for myself. I continued to live with this family for ten years.

My new little sister was glad to have me; she was nine years old. Because I was her teacher at school as well, we had to create boundaries, but we were happy with each other. She had her bedroom which she had to clean and maintain in an orderly manner while learning simple house chores as well. We were free to enter each other's bedrooms with discretion. I never returned home which annoyed my mother very much, but I thought it was best for my development. I would arrange to meet my parents at a restaurant or park in the city after work. We would meet and chat, eat and have fun, and then I returned to my new living place that my God had created.

In retrospect, this early experience taught me that sometimes prayer alone does not work. We need to apply God's Word where it hurts. If I had not changed my sulking, sorry for me, and disappointing attitude by reading God's Word and applying it to my situation daily to renew my mind and allow *"the joy of Lord to be my strength"* Nehemiah 8:10, I would have missed my blessings and my future might not have been so bright. My deliverance took some time but when it did occur, it was swift and there was no confusion nor sorrow. God did everything in a timely and orderly fashion. I also learned that nothing is too hard for God. For example, when my friend's mother asked for my assistance with her granddaughter, I became fearful to talk to my parents about such a situation, but God intervened on my behalf.

I would like to thank Almighty God for accepting me as His child, and for the guidance, provision, and protection He has provided throughout my life. There were many times when miraculous things happened in my life, but they always happened in God's timing with His divine intervention because He is always right. I would also like to thank Him for His Joy which is a blessing only He can give. It's a joy that does not discriminate or condemn but brings true happiness and contentment.

If you would like to experience this God-given joy and peace in your life, please pray the following prayer:

Dear Heavenly Father, you are the Alpha and Omega, the beginning and end of every aspect of my life. So, I give praise and honor to your Holy name. I ask for forgiveness for my sins and for you to come into my heart and make me a new person. I thank you for accepting me as your child. Also, please take care of all negative emotions and situations in my life that are distracting me from achieving your goals for my life. May your will be done. Amen.

 Sharon Walters was born in Guyana, South America, where she attended elementary through to high school during her early years. She later attended the Cyril Potter College of Education (1978 – 1980) obtaining a Trained Teachers' Certificate, a Certificate in Computer Technology from The Technical College of St. Vincent and the Grenadines (1993 – 1995), and attended the Practical Nursing Programme at Mohawk College of Applied Arts and Technology in Hamilton, Ontario (2012 – 2015). Sharon currently resides in Canada with her three children.

CHAPTER TEN - Lisa Patrick

...But God!

Ring, Ring!

"Hello?"

"Hi, Lisa. Do you have a moment to speak?"

"Yes..."

And just like that my world changed!

Okay, okay, let me start from the beginning...

"FOUR, FIVE, SIX...what is that?" I wondered to myself as I rubbed my hand over the side of my leg for the umpteenth time. I was just finishing up my second rep of squats and found a hard spot just above my knee on my left thigh. I cautiously checked the opposite leg; it didn't feel the same. *"I better get this checked*

out," I thought as my mind reverted to my grandmother who had lost her entire leg prematurely.

Heading to work the following morning, I remembered the clinic across the street. Not wanting to waste any more time, I took an early lunch and headed straight over. Thank God there was an opening. After explaining my dilemma, sadly, I was met with sarcasm from the doctor who told me that I worried too much and that it was more than likely just a muscle knot.

Considering this was only my second time visiting the clinic, I was unsure why he thought he knew me so well. He didn't even examine the area, not even a touch. Ignoring his remark, I asked him to send me for an x-ray or something. He chuckled, telling me it was unnecessary. I was indignant. Seeing the look on my face, he told me I was being overly dramatic and fearful. Narrowing my eyes at him, I was about to tell him something "DRAMATIC!" and right then the Holy Spirit impressed on my heart, *"Lisa, that's not Christ-like!"*

The LAST thing I wanted to be was Christ-like! But I stopped, paused, shifted my weight to the opposite leg, and breathed. Trying to muster up a smile through my gritted teeth, I said, *"For your information, I am not fearful! I am being cautious due to my family history."* He chuckled and suggested I get a bone x-ray which I found out at my follow-up appointment was negative. Smirking, he responded, *"See, I told you, it's nothing more than a muscle knot. It will clear up in a few days."* Annoyed, I thanked him (for what I don't know) as I walked out of his office frustrated, promising myself never to return. Walking back to work, I prayed, *"Lord, please help me find a better doctor."*

A few days later, a family friend suggested I go with her to her doctor and let him have a look. *"Besides, the most he could say is no,"* she joked. Though he wasn't taking new patients, he decided to examine me and wasted no time sending me for an ultrasound. Leaving the doctor's office, I was both nervous and relieved; grateful I was finally going to get some answers. A warm calm came over me as I remembered the scripture from Isaiah 26:3. *"You will keep (them) in perfect peace all who trust in you."* Unfortunately, the results came back inconclusive. The doctor shared his concerns and ordered an MRI. The pandemic backlog caused a two-month wait. At the appointment, the attendant shared it would take seven more days for the results. My calm persisted.

The morning after the appointment, I woke up restless, anxious, and not quite myself. I didn't want to get out of bed. I tossed and turned for some time trying to talk myself out of going to work. Remembering I had some overtime, I decided to go in later. I made it to the car, and just then my phone rang. I saw that it was the doctor's office calling.

"Hello?"

"Hi, Lisa. Do you have a moment to speak?"

"Yes, Doctor go ahead…"

"The results are back and Lisa…as I suspected, you have a tumor." The doctor paused and then continued, saying, *"Also, looking at the blood work, it's malignant and aggressive. We need to act now!"*

At that moment, everything slowed down. *"No, not again!"* I heard my mind scream. 2021 was proving to be quite a year. We almost lost my mom in January and my dad was just diagnosed with an illness two days prior.

One tear rolled down the inner corner of my right eye, coming to rest just above my upper lip. My eyes went blurry as everything around me faded. I could hear the sound of a car horn in the distance. My heart rate increased, seemingly growing louder with drum-like beats in my ear. I felt like all the air was leaving my body and there was nothing I could do to stop it. Then I heard it, like a soft caress. I searched my mind for its location. There it was again, a still small voice, a whisper – calling me, reassuring me. As the voice became clearer, my heart realized it was the Holy Spirit saying, *"This too shall pass!"*

Before my mind could formulate panic, I could feel trickling drops, like warm summer rain slowly saturating as it spread from the top of my head, rolling downwards. My feet tingled as the same feeling made its way upwards, the two converging, intensifying, and gradually consuming me.

"Wait a minute, I know this feeling!" I thought to myself. Not quite as extreme but still familiar, always present in moments of frustration. As the feeling permeated my being, the warmth restricted my mind from going down a dark hole.

"Lisa? LISA, are you still there?"

Hearing the urgency in his voice jarred me out of thought. I answered quickly, *"Yes, I'm here, Doctor."* After reassuring him I was fine, we made plans for the next steps.

As I got off the phone, my mind instantly drifted back to the feelings that now dominated me – feelings of repose and calm.

In my heart sang my comfort scripture, Psalm 46:10, *"Be still and know that I AM GOD!"* I continued to allow my mind to travel desperately where these feelings led. I could discern the safety thereof and I wanted more. Not wanting to hold back any longer, I surrendered to its all-consuming presence…Aaah Peace!

What I didn't know at the time was just how much this one experience would alter my outlook on life. It would increase my faith, reshape my speech, and revamp how I lived everyday life.

I sum up the next few months as heavenly acceleration and favor. I received a referral for the oncologist and was placed on the waitlist. To my surprise, I received a callback two days later reassuring me my referral came as a high priority. The following week I was in for an assessment, with a biopsy shortly thereafter.

By this time, the mass had grown aggressively from my knee to my hip, wrapping itself around my bone, entangling itself with my nerves and arteries, and causing anemia. It also occupied two of my four muscles, hampering my ability to walk. My surgical team shared that surgery was the best option as they feared I would be left with only 30% mobility, possibly bound to a wheelchair or at best a walker for life. Hearing their report, I took it to the Lord.

A few days later I received a call from the lead surgeon opting for a different root. Instead of surgery first, I would start with five weeks of radiation treatment with no need for chemotherapy. During treatment, physically I felt awful, fighting fatigue, excessive nausea, and emesis; spiritually my peace increased. My attendants asked, marveling at my constant happiness and lack of pain. I finally shared with a cheeky smile, *"This is what the joy of the Lord looks like."*

The final tests were in and surgery was set for the New Year. On January 9th, four days before my surgery, I was lying in my bed when I heard the Holy Spirit say, *"We are about to do surgery."* The voice was so audible that I jumped up looking around. Just then a searing pain entered my upper left thigh. It lasted just under a minute and then it was gone. I lay there a little stunned at first as feelings of gratitude inundated my heart.

Friends and family continually comment about my calmness. I can sum it up in two words: BUT GOD! For all the times I've told others to trust God, pray, and take Him at His Word, now was my test. God has shown himself strong many times in my life, but this was the **big** one! This reminded me of every lesson I've learned since coming to Christ. Everything I've heard, preached, prayed, taught, read, and experienced came down to this moment. Did I believe Jesus **for me**? If so, then my **attitude** needed to show that. This was my turning point!

So Yes, I believe in His blessings, promises, and healing written in Deuteronomy 28:1-14; yes, to Isaiah 53:5 gifted to us through the love and blood of Jesus Christ; yes, to Philippians 4:8 keeping a positive mindset. The truth is, these promises and many more are for **everyone** willing to say **yes**.

I've heard it said when you use the word but in a sentence, it negates everything said before. When I got ill, something **shifted** in me. I was faced with my **mortality**. With all the emotions pounding at my door, I could have rolled myself into the fetal position and cried, asking, *"Why me?"* But the only answer would be, why **not** you? Jesus never promised that we would be exempt from trials and tribulations. What He did promise is He's always with us and to cast our cares on him. And before you think this is my strength, know that this has nothing to do with me **but** is solely on the one that holds **our** future.

We will experience hardships and perplexing circumstances, even to the point of death, but we must hold tight to God for our deliverance. Regardless of sickness and fear, undeterred by frustration or pain, despite the doctor's report, we rejoice that we have a Father who cares for us. So, I say **BUT GOD!**

In the gospel of John, Jesus tells us not to fear because He gives us His peace. You too can access the Father's peace today through His son, Jesus, by making him Lord over your life. The choice to believe God is **ours**! Matthew 6:33 tells us it's only when we seek God and His kingdom that we gain access to his benefits and blessings. My confidence in God is empowered by knowing **nothing** surprises Him. He is all-knowing, always present, and all-powerful. Whether He chooses to take me home or heal me here, I am **always** in good hands. **HIS HANDS!**

It has been a few months post-surgery and my doctors and physiotherapists still marvel at the speed of my recovery. What should take two years is being done in months. Besides slight discomfort, I've never had any pain during this process. One of the surgeons called to share his thoughts, even praising God with me; telling me they were shocked at what they saw. Despite all the tests showing the mass entangled around my bone, muscles, and arteries, cancer had only infected one muscle and all they had to do was scoop it out.

Even here at the rehab center, the doctors admire my wound, all done in a straight line; gathering various colleagues to examine me. I asked the nurse what the big deal was. She commented that usually, the post-surgical site is zig-zagged, keloid, raised-raw, and altogether angry-looking. How the doctor managed to get mine flat and in a straight line is to be applauded and the fact I feel no pain is incredible because most patients usually live on narcotics for several months. The Lord is using each visit to share my testimony, salvation in Christ, and His goodness in the land of the living.

I still have one dilemma I'm wrestling with. For the sake of others, should I return to the first doctor with my report?

Can you have peace amidst a storm? Cancer survivor and first-time author Lisa Patrick testifies, *"Yes, you can,"* in this anthology. With over twenty years of experience in social services and travel, Lisa credits her faith in Jesus and many healthy relationships for her joy. *"You don't have to be plagued by fear and indecision when you lean on Jesus. Death and life are in the power of the tongue. You shall have what you say!"*

CHAPTER ELEVEN - Karen Mighty

Unbothered

I would be lying if I said that I never look at the clock on the wall anymore. Experience has taught me to ignore its ticking. I was once so focused on getting things done within my timeframe.

A lifetime of lessons has taught me that it's all about God's timing.

I recovered from a car accident where I was told that I would never walk again. After seeing how God brought me through, I still can't believe that I thought God needed my help in planning my life.

I wanted to give myself the life I never had as a child, and I was determined to make money. All I did was work. Reluctantly before my shift, I went to a birthday party. I enjoyed being around young people who were yearning for God. I didn't know this area of town. It was dark and I was lost. I saw two headlights that looked like eyes. The devil laughed loudly. I screamed out, *"God, I'm scared!"* and clutched the wheel. God told me, *"Go back. Do not continue on this path."* So I did and I saw city lights. I was so relieved.

That was the first time I heard God speak to me.

Then suddenly – black ice. I'm in the wrong lane and I see cars coming at me. I look past the Bible on my passenger seat into the oncoming headlights.

On my road, there was a Good Samaritan who covered me with coats and assured me that my daughter had not been in the vehicle with me. The ambulance attendant commented on my bible and smiled. *"Your angels were with you."*

A fractured left ankle, right arm, and sprained left arch on foot. Operation room lights and a recovery room filled with prayers and testimonies about how God revealed my accident to my church sister. Laying there physically broken, I felt filled with God's love. I worshiped in my hospital bed until the painkillers knocked me out. When I woke up, the same arm that I had held up to worship with the night before was locked at the elbow and my fingers could not be released from a fist. There was significant nerve damage, and I could feel nothing but numbness and pain. I heard the devil laugh again.

Doctors were perplexed. Surgeons and specialists were curious and confused about my arm. I was told I would never use that arm to write again, and I would need years of physiotherapy to learn to walk again.

God had me on my back for six months. There was a hospital bed, a wheelchair, and a walker in my room. I had nothing to distract me from spending time with Him. He spoke to me and woke me out of my sleep with revelations for myself and others. He replayed the whole accident and that experience let me know that I was chosen by God. The devil wanted me and God said, *"No."* I still remember the two headlights on the hill, the laughter, and me screaming to God. And His answer to the devil was no. His mercy said no.

Years later in my search to find the "what next" in my life, I didn't ask God what his plan was for me. I didn't seek Him in my quest to find what next. Instead, I planned, plotted, and eventually wrote my own narrative. I am so thankful that God had a plan and a purpose for me because my plan did not work.

I was looking at the clock and saying, *"I'm getting old." "I want another baby." "God, where is my husband? If you don't send him soon, I may have to help you."* After being healed from my accident, I felt that an all-knowing God actually needed my help.

I still remember the tears that fell when they told me that my almost two-year-old son had autism. Though my mind was strong, my heart was weak. I cried a fountain of tears when no one could see.

Do you ever ask yourself, *"Why me, God?"* I still do.

Life with autism impacts everyone, not just the child who can't speak, has trouble self-regulating, and needs to be taught the same skills over and over again – daily. It's frustrating, tiring, and abusive.

If you fail to look closely, you see no rewards.

Everyone told me that they admired my strength. But I didn't want to be strong…through the phone calls from school, the acting out while I was driving, or even the piles of CRAP that were left for me to clean up. I didn't want to be strong in the grocery store when critical eyes watched as I had to leave quickly before an escalation occurred. I certainly did not want to be strong when years of marriage dissolved into a sea of anger. They say anger is an energizer. I was definitely energized.

I watched as hours turned to days that turned to weeks and each month just felt the same.

Time was passing. The monotony was just getting annoying and depressing. I needed something more than cocktails, shopping sprees, and regret to numb this pain.

When my anger turned to unbearable sadness, I prayed.

When I look back through time, I am amazed by how God had His awesome hand all over my life. I remember in college being so annoyed about my job placement with children who had severe mental, health, and behavioral challenges. I didn't ask for that. Whose big idea was that? It was God's. He was preparing me then for a lifetime of challenges. He was building in me skills that I would need as a parent.

It's difficult to give you an accurate picture of what goes on in my day-to-day life serving a child with autism. If I told you, perhaps some days you would admire my resilience while others would judge or scold me. Autism taught me the meaning of unconditional love. What it means to serve and get little in return.

There are certain things you will not know how or why until later when God reveals to you that **HE** was working all things for your good. Working is a verb. It is an action word and is present tense. Time after time, God showed me how actively present He works all things together for my good.

Do you ever feel the need to be rescued from yourself, from your thoughts, from your words, from your actions? Looking back, I see how many times my mind was my biggest obstacle and in order to overcome it, I would have to change my thoughts and speak life into my situation.

I always prayed that my non-verbal son would speak. I'm not sure exactly the moment that it dawned on me that communication is more than words. Perhaps it was in my moaning to God when I felt so low.

Whenever the revelation was, my prayers changed. I started asking God for understanding. Not just for me to be able to understand my son but for him to be able to understand the world around him.

It's funny how God doesn't take you from here to there until you learn to be happy in the here. Until you truly appreciate that "**THIS** is the day that the Lord has made" and rejoice and be glad in **IT**. Be glad in the **HERE**. Even when it's overwhelming and unbearable. Know that God is with you and is taking you through the process. Grow in the here so that God can build in you what is needed for what is coming.

The time between midnight and daybreak was when I realized that my life was not about me. Serving and possessing the fruits of the spirit was more important than my five-year plan. That's when I realized that God had given me the desires of my heart. My heart desired God, his Holy Spirit, peace, and love. I wanted to hear from God, be in His presence, and manifest the fruits of the spirit.

There are still very difficult days. Times when physically, emotionally, and mentally I feel weak. Times when in the absence of words, I cry out to God. If God did not keep me wrapped in His grace, I would be lost – a mere shell of who I am supposed to be.

Autism was God's tool to teach me unconditional love, selflessness, gentleness, and patience. So now when I ask God, *"Why me?"* He whispers, *"So I can build the fruits of the spirit in you, Karen, so that when I look at you, you can be a reflection of me."*

I would never dedicate a chapter to the time in my life called marriage. In fact, if I could rename that time, I would probably call it "lesson learned."

There is something to be said about a child who grows to be a woman who struggles with feelings of abandonment, rejection, and loss. There is much to be said about how not having her father in her day-to-day life may have influenced her view of men and impacted how she navigates a simple but complex thing called relationships.

Over time God has changed my childhood perceptions into adult realities and I have learned to forgive. I have recognized that when a man puts God first in his life, he is governed by the principles that help to make a relationship more sustainable. I have concluded that I can only submit to a man who submits to God. When the fruits of the spirit are what a man uses as a compass for his life. I can be led by such a man. I am the best version of myself when by my fruits he knows me, by his fruits I know him, and together we reflect Godliness.

So, what now? Time is a teacher and though some lessons took longer to learn, I know that love and hate cannot dwell in the same place. Hate consumed me and one day I woke up and wanted to be more than hate. I wanted to be love, for my God is love.

I prayed for God to take away the anger of unfaithfulness, selfishness, and the regrets I felt from living years in a relationship that I knew was not compatible with who I am. And **HE** did. God showed me that all things work together for good for those who are called. Even the ones we resent. Some of them are called and God is working all things together for them too.

I felt a burden was lifted when I had a renewed spirit about my childhood and my chapter called *Lesson Learned*.

Through it all I have learned that faith and fear can dwell in the same place. I must trust that God's no will always lead to a better yes. God's timing is not in my timelines but His plans for me are perfect.

So now when I hear the ticking hands sent to remind me that time is moving quickly, I am unbothered.

Karen Mighty has been a child and youth advocate for over twenty years. She used her passion for the Word to teach at Sheridan College and mentored 3rd year practicum students. Recently, God has ordered her steps in another area of her passion, and she works to promote equity and belonging in children's mental health centers. Mother, daughter, sister, friend. God has opened doors for her to serve in mentorship, counseling families, and analyzing policies.

CHAPTER TWELVE - Koreen J. Bennett

A Blossoming Caterpillar

Have you ever watched the stages a caterpillar goes through to become a butterfly? Have you questioned the stages, asking what would happen if, along the process, one of the stages did not happen? It would only take one misstep to change the results of how this butterfly would look and/or turn out to be.

And so, it is with life. Would you say that your life could be looked at as how the caterpillar goes through its own personal transformation? What is taking place during your season of Transformation? What is transformation? How are you perceiving your journey? What is your perception of being empowered and being transformed?

I am not sure if you are like me. But there are so many questions running around in my head. As I start thinking about a word like transformation and being empowered, my mind starts asking questions, which then leads to other questions (like those I posed just moments ago). I believe it could also be my nursing antennas coming out. I needed to truly figure out what it meant to be empowered and transformed. Did I feel empowered during my journey of transformation? Had there been a profound moment or moments of transformation in my life? Was it a struggle? Yes. Absolutely. Did I think I could stand tall, or did I succumb to the emotional, mental, physical pain, and spiritual fight to get to the end stage of my transformation which included spirit, mind, and body?

These past four years have been a season of traumatic events. A whirlwind of thoughts and emotions. I felt angry, discouraged, disappointed, and feelings of being lost. It was very difficult to mentally and emotionally go into 2019. I felt as if I was leaving my first-born son behind in 2018 (he passed away on September 8, 2018). I was physically going forward without him but could not mentally and emotionally. The year 2019 felt as if I was walking in a fog. It was as if I was in a bubble. I lost confidence in who I was and my purpose on this land seemed unimportant or needed. The world as I knew it was now like being in a foreign land not knowing the people, the language, or the surroundings.

The year 2020 was a season of being in a cocoon. I needed to be sheltered from the environment of doom and pain that I was experiencing externally and internally. I was at a stage during my transformational journey that was either going to end in a downfall or me coming out in victory. Was I going to be stunted and marred for life or come out a beautiful butterfly? This was the beginning stage of the healing process. God needed to surround me and quiet me in a way to begin His transformation. This beginning was assessing and evaluating my life, and what I deemed it to be which was far from beautiful. I was asking myself if I was living my true authentic self. Did these titles of wife, mother, daughter, sister, friend, or nurse define me? This was a process of taking me to the next level of spiritual development and renewing my mind and spirit. Healing needed to take place – a shift in how I thought and spoke was going to take place. A strengthening of my thoughts and a change in the words I spoke to myself had to take place.

The Holy Spirit was now leading me through this transformational journey or stages that I was going through. I did not understand this journey at first. The past few years had so much trauma and at times, I asked, *"What am I doing with my life?" "What is going to make me happy?" "What do I need to do to fulfill the purpose of my life?"*

Every stage was crucial to get to the next stage. What was my identity in Christ not just in my surroundings and in my community? But what was Koreen's purpose on Earth? When I felt a pulling that I needed to be at another level, it was because I was at a stage for too long. I was in a place of mourning over the passing of my son and my baby sister, and all the other things in my life felt "stuck." This was not good either because remaining in a place or situation for too long can bring added anguish and pain. It can prevent growth and the move to your next level. When is it too long to remain and how do you know when you need to move?

When you hear the word transformation, what comes to mind? My thoughts are that there is a 360-degree change, most times for the better. A true transformation brings forth a change – a noticeable difference. Sometimes the transformation is so perceptible that it takes you off guard and you can't keep your eyes from constantly steering as you enjoy the beauty of this incredible change.

I do want you to remember that transformation is not an overnight thing – at least a true transformation. It is a process; it requires some changes which can be outright painful. Allowing the process to happen is a struggle at the beginning. It is not an easy journey especially if you are not going through or you're fighting the process. It is like having a tug-of-war with God. Trust me, you are not going to win that tug. This is a time of renewing the mind and heart. Acts 3:19 says:

"Repent then and turn to God, so that your sins may be wiped out, that times of refreshing may come from the Lord."

It is a time of being broken and rebuilding. It is never an easy place to be. Forgiving yourself and others, and being patient with yourself and others is part of the process. Remember to breathe. Inhale and Exhale. Seriously. Do it. Inhale (counting 1, 2, 3, 4, 5) and exhale (1, 2, 3, 4, 5). Not going through the process can also result in prolonging your journey leaving you in a stagnant frozen space. Remember the stages that the caterpillar has to go through to become that butterfly? One missed stage and the end result can be a butterfly with one wing versus two. However, when the process is complete, you get to the last stage and you see the finished results. Wow! Look at the Divine Design that is before your eyes. You can't help but be empowered firstly by the process and then by seeing the finished product or results. That transformation does something to your mindset. It gives you a brand-new perception, a different angle (a bird's-eye view) of your environment and life as you know it.

Being the compiler of my new book *Oil of Joy: Stories of Faith's Healing Journey Through Grief,* which was published by LWL

PUBLISHING HOUSE, helped me do much soul-searching and progress with my healing journey. Going through my transformation revealed how strong my faith in Christ is and will continue to be as I keep Him close. Jesus has been my greatest supporter and has been with me down in the valley and upon the mountaintop multiple times during this journey of transformation.

I did not always see myself transformed, not even empowered. I struggled with myself for years: how I looked to myself and how I looked to others. My perception of myself was low many times (lies I listened to from The Destiny Killer). I wanted to please everyone and be all to everyone around me. That can be such a huge pressure and it became a heavy burden to carry. Transformation brings an assessment and evaluation of your life. It is a renewing of mind, body, and spirit (2 Corinthians 5:17). Know that God is with you during every stage, overseeing the intimate details, and reminding you of your purpose. Maintaining a renewed mindset and heart-set requires reading the Word and speaking the Word of God over your life and your loved ones daily (and the days and months when you can't read or speak, have the Word playing in your ear). Tell yourself that you are Fearfully and Wonderfully made (Psalm 139:14 KJV). You are created in the image of God (Genesis 1:26-27). That is what His Word says about you and me.

To you, the beautiful reader, my prayer for you to remember that this is your journey and God will be alongside you helping you become the vessel that he is molding you to be for Him – to use you to pour into someone else's life. You are strong because God says so. You are going through this time of unknown and maybe even unimaginable pain and loss. Know that you are in the palm of His hand and God would never leave you or forsake you. His words in Jeremiah 29:11 say:

"For I know the plan I have for you, declares the Lord, plans to prosper you and not to harm you, plans to give you hope and a future." (NIV)

Another version says:

"For I know the thoughts that I think toward you, saith the Lord, thoughts of peace and not of evil, to give you an expected end." (KJV)

God knows who you are and what you are able to handle for Him to take you to your next level. He wants his eagle to be able to soar above all obstacles and fulfill your divine purpose on this land. Praying was not always easy for me during my journey of transformation. I believed in the Lord Jesus. I knew he was present, however, when I was experiencing all the emotions and feelings and mustering up all the energy to go through the rollercoaster of my life, it was difficult to get into His presence. There were moments during the grieving process and other life situations where I remained in a space for a time. I want you to know that even though the journey is hard to go through, you can do it. You can make it to the final caterpillar stage. The transformation was never meant to be easy, but it is truly worth it especially when not only you, but others see what the Lord has done. I encourage you to stay the course, seek the Lord (Matthew 6:33), and he will guide you through life's ups and downs. Even when you may not feel him, He is there. Even when you are facing challenging seasons, keep holding on.

Through the loss of my son, experiencing COVID-19, dealing with financial hardship, the loss of my baby sister, COVID again, and a recent house fire, I have experienced transformation and it is empowering me to keep going forward for my family and myself. Is it easy? Absolutely not! But I can't wait to see my beautiful wings at the end of this journey. Philippians 1:6 says:

"And I am sure of this, that he who began a good work in you will bring it to completion at the day of Jesus Christ."

I would love for you to say this prayer with me. I wrote this for you who may not know the Lord Jesus and for you who just need to renew your relationship with Christ Jesus.

Almighty God. You say I am Fearfully and Wonderfully made. Your Word says I am created in your image. I ask you, Lord Jesus, to come into my life and transform me. Change my mindset and heart-set, Lord God. I have not always done right, and I place all my sins and wrongdoings at your feet now. I love you and I need you, Jesus. Thank you for empowering me and transforming me to be that light for your Kingdom. I accept you now as Lord and Savior over my life, forever. Amen.

God bless you and your journey.

I can't wait to see your beautiful wings.

Koreen J. Bennett is a wife, mother, grandmother, Kingdom citizen, Registered Nurse of eighteen years, entrepreneur, and best-selling author 4x with LWL PUBLISHING HOUSE. She loves the Lord Jesus and her desire is to inspire, encourage, and empower those she encounters.

CHAPTER THIRTEEN - Rev. Carolyn J. Anderson

Empowered to Be Who You Were Created to Be

"God is in the midst of her; she shall not be moved; God will help her when morning dawns." Psalm 46:5 (ESV)

"God lives here, the streets are safe, God is at your service from crack of dawn." Psalms 46:5 (MSG)

"God [is] in her midst – she is not moved, God doth help her at the turn of the morn!" Psalms 46:5 (YLT)

"God in the midst thereof shall not be moved; God shall help it early in the gray morrow tide. (God is there in its midst, and that city shall not be shaken, or destroyed; God shall help it early in the gray morning/at the break of day.)" Psalms 46:5 (WYC)

You will bring **GOD** good and not harm all the days of your life! Strength and dignity, and she will **LAUGH** at the time to come! Begin to laugh now at the devil, at the pain he tries to bring, and the limitations of femininity that we **THINK** we must live within its boundaries! You are precious and **PRICELESS!** The devil cannot afford **YOU!**

Therefore, you laugh without fear of the future! Because you can do **ALL** things through Christ who is strengthening you **RIGHT NOW!**

Dress **YOURSELF** in strength against the wiles of the devil. Just like you pick out the correct pearls to wear with your favorite frock, so can you pick out the Word of God that will bring you encouragement in the time of trouble and challenge. For you are **STRONG** and you will do **GREAT** exploits – because God's got you in the early morning, before you realize that you really need the one who sees and knows you for real. There are many capable women, but you surpass them all.

How? I am so glad that you asked. There is no one but you to do what only you can do because there is no one even **CLOSE** to being you! When you really inculcate this into the depths of your being, you will realize that you **MUST** accept your assignment to be **YOU**. If you choose **NOT** to be **YOU**, then that space, that directive, that assignment will go unfulfilled – forever. Oh, that knowledge doesn't feel good, does it? Well, my sister, my friend, you have no other choice. If you **DON'T** do it, who will? So, face the fact, my friend. Realize that there is no one else. When the President is sworn in, he becomes the President and there is no one else able to take his place while he lives. While you live my friend, who will take your place?

There is no one but you. The empowerment in this instance is the recognition of the reality of the fact that it's all on **YOU**. Yes. **YOU!** Nobody but **YOU.**

So, now that we have settled that, what do we do? We must find out our marching orders. We must identify who God has called us to be, and what God has assigned us to do.

How Do We Find Empowering Strength?

"As a man (woman, boy, or girl) thinks in their heart, so is he/she." (Proverbs 27:3)

So, this lets us know that the bottom line is that of a "heart issue." Create in me a clean heart, Oh God, and **RENEW** the right spirit within me. Look at the word "renew." "Re" means to do again and "new" is simply something freshly unknown to us. So, we realize that we were new, fresh, unfiltered, and unbothered at birth, physically and spiritually, into a brand-new world unknown to us before. And in some way, we have gone astray, lost our newness. That baby smell is gone; we have a different odor…of failure, self-doubt, unbelief in our gifts, mistrust in the compliments of those who observe greatness inside of us. We make a choice **NOT** to believe them, not to receive truth as God speaks through them the reality of the greatness of His creation inside of you, the only you that **IS** you! How sweet is that?

Now, aren't you beginning to feel special? Well, God has been attempting to get you to understand who you are for a long time. He made you and **ONLY** you. You are the only you that will ever be **YOU!** It took me such a long time to realize, so I am not mad at you – it takes us all a spiritual minute (one day is as a thousand years to God). Wow! Now that is a **REALLY** long time that we might go without realizing that we are **REALLY** somebody special.

You do not have to accept the first thing that comes your way. You do not have to accept the first man, the first job, the first bouquet, the first anything because you are worth it, my friend. So, now that you are beginning to realize just who you are, don't you feel a little better? You feel like putting on your best dress and taking a strut down the avenue of life to show off the beauty that God created inside of you.

You go girl!

There is nobody who can strut your stuff because you are the only one with ownership of your gifting, your calling, your anointing, your posture and position in life, your love, your caring, and your giving the way you do it. There is no one to fill your shoes. So, what can we decide to do about this **GREAT** gift that we own? Let's return again to our first text, Psalm 46:5:

"God lives here, the streets are safe, God is at your service from the crack of dawn." (MSG)

The Message Bible so clearly reassures us that even if we live alone, God is not only in the house with us, but he is also servicing us by working while we sleep to make sure that the streets of life that we are assigned to journey down are safe for us. Even though the commentaries state that this text was directed toward the safety of Jerusalem, for our subject on empowerment, we desire to join the interpretation of the Message Bible that substitutes the word City for Her, and even though each of us is truly a city of our own, we are complete, housing within us everything that we need to make it.

Even as I write this, I am being personally encouraged that God's got me as well. How about that? As we look at a map and observe the many cities within so many countries, states, counties, provinces, and townships, each has what they need to make it as far as stores, libraries, etc. Each of us also has housed within ourselves the information we need and the library of the Holy Spirit allows us to pick what we need – free of charge – and take it with us.

"Take the Lord God with you everywhere you go" is an old song sung by our Pentecostal brothers and sisters, and is a very true statement. When we realize the richness of our lives, the wealth of the power invested inside of us by the Lord Jesus Christ, how can we **NOT** run on to see what the end shall be? How can we **NOT** be all that we can be in the army and service of the Lord who has made us uniquely different and special, and there is **NOT** another copy anywhere in the world.

I am sure that you have heard the thought that everyone has a twin somewhere, but the reality is that even twins carry a separate DNA. So, there is no way to get away from the fact that *"Jesus Loves Me, this I know, for the Bible tells me so."* Jesus loves you my friend just the way you are, but He loves you **TOO MUCH** to leave you and me that way.

> *"For eyes have not seen, neither have ears heard, neither has it entered into the heart of man all that God has in store (prepared) for those who love Him."* (1 Corinthians 2:9)

I invite you to repeat that last sentence again and put your name in it. This time, repeat it **OUT LOUD** to yourself so that you can hear it and scream your name in it. I pray that by now you are, first of all, convinced that you are fearfully and wonderfully made! Great are the works of God! Great things God has done when He shaped you in your mother's belly. Even if you do not know your mother, you know the One who placed you there – God Himself. God **ALWAYS** knows what He is Doing! God cares for you first and foremost. **He NEVER** leaves us alone. He made you the shape, the shade, the form, the intelligence that He wanted you to be. Rest in the fact that you are the BEST you God could do. Be empowered with the knowledge that there is only you, and if you do not do what you are assigned to do, then who will?

Now, it is time to:

GIRD YOURSELF WITH STRENGTH AND MAKE YOURSELF STRONG!

What is our next assignment? We will *"call those things that are not, as though they were"* (Romans 4:17). I speak of the things that we will not accept about ourselves, that we are not anointed and appointed, that no one wants to hear what we have to say, that the gift of creativity that we have is not as good as the next person. Whatever you have accepted to be the you that you see is not real, so that is what "is not" in our lives, and we will then, through the empowerment of the Spirit of Christ, "call" or "speak", or even "declare" who we are in Christ – who God made you to be, the only one that is you, by the way.

I keep repeating this because the travesty is that we have never really accepted the responsibility of shouldering the calling that we carry and realizing that like Jacob's coat of many colors, it was the only coat that looked like that. You are the only one of you – and to totally accept that fact and put on the cloak of the responsibility, giftings, and blessings that accompany our particular calling is the empowerment that God sent Jesus to assist us with. It is what the Holy Spirit is assigned to do and to be in our lives. Please know that you are NOT alone in this assignment of life, for the assurance that *"I will never leave you nor forsake you"* (Joshua 1:5 NIV) is the security that we need to accept our assignment and then, as the old folks used to say, *"Run on to see what the end shall be!"*

God recognizes our insecurities, our doubts, our fears, our self-hatred, self-loathing at times. God knows that we are imperfect beings, and God sent the Comforter, the Paraclete, the Holy Ghostbusters, to push, prod, and encourage us into the *"this is that which was spoken by the prophet Joel"* (Acts 2:16 NIV) place of totality in our lives, the place of harmony when our spirit is one with God. Now, don't get it twisted, *"In this world we SHALL have tribulation, trials, tests,"* but God said, *"But I have overcome."* Remember our opening text? God is at your service from the crack of dawn. While you are asleep, God is working on your behalf. And now, my friend, that is where trust comes in. That is where you and I learn to lean back and depend upon God to be our "catcher" when we feel that we are falling. There is an exercise in trust that I am sure that you are aware of; when one is told to lean back and fall into the arms of another who has promised to catch us! Well, that is our big God – He will **ALWAYS** be there to catch us when we fall from the place that we were called to be. When we miss a step, and falter, and doubt, God is there always, and so we trust, and so we grow, and so we go toward what was intended for us before birth – the one assignment that you already know that you MUST do. If you are saying that you do not know, then, I am here to encourage you, my friend, that you really do know somewhere deep inside yourself, you have always had a desire from childhood. I encourage you to go back and spend some time with yourself, reaching back to those very early dreams, to do hair, to drive a fire truck. Only you know the dreams of your childhood. That is what God planted inside of you and now releases you in the name of Jesus to do it with all of your heart.

You are the called, you are the anointed and appointed, you are the city that God says, *"shall NOT be shaken or destroyed."* God is there at the break of dawn – when you first arise; God is there is usher you through, to accompany you as you go about the assignment that **ONLY** you have been given.

My friend, accept your assignment and be empowered in the name of the Lord to do **GREAT THINGS!**

Rev. Carolyn J. Anderson is a music educator and ordained minister, leading a very full life of transformation, creating, and defining visions that support the development of ministry in the arena of music, arts, and the spoken word. She is a gospel musician, preacher, recording artist, and a believer that God desires for His children to enjoy full sensory ministry! The legacy that Carolyn desires to leave is a life committed to simply loving people to Jesus Christ!

   Musicallife4u@Yahoo.com

CHAPTER FOURTEEN - Alicia Grant

His Spirit Lives Within Me

I was a happy child growing up. But then at the age of seventeen, my happiness went downhill as I started battling depression. I suddenly felt unloved even though I knew I was loved by my family. The devil made me believe that I wasn't. He would cloud my mind with negativity and I started hating myself. The words *"Why were you born?"* would constantly plague my mind. It reached the point where I no longer wanted to be alive. I started dwelling on how I could take my life. Even though the thoughts were going through my head, for some reason I could never find the courage to do it. I became an addict by consuming a lot of pills, at first to overdose, then just to feel high.

I hated myself. If I looked in the mirror, I would tell myself how ugly and stupid I was, and no one would ever love me.

When I moved to a different county, I thought things would be different; things would be better for me. I thought I would start loving myself again, but I was still feeling numb. Something was still missing. I had a relationship with God but I never had a real encounter with Him. I started dating to fill that missing piece, but I was still not happy. I hated myself even more because that's not what I wanted. I didn't want a relationship with a man; I wanted a relationship with God. Along with taking the pills, I would cut my wrist.

One day, I got overdosed and was hospitalized. I could hardly speak; my short-term memory was gone. My sister heard that I was in the hospital and she came there. When she saw me, I could tell she was worried. I looked at her and told her not to worry because *"I'm going to die."*

My sister spoke into my life that day. *"Alicia! You shall not die but you shall live and declare the works of the Lord"* (Psalm 118:17). She may not know what she did that day, but God was using her to speak life back into me. When I came out of the hospital, I stopped taking the pills but I was cutting my wrist more frequently. I got depressed even more: I was empty, I was lost, and I needed to find peace.

One day, a church friend asked me the question, *"Let me know something about yourself that you love?"* I couldn't find anything that I liked, never mind loved. I hated just the thought of being born. Not knowing God was ready to make a shift in my life, I started looking in the mirror just to find something about me that I liked. I caught a glimpse of my eyes and I started telling myself I liked my eyes; they were beautiful. Every day I would look at myself and speak about my eyes. Then I realized that I have a beautiful smile. I now could feel a big difference – something in me was shifting. God was allowing me to acknowledge how beautiful I was. I could feel a breakthrough coming.

Daily I would look at myself and instead of saying how ugly I was, those words changed to how beautiful I was because I started to realize how beautiful I really was. I started speaking over my life.

"I will praise you because you are fearfully and wonderfully made; your works are wonderful, I know full well." Psalm 139:14

Oh, how I felt a purpose for being alive, and I started believing in:

"For I know the plans I have for you declares the Lord, plans to prosper you and not harm you, plans to give you hope and a future." Jeremiah 29:11

"Come to me all you are weary and burdened, and I will give you rest." Matthew 11:28

I started going to God. I cast my care upon Him because He cares for me (1 Peter 5:7). I no longer hated the way I looked; I was seeing God's beautiful creation.

When you begin to trust God and His words, it starts to make a big difference in your life.

"Trust in the Lord with all your heart, and lean not on your understanding; in all your ways acknowledge Him, and He shall direct your paths." Provers 3:5-6

I started trusting in God's words because I wanted to be closer to Him. I wanted to have an encounter with Him. I want to be free from depression. The more I studied His Words, the closer I got to Him to have an encounter with Him. I can now say I have a personal relationship with God. I've encountered His love and His mercies.

It wasn't an easy journey to get close to God. It took everyday encouragement and discipline in order not to go back to the dark place I had been. I had to have everyday communication with God, reading and meditating on His Words to get me on the road of deliverance and having the encounter I needed with Him.

> *"The Lord turned my wailing into dancing, He removed my sackcloth and clothed me with joy that my heart may sing His praises and not be silent."* Psalm: 30 11-12

When you are free from the bondage that held you as a prisoner for years, you have to learn how to remain free. The enemy doesn't like that I'm no longer a slave to him, and sends distractions my way because he wants me to go back to that place where he can control me. He doesn't want me to get closer to God because he knows once I'm there, he no longer has a grip on my life. To remain free from bondage, it took a deeper commitment with fasting and prayer. Instead of dwelling on the past, I meditate on God's Words.

> *"It is for freedom that Christ has set us free. Stand firm, and not let yourself be burdened again by a yoke of slavery."* Galatians 5:1

I let Psalm 118:5 be my everyday cry:

> *"I called upon the Lord in distress: the Lord answered me and set me in a large place."*

Being free from bondage took a deeper connection with God

and that takes everyday practice. It wasn't easy, but everyday reading of God's Words makes it easier and becomes natural. Speaking daily in my life that "I am free from the bondage of hating myself" was also a big help because I never want to go back to the dark place I was. I would dig deeper into God's Words, searching through scriptures for encouragement. As I searched, I came across Isaiah 41:10:

> *"So do not fear, for I am with you; do not be dismayed, for I am your God. I will strengthen you and help you; I will uphold you with my righteous right hand."*

I would let those words sink into my spirit. The Holy Spirit led me to (Joshua 1) and I will meditate on it day and night.

In verses 7 and 8, it says *"Be strong and courageous"* and then in verse 9, God asks the question:

> *"Have I not commanded you to be strong and courageous? Do not be afraid; do not be discouraged, for the Lord your God will be with you everywhere you go."*

I knew the Lord was speaking directly to me. I needed to trust God and His Words.

I would like to encourage someone today who is battling depression. It is impossible to be in the presence of God and not be changed. You have to change your way of thinking. The enemy attacks us through our thoughts and once he gets us to start thinking negatively, he holds us there until we are back into depression. Don't allow the devil to attack your thoughts; don't allow him to steal your joy. Pull yourself up. God did not create you to be depressed. He didn't create you to worry. For too long the enemy has had you in bondage. Yet, today you are coming out; today you will be free; you will no longer be a slave of fear, a slave of a worrier, a slave of depression, but you will be a slave of happiness, a slave of prosperity, a slave of God.

If you are battling depression today, God will wipe every tear from your eyes and give you deliverance. There will be no more death, no more mourning, no more pain; just trust in His Words. Trust in the process, even though it seems forever. Don't give up because a breakthrough is coming. You may not see or believe it, but it is coming. Claim your deliverance in Jesus' name. Do not lose hope. Though your outer self is wasting away, your inner self is being renewed day by day. God is always with you and He will never leave you. Remember, it is the Lord who goes before you. He will be with you; he will not leave you or forsake you. Do not fear or be dismayed.

> *"God sees all your tears and He knows all your struggles; He wants you to come to Him with your problems, he wants to heal you and set you free. Don't be afraid to give it all to Jesus. Submit yourselves to God."* Hebrews 13:5 (ESV)

> *"Resist the devil, and he will flee from you."* James 4:7

> *"Be alert and of a sober mind. Your enemy the devil prowls around like a roaring lion looking for someone to devour. Resist him, standing firm in the faith, because you know that the family of believers throughout the world is undergoing the same kind of suffering."* 1 Peter 5:8-9

Surrender your all to God; hold back nothing from Him. God wants your all. He wants you to surrender to Him and He wants to set you free from bondage.

Prayer

Father God, I humbly come into Your presence. I ask that You look beyond my faults and see my needs. Lord, I come to You because I need to be free from the bondage of depression that's had a hold on my life for many years. Lord, you say anything we ask in Your name it shall be granted to us. You did not give us a spirit of fear but gave us power, love, and self-discipline. So, I come to You with my needs. Lord, I ask that You turn my mourning into dancing. I want to be able to smile again. Take my sackcloth and clothe me with gladness. Lord, I cry for help because I can't do this on my own. Take full control of this situation. God, I surrender my all to You. Only you know the darkest place in my heart. I ask that you replace my struggles with joy so I can rejoice again. You say in Your Words that those who hope in You will renew their strength, they will soar with wings like eagles; they will run and not grow weary, they will walk and not faint. Lord, there is nothing that's too hard for you. I believe that You can turn things around for me. You say if we have faith as small as a mustard seed, we can say to the mountain move and it will be moved. Lord, I have faith that this depression will no longer be. I have faith that I will be renewed and set free. I speak into my life today that the devil no longer has a hold on me and I am free. God, take full control of this situation and make me whole again. I leave everything in Your hands, and I call it done in the mighty Name of Jesus. Amen.

Scripture Verses for Being Free from Depression

Deuteronomy 31:8   John 16:33   Psalm 23:4   Psalm 9:9   Psalm 40:1-2   Psalm 34:18   Psalm 55:22   Psalm 46:10

Alicia Grant is a retail manager, a singer, and a songwriter who loves the Lord with her whole heart. She is currently residing in the Cayman Islands. Alicia has held various positions as a youth and children's choir director, assistant choir director, as well as Family Training Hour (FTH) president and secretary in Jamaica and the Cayman Islands. Her main purpose is to win souls for God's kingdom and encourage the vulnerable through her music.

 azaniahgrant@yahoo.com

CHAPTER FIFTEEN - Jasmin Cher Monasterial-Baguio

Empty No More

One day I was sitting in my car after registering my daughter to be baptized in the Catholic Church when a question popped up in my mind and heart. *"Why do I feel so empty?"* I had everything I needed in life: my children, my husband, a roof over my head, and all the basic things I needed to live. At some point in my life, I thought being wealthy or having more money would make me happy. I pursued many business opportunities and had little success. Then another question came to my mind. *"What is missing in my life?"* As I thought about this question deeply, a small gentle voice said to me, *"God is missing in your heart."* I was a little surprised because I had attended church all my life. I thought I knew God. But I was wrong because I did not know him personally. I learned some things about Him that were taught to me by my parents, teachers, the church, religion, and the world.

It was like a light bulb went on inside of me. The revelation that I didn't know God for myself is why He was the missing piece of my heart and life. This revelation was my AH-HA moment. So, I decided I would find God and get to know Him for myself.

I did not know the wild journey that lay ahead of me.

As a young mom of three at the time, I did not have any close mom friends. One day, an old schoolmate messaged me on Facebook. Although we were not friends back in school, I was happy that she was also a young mom like me looking for fellowship. Little did I know that God planned to draw me closer to Him. My schoolmate already had a close relationship with the Lord. Intrigued and interested were the words that described how I felt about having a relationship with God. My schoolmate invited me to check out her church called ACTS which launched on the day I gave birth to my fourth child. At the time, I was still hesitant because of my Catholic background. Afraid of what my family would think, I waited for the right time. It was January 2016 when I was walking around the mall with my mom. Then a thought hit me! It was another light bulb going on. I decided that I would cut off listening to worldly music and focus on Christian Worship music. I started to open my bible and read it. Then I started talking to God like I would talk to a close friend. Finally, I chose to check out ACTS Community Worship Centre for myself. As I stepped into the church, I heard the beautiful worshippers singing to the Lord. There was something different about this church. I could feel something. I did not know that I felt the presence of God in the church. Many thoughts were coming into my mind. Some were negative thoughts because I came from a religious background. But the presence of God outweighed the negative thoughts. I went the second time and got prayed over by the pastor. As she prayed for me, I felt flutters all over my face. That was the Holy Spirit, but I did not know Him at the time as yet.

One day I was driving on the way to my next client. I was tuning into my worship music while trying to find my client's house in the countryside. The day was Good Friday, a dark and gloomy day. I started talking to God while still driving around looking for my client's home. I thanked God for keeping me even though I was at the end of my rope. Life was full of ups and downs. I felt like there were more downs than ups. I was pouring my heart out to God. Then all of a sudden, out of my belly and mouth came the loudest Hallelujah ever! BOOM! The Spirit of God fell upon me like a HUGE TSUNAMI WAVE of PURE LOVE! I felt the tangible presence of God with every fiber and cell of my being. It was so beautiful, yet too magnificent to describe. It was the sweetest and most satisfying love I have ever felt and experienced. Amazed and in awe that I found God Himself! He does exist! His Word was and is true! Jeremiah 29:13 says,

"You will seek me and find me when you seek me with all your heart."

This verse was the truth because it happened to me. I was overwhelmed with tears of joy. Right there, I accepted and confessed Jesus Christ as my Lord and Savior. I chose to turn away from my sinful ways and decided to follow only Jesus. My Heavenly Father was right there in the van with me. He lavished me with His agape love and forgiveness. Every emptiness inside of me was gone. I was full of God's joy, peace, and love. The Holy Spirit was now living inside of me. I went from being empty and like the walking dead to full and alive in the spirit. I became born again because of Jesus Christ, my Lord and Savior.

I knew that I was not the same Jasmin. My heart and life were now on fire for God. The presence of the Holy Spirit was on me as I was driving to my destination. At her home, I told my client how God loves her and every human being He ever made. I testified who Jesus Christ was, what He did for us on the cross, and that He rose from the dead to give us new life in Him was true. After work, the Holy Spirit led me to visit family and friends to testify of Jesus Christ and my encounter with God in my van. I knew not many of them truly believed me. But it did not matter because I was finally **ONE** with My Heavenly Father God. I found the **GREATEST TREASURE** anyone can ever find. The greatest treasure was God Himself, **THE FULLNESS OF GOD**. I felt ever so **LOVED, ACCEPTED**, and finally **COMPLETE**. From that day forward, I started serving God and following Jesus Christ. Forming a close relationship with the Holy Spirit was my priority. He would download the Father's heart each time I made time for Him and His Word. Miracles, signs, and wonders followed me even to this very day. Healings took place within me, my children, my clients, and many others through faith-filled prayers and declarations of God's Word. I realized that I was now in alignment with God and His purpose for me. If I could tell you all that **He** has done for me up until now, I would need a whole book to write it down.

The most important thing to me is who God is to me. He is my Heavenly Father, known as my Daddy, Abba GOD. He is my husband, my rock, my provider, my shelter, my shield, my fortress, my hiding place, my healer, my deliverer, my protector, my peace, my joy, my strength, my love, and my everything. Jesus Christ is my Shepherd, my Lord, my Savior, my saving grace, my brother, my daily bread, my fountain of living water, my light, and my salvation. The Holy Spirit is my Sweet Holy Spirit. He is my comforter, my teacher, my counselor, my guide, and my best friend. Every day as I choose to walk with the Holy Spirit and follow Jesus Christ, I receive more revelation of His Word and His Will for us. This is my Christ-empowered transformation. I have been set free from addictions to skin picking, gambling, and playing video games. I had low self-esteem and hated myself. I did not believe I was good enough, beautiful, intelligent, and all that God created me to be. Today, I have the mind of Christ. I am a new Creation in Christ; old things have passed away. I can do all things in Christ who strengthens me. Since accepting Christ, my life has never been the same. It is one million times better because I am doing this beautiful life with God right by my side and His Spirit living inside me. He has carried me through the storms of my life: from a difficult separation with my husband to emotional and health challenges. Today, I thank and praise God that I am still standing and walking by faith. I am stronger than I was. I am Christ-confident. I am learning to love myself the way God loves me and sees me through His eyes. I am a thriving mother of five beautiful children with a successful career as a school bus driver. I am truly blessed to lead worship at ACTS Community Worship Center and serve the Lord there. God put His fire and passionate love within me to distribute to every person He puts in my path. I am His Fireball and Evangelist Jasmin. I am finally FULL-FILLED and empty no more! HALLELUJAH!!

From the day I started to know God for myself, I realized there are no "accidents" or "coincidences." I now believe in "God-incidences" (refer to Psalm 37:23). They are encounters set up by God. As you read this, I know God led you here because He knows you very well (Proverbs 16:9). He made YOU fearfully and wonderfully in His image (Psalm 139:14, Genesis 1:27). He knows the number of hairs on the top of your head (Luke 12:7). How amazing is that? God said in His word that He knew YOU before HE FORMED YOU in YOUR MOTHER'S WOMB (Jeremiah 1:5). He has chosen you to be born for such a time as this. You have an assignment on earth before you go to be with our Lord in Heaven. At the same time, He gave you the beauty of free will. It is up to you now to seek Him with all of your heart so that you can also find Him as I did. He desires our hearts and to have a relationship with us. Just like we have parents and family here on earth, God the Father, Jesus Christ, and the Holy Spirit are our true family. Our Heavenly Father has adopted us back into His family because of what His Only Begotten Son Jesus Christ did for us (Ephesians 1:5). He has forgiven us of all our sins and removed all barriers to having a real loving relationship with Him. Nothing can separate you from the Love of God! (Acts 13:38-39, Romans 8:31-39).

Thank you for taking the time to read my story. I thank God for you and your life. God has a great plan for you – bigger than you can imagine! If you are open to receiving the Lord Jesus Christ in your heart and life and want a real relationship with our Heavenly Father to be full of His love, then you can pray this with your whole heart.

Dear Heavenly Father, I thank you for this special time to come to know you for myself. I thank you for keeping me through the good and bad times. I thank you for my life. I thank you for all that you have done for me. Father God, I humbly ask you for your forgiveness for all my sins and mistakes that I have made in my life. (Let the Holy Spirit lead you to confess any specific sins). I confess and believe that you did send your only Begotten Son, Jesus Christ to suffer, die on the cross for all my sins, and rise from the dead to give me new life. Dear Jesus, come into my heart and be Lord over my life. I turn away from the world to follow you from this day forward until I go to be with you in Heaven. I ask you to fill me up with your Sweet Holy Spirit. In your precious name, amen.

Jasmin Cher Monasterial-Baguio was born and raised in Hamilton, Ontario, and is a mother of five beautiful children. Fireball Jasmin is what her church family calls her because of her passion and love for Jesus Christ. She is currently a lead worshipper at Acts Community Worship Centre in Hamilton. Fireball Jasmin enjoys being a mobile evangelist for Jesus Christ while driving the school bus, worship flagging at a park, and wherever she goes.

- Jasmin Cher (Fireball Jasmin)
- Abba's Gifts by Jasmin Cher
- Fireball Jasmin
- Fireball Jasmin

CHAPTER SIXTEEN - Lisa Simpson

I'm a Survivor

Hi everyone! My name is Jonah. And I'm a track star!

I am going to lie to you.

I am going to lie and tell you that it is easy. I am going to lie and say that going through the warzone in your mind, your heart, your soul, and your body does not hurt. I am going to lie and tell you that as you stumble through life's curveball battles, it becomes easier.

I am going to lie because it is simpler to lie and put on a good face than to tell the truth.

It is easier to keep the pain locked away on the inside and pretend that you are always strong.

It is easier to lie and pretend to be strong, pretend to have it all together than admit you need help and you are not doing well.

Well, isn't that what everyone wants to believe and think about you?

Living a lie makes it easier to live.

I'm a runner, not a fighter. Yet somehow, I always keep getting pulled into battles. Battles from which I cannot run. Battles that keep coming after me, repeatedly until I stop running and fight the war – with myself.

There is an old saying: *"Belief kills and belief cures."* Now, I understand this to be true. You manifest what you believe. If you believe you are not enough, that you don't deserve the best, then you will never be enough, not even for yourself and you will never be able to receive the best even if it is handed to you. If you believe that you are not worth it, and you get to a point where you don't have the strength to fight for yourself, to fight for what you want, to stand up and declare that you want more out of life than you are currently experiencing, then you will continue to live a sub-par life; a journey that you really do not want, nor will you enjoy. One in which you are not engaged, leaving you unhappy – not only with yourself but with everything around you.

Living a lie. Living someone else's dream. Living in everyone's shadow. Living a life consumed with fear and scarcity.

Wait…let me correct that. I never felt as if I was living. I always felt as though I was existing. Moving from moment to moment and tuned out day by day. I had this deep desire in the back of my skull demanding more from life, but so beaten from my experiences that I did not have the strength to fight.

I felt as if I was a burden to everyone, including myself. Never feeling as if I could or ever would get life right. Never feeling as if I fit in anywhere so I did not go anywhere. Making myself as small as possible to not be noticed or called upon. Having skills, personality, and charisma but afraid to show it. Praying for the depression to end in the only way out I thought was possible, the only way out I believed would make life easier for everyone – death.

> For most of my life, I've wanted to die,
> I'm tired of feeling alone,
> Tired, depressed – angry, oppressed,
> For my sins, I can never atone.

> For most of my life, I've wanted to die,
> A vestige of hope has kept me alive,
> Battered and bruised, I've been beaten until,
> The only thing left to do is survive.

> In the fathoms of depression, I hold on to fear,
> Hanging my head down in my shame,
> I thought I could beat this; I thought I knew how,
> Time out! I need a breather from this game.

> For most of my life, I've wanted to die,
> This pain keeps drenching my bones,
> "You're depressed because you want to be…
> Snap out of it my dear,"
> Empty comfort has left me feeling broke.

> For most of my life, I've wanted to die,
> I don't know what I haven't been through,
> The one thing keeping me alive right now,
> Is only what God had to say.

> But now…. I want to live!

Where my unhappiness began, I am not able to say. I don't remember much of my childhood and honestly don't know if I even want to remember. I do, however, know where my happiness, my true happiness, began.

It all started with a thought – *"I want to be happy!"* I was tired of how I was living. Everyone on the outside thought that I was happily married. I was always laughing, smiling, joking around, making everyone else happy while I was dying inside.

Don't get me wrong, my change didn't happen overnight.

Day by day, as I fed my soul with encouraging food for the soul, the thoughts developed and persisted, that my life could be better. Things could be different. In fact, if I were to truly be living as a Child of God, things ought to be different. Hence, I was not able to give up. Somewhere deep down inside me, the Spirit that I had would not allow this mere existence to continue forever.

The Word tells us that God will make even our enemies be at peace with us but sometimes the enemy that we need to make peace with is ourselves. Sometimes we can be our own worst and greatest enemy.

Making peace with yourself comes with only one rule – you must be willing to look yourself in the mirror and be brutally honest. Yes, it will hurt. But anything that is good for you will cost you…something. You finally wake up and decide one day that enough is enough. Everything that you have been doing does not seem to be working and no matter what, you just can't get it in you to give up. And the most important question to ask yourself is this: *"Are you willing to pay the price to receive the life you desire, deserve, and require for you?"*

Your new life will come at the cost of the old one. If you want a new way of thinking and being, you will have to start thinking differently and become a whole new person. You can't have a new life, and create a new way of living and thinking while still holding onto the old. Unless you want to continue living in the same cycles that broke you instead of you breaking free. One must go, and you are the only one who gets to make that choice.

This time when you make a choice, choose not to prolong your suffering.

My Reason

When someone asks me why
I reply,
The reason is me!
When I look in the mirror,
I want to see,
The person I need to be,
A whole new…kind of me.
And so….
I must do this,
For me!
Changes must come my way,
Then I can never say…
I never did it…
And I did it…my way…for me!

I got married. Then I got divorced. We were together for ten years until I decided I could not continue living a lie. I was holding on the best way I knew how. I fasted, prayed, read my bible, spun around in a circle three times, got counseling – and still nothing worked. What hurt the worst was not being loved, respected, and cherished in the way that I needed to be. Which I desired to be.

It didn't matter if or how I expressed my feelings. It didn't matter how much I expressed my past or present hurts. The person I was with did not have the capacity to render me perfect love. A love that was unconditional. A love that was patient and understanding. A love that was kind and compassionate enough to hold my broken pieces and help me to heal.

Each time I would bare my soul, a little at a time, it would be weaponized and used against me in the next disagreement or opportunity to break me down, bit by bit. There just never seemed to be any lasting peace, and it made me weary. Each episode reminded me of my abusive childhood, a place where I never had a voice, my feelings did not matter, and I was always required to put everyone's needs above mine. Not only did I simply accept abandonment and rejection from those closest to me, but I made it into a shield. Unable to recognize love and acceptance, I despised my heart for feeling and would rather abandon and reject others before they had a chance to do it to me.

So, I ran!

And I just kept on running.

Running away from my fears of not being loved, appreciated, and accepted. Running away from my hopes, dreams, and innermost desires. Running from my demons, my insecurities, my imperfections, my anxiety, my fears. But no matter how fast or how hard I ran – they were all always there.

Until that fateful day conversing with a dear friend who said one thing that upended my entire life.

"Why don't you just stop running?"

Based on the conversation we were having at that moment, I understood what was meant. But those words struck a chord that resonated within me, and I started to seriously examine my life.

I had finally stopped running.

And it was scary. Because now I had to stop and face everything that I had been running from all of my life. I had to finally have a complete reckoning with myself. Instead of avoiding all the ugly things, the things and thoughts that made me uncomfortable, I had to deal with them. Instead of pretending as though everything was going well and I had it all under control, I allowed myself to let go of the fantasies of living in a happily ever after with the person I was with because I had known the truth all along that it was never going to happen. I had to also discard some of my Christian teachings that God does not allow divorce and if I got divorced, I would be stepping outside the will of God and He would be upset with me. I had to get comfortable with the thought that I would become an outcast in my church and my family. Everyone thought I had the perfect husband and the perfect marriage, so how I upset this illusion.

Then I had to contend with the thought of what people said about me. What would they think about me?

Then I had to learn to quiet the loudest critic. Myself, and what I thought about me!

How many times I cried and wondered, *"Am I doing the right thing? How will I do this? How will I be able to manage on my own?"* I already felt like a failure and here was one more thing to add to my list. Swirling doubts rising like a vortex with its only aim to swallow me, trying to pull me back into a space from which there would be no escape.

But God had other plans.

I heard Him clearly one day when I was about to lose my mind. That still, calm voice within giving me a choice. A choice between life and death. A choice between love and hate. That day I chose love. Because God loved me first and He is showing me in every situation I find myself in, that He continues to love me and wants to see me happy and live the abundant life which he has prepared for me. And every day I will continue to love…me.

I Love Me

I love me…
All my faults, my flaws,
Even my insecurities,
Everything that makes me who I am,
Everything I want to be,
My past, my present, my future,
All goes into loving me.

I love me…
You don't have to love me,
They say that your love is extra,
An addition to my rendition,
Of the love God placed in me,
For me – to love me,
Totally!

I love…me!

Alesia (Lisa) R. Simpson is an Honors Graduate of the Social Service Worker program at Humber College and is currently working as a Social Service Worker. She is pursuing a Hons. Bachelor's Degree in Counselling Psychology and working towards becoming a counselor in her community. Lisa is also an Ordained Pastor whose vision is to see others grow and excel in life.

CHAPTER SEVENTEEN - Reverend Alice Blaylock

How I Weathered the Storm

Whether we like it or not, storms are a part of life. It's not the category of the storm that we should concern ourselves with but how we weather the storm that matters. My marriage was ending, and I didn't know how I was going to survive. I was a stay-at-home mom with three young children. I thought I was doing everything right. I believed in God and considered myself to be a godly woman. Not only did I attend church regularly, but I was also a leader in my church, so why was this happening to me? Why was my marriage falling apart and how would I ever make it alone? I couldn't see past the "right now" to even consider what was yet to come. I just knew that my prayers would be answered and that my marriage would be reconciled. It was during this storm that I understood the meaning behind "What doesn't kill you makes you stronger." It was during this storm that I learned that no one is exempt from heartache and pain and it's our response that will determine our survival.

I found myself using the rain to camouflage my tears, wondering where God was. I had to decide if I was going to dance in the rain and live or if was I going to let the rain consume me and drown. I decided to dance, and as I began to dance, I realized that God was my partner dancing alongside of me. It was by His grace that I was able to gracefully endure the ending of my marriage. As the rain fell, I realized I was rooted in a solid foundation growing with an unwavering peace that surrounded my very presence.

It would have been so easy to look at my failed marriage and be convinced that God had turned His back on me. My husband and I knew who God was. As a matter of fact, we went to church on our first date so I could meet his mother and grandmother. He and I were believers, but we didn't make room for God in our relationship, and when things got volatile, we could not see past the hurt and disappointment we both invited into the situation. Neither of us really wanted the divorce, but neither one of us was willing to do what was necessary to make the marriage work. We didn't want to change our selfish self-serving ways and the thought of being transformed was a concept that we didn't understand. With my husband, it was, *"When God wants me to change, He will change me,"* and with me, it was, *"Well, God will make a way. I will just ride this out and pray for the best."* Never did we think to ask or consider what God wanted from us or for us to do to make our marriage work. We thought that merely making our presence known in church would be enough, but it was going to take more than just going to church. We would have to be willing to surrender our worldly deeds, thoughts, and actions and pick up God's armor to lay the foundation for our marriage to work. We were not willing to make any Godly sacrifices to make the marriage work and wound up sacrificing our marriage.

God has the authority to use our storms to reinforce the need for us to have a relationship with Him and it's that relationship with Him that will get us through the storms we face in this life. I found myself alone and broke after my divorce, with no job, no employment, the house was under foreclosure, and I had three small children to provide for. I think those were good enough reasons to surrender but I couldn't give up. Fear of the unknown made decision-making for the future difficult, but I had to pull out my faith and trust God to catch me and keep me in step as we danced during the storm. What other choice did I have? It was do or die. Taking that leap of faith, I found that there was something better on the other side! I was determined I was not going to be the victim and cry "Woah is me," but I was going to dance sometimes with tears that watered the seeds for my blessings.

Change is difficult no matter what the reason is for it. I had to focus on the needs of my children and allow myself time to heal. No matter how scared I was of the process, I had to believe that God would be there and provide all my needs. I had to change my attitude and humble myself to accept that I needed help. Asking for help and being transparent about needing help was one of the hardest things I had to do. That first step was the most difficult, as I battled with all the impossibilities of my success without my husband. It was then that I began to appreciate the value of wisdom, and as I pursued it, it embraced me. Scripture was my source for understanding it. It helped me make wise choices and commit to sticking to doing the right thing no matter the circumstances I was facing. I had to put my full trust in God, step out on faith, and move with God's grace. And as my faith grew, God's love filled me up and poured out provision as I navigated through the storm. Is not God the creator of heaven and earth and everything thing within, so why wouldn't I trust Him with what was going on with me? It was this storm that drew me closer to God, keeping in mind that God can orchestrate things for His glory which puts us in a position to receive His favor. All we have to do is believe, be faithful, and be obedient to his authority over our lives.

I was determined to move forward with my life. I redirected my focus to a greater need than the one for myself – the needs of my young children who relied on me to care for them as they were under the umbrella with me during the storm. Focusing on them diminished my pain and all of those "woah is me" thoughts that I mentioned earlier. Once I had a realistic view of my circumstances, I was able to put things into perspective and solutions came into view. There is no greater release than realizing that a problem was not as overwhelming as it seemed in someone else's distress. I was no longer afraid to reach the light at the end of the tunnel for fear that it was an oncoming train. I told myself that I would not become self-consumed when a storm came and by focusing on the needs of those who depend on me cultivated my healing by giving of myself. Once I redirected my focus and stopped complaining and being resentful of my circumstances, I began to glean from what life had to offer me. I trusted God for increase and favor as I moved forward day by day. I gained a new appreciation for God's new mercies and when storms come my way, I welcome them as opportunities for joy, understanding that when my faith is tested, my endurance has a chance to grow. I gained an understanding that in those times of testing were opportunities to strengthen my character and sanctify my spirit. I learned to pursue change and not run away from it. If moving to a different environment is necessary to get past the situation, move and do not look back. I learned the importance of nurturing a grateful spirit during my storm, reminding myself that there is always someone who is in a worse storm than the one I am in. Being willing to do something I have never done to get something I have never had has become second nature for me. I am no longer afraid to step out of comfort to discomfort to secure peace and protect my joy. I am no longer afraid to be vulnerable and transparent with those whom God has placed in my life because one of them could be the source of a blessing.

During my marriage, I always wanted to make sure that my husband and children were taken care of, and I never put focus on my needs. I felt that if I did anything for myself, I was being selfish. So many married women feel that way and their marriages wind up failing as they start feeling resentment towards their spouses and children and their lives become void of joy, hope, and eventually love. I was blessed to have a relationship with God that reminded me that joy comes from within, and no one can give it to me or ever take it away from me. When my next chapter as a single woman began, I held on to the joy of knowing that I was chosen. I have unwavering hope for the future knowing that Christ is coming back to get his beloved and I am living my life on purpose with purpose to secure my life in eternity with Him trusting the fact that God does not make promises He does not keep! He promised to never leave me nor forsake me, and if I love myself the way God loves me, I will not be a victim who allows or accepts love from anyone who offers less than that!

My children may have grown up in a home without a biological father present, but their heavenly father provided for them and for that I am grateful. I am a living testimony that there is nothing more powerful than a praying mother and I will always pray and give God the glory for blessing and keeping us. Our needs were always met, and I was always available when they needed me. I always compared myself to the Proverbs 31 woman and always felt I fell short because my marriage failed. I realize now that I am in a relationship with God, and by putting His will and call on my life as a priority, I am that Proverbs 31 woman. Each day I embrace as another opportunity to embrace God's love for me and extend that love to others.

My marriage may have failed but the experience is one that I am grateful for, and I have no regrets. I acknowledge that grace and peace are mine in abundance through the knowledge of God and of Jesus Christ, our Lord and Savior. I accept God's divine power that gives me everything that I need to live a life of godliness. My knowledge of Him who called us by His own glory and goodness has given me His very great and precious promises so that through them, I may participate in the divine nature and escape the corruption in the world caused by temptations of the flesh. For that very reason, I make every effort to add to my faith daily – goodness, and to goodness – knowledge, and to knowledge – self-control, and to self-control – perseverance, and to perseverance – godliness, and to godliness – brotherly kindness, and to brotherly kindness – Love. For I have learned from Peter 2:1-8 that if you possess these qualities in increasing measure, they will help keep you from being ineffective and unproductive in your knowledge of the Lord Jesus Christ who is your protection in even the worse of storms. Remember Jesus was sleeping unbothered in the boat during the storm. This is an example for us that we should have steadfast unwavering faith strong enough that we should not only weather the storm, but we should be able to look in the eye of the storm and know that there is peace on the other side of it.

All we must do is navigate through the storm with Jesus!

Reverend Alice Blaylock-Pitts has her degree in Christian Ministry and is the co-owner of Laced Up Dance Studio. She's an Avon and Mary Kay Independent Consultant and a licensed insurance agent. Alice has three adult children [Alex-Anthony (wife Andree), Ariel, and Amari] and four grandchildren. She is passionate about making a difference, believing that through Christ, we can have an abundant life. Alice considers it a blessing to help others on their journey.

CHAPTER EIGHTEEN - Patria Robert Francis

God's Amazing Love

As a rule, the first thing I would do each morning is go into the bathroom, stand in front of the mirror, and say, *"Wow, this girl is getting prettier every day. Lord, I love you! Thank you for waking me up again another morning! I thank you for waking up all my loved ones another day."*

Usually after my morning routine, I would begin my devotion and lift up my voice in praise and admiration towards my Heavenly Father. I then would immediately get my Bible out and start reading His Word, meditating on the scriptures that I had read, and admire how much He has been so good to me.

Many times after doing my devotions, I would find myself lifting my hands to the heavens to make declarations each morning. For instance, *"Lord I am blessed, I am the head and not the tail, I am above and not beneath, I am anointed, I am sanctified, I am healed, I am prosperous, I am strong and most of all I am gloriously saved and washed in the precious blood of the Lamb."*

This is when my life all changed. It began one Wednesday morning. I woke up and did my usual routine to start my day because I didn't like to take any nonsense from that liar, the enemy. I had my breakfast and then started getting ready to go to my senior's luncheon at church for the afternoon.

I was one to take the bus to wherever I had to go. So there I was, on the bus enjoying the scenery along the way until it was my time to ring the bell for my stop. In the meantime, I waited for the bus to come to a full stop and for the door to be opened so that could I step down off the bus to be on my merry way. As my feet touched the sidewalk, I decided to wait for the bus to pass me, like always, so that I could cross the street. But for some strange reason, the bus driver took longer than usual to drive off. I proceeded to look on both sides of the road to check if any vehicles were in sight. It was very clear for me to cross over to the other side of the street. However, as I started crossing the road, the Lord showed me what was about to happen. It was at that moment the bus driver decided to drive off. All I felt was this big heavy rush on the side of my face. I then cried out, *"Lord Jesus, help me!"* That's when I realized I was underneath the bus.

As a result of that, I began to feel a great amount of pressure on my chest and my shoulder. It was the wheel of the bus that was on me. At that moment, I was gasping for air since the bus was on my abdomen. From a distance, I could hear the voices of individuals from the church. Afterward, the bus was moved off of me, which gave me somewhat of a relief. Above all, the last thing that I could remember was the sound of the siren. Furthermore, I knew nothing else after that. It seemed that I had passed out because of the traumatization that I had experienced. If it hadn't been for the grace of God and the prayers of my church family, I would not be here today.

When I eventually opened my eyes, it was brought to my attention that I had broken ribs, a broken ankle, and surgery on my left leg. It was my understanding that I had about four surgeries to try and mend the injuries. As I tried to comprehend what had happened to me, I came to the realization that my whole body was in a tremendous amount of shock from the accident.

Immediately, it started to make sense. It was the enemy trying to take me out again, for the third time and last time. I knew that the enemy was after me because he already made two attempts and I told him that he should have gotten me the first time when he had the chance. Although he had tried to take me out, this would not discourage me from serving God.

You see, I am not the same person as I was before the accident. I am more determined to press on and not look back. I am so empowered more than ever to serve God come what may! I refuse to let this season of my life hold me back from what God has for me and what He has called me to do. Three times the old slew foot devil tried to tempt my Big Brother Jesus, but my Jesus did not yield to his temptation, so it is with me – I will not be tempted to give up on life because of this new season that I'm in.

"Then was Jesus led up of the Spirit into the wilderness to be tempted of the devil. And when he had fasted forty days and forty nights, he was afterward an hungred. And when the tempter came to him, he said, If thou be the Son of God, command that these stones be made bread. But he answered and said, It is written, Man shall not live by bread alone, but by every word that proceedeth out of the mouth of God. Then the devil taketh him up into the holy city, and setteth him on a pinnacle of the temple, And saith unto him, If thou be the Son of God, cast thyself down: for it is written, He shall give his angels charge concerning thee: and in their hands they shall bear thee up, lest at any time thou dash thy foot against a stone. Jesus said unto him, It is written again, Thou shalt not tempt the Lord thy God. Again, the devil taketh him up into an exceeding high mountain, and sheweth him all the kingdoms of the world, and the glory of them; And saith unto him, All these things will I give thee, if thou wilt fall down and worship me. Then saith Jesus unto him, Get thee hence, Satan: for it is written, Thou shalt worship the Lord thy God, and him only shalt thou serve." Matthew 4:1-10 (KJV)

You may ask the question, *"Why?"* It is because my Bible tells me that I am more than a conqueror and will not be defeated! Never, ever! In Jesus' name! I may have some challenges every now and then. For instance, in this new season, I had to learn how to sit up and walk all over again with the help of my spiritual daughter and with a walker too. This new challenge has been painful, scary, and overwhelming at times, but with God's grace, I am able to overcome it all.

 Although I may have to limp with my left leg, I'm still able to do certain chores around my home for myself like preparing my own meals and light cleaning, the rest of it is taken care of by someone else. So, indeed I am really blessed and highly favored. I am really amazed at how God has brought me through this season of my life. I can certainly say that my God is a great big, wonderful God!

You may be wondering how I became so empowered. I have seen God's amazing love, grace, and deliverance in my life so many times. It was as if I had met my dear Savior on the road to Damascus just like how Paul had met him there. Jeremiah stated that it was like fire shut up in my bones and I just could not hold my peace.

Being a child of God and knowing who I am in Christ has empowered me to be all He has created me to be. Spending time in prayer, reading His Word, and listening to Him has given me the empowerment to put my foot on the devil's neck by saying with authority, "It is written in Jesus' name that I am healed, I am victorious, I am stronger!" You know something, I just feel the urge to stamp the devil's neck right now and crush his head another time.

My God has transformed me. He has removed the fear that I had as I started on this new journey. He has never left my side. I know deep down within my heart that I never would have made it without Him. Therefore, I will continue to live this new life that He has given to me. I continue to trust this same God that I've known since 1974. He is the Father who never failed me, even though I have failed Him many times, yet, He has never once failed me. When I may feel that it is getting late to hear from Him, He shows up right on time.

Although this journey had been rough and painful at times, God made it His duty to transform me into who I am today.

He has given me His peace which passeth all understanding because I have kept my eyes on Him. Therefore, He will keep my heart and mind in perfect peace. It is the greatest feeling to know that He's got my back. I know that I am not alone because God is walking with me through this season now. He sees and understands the pain that I go through more than anyone in this world. I am not afraid to tell of His love for me and what He has done for me to this day. I know I have a personal relationship with Him and that will never change.

If you would like to experience being transformed, ask your heavenly father to forgive you of your sins, repent from all unrighteousness, and allow Him to be the Lord of your life. Spend time reading His word daily, listen to His still voice, and talk with Him. When you don't know what to say, just remain quiet and be still He loves that. He knows your heart.

"and said, Naked came I out of my mother's womb, and naked shall I return thither: the LORD gave, and the LORD hath taken away; blessed be the name of the LORD." Job 1:21 (KJV)

"In thee, O Lord, do I put my trust: let me never be put to confusion. Deliver me in thy righteousness, and cause me to escape: incline thine ear unto me, and save me. But I will hope continually, and will yet praise thee more and more. My mouth shall shew forth thy righteousness and thy salvation all the day; for I know not the numbers thereof. I will go in the strength of the Lord God: I will make mention of thy righteousness, even of thine only. O God, thou hast taught me from my youth: and hitherto have I declared thy wondrous works. Now also when I am old and greyheaded, O God, forsake me not; until I have shewed thy strength unto this generation, and thy power to every one that is to come. Thy righteousness also, O God, is very high, who hast done great things: O God, who is like unto thee! Thou, which hast shewed me great and sore troubles, shalt quicken me again, and shalt bring me up again from the depths of the earth. Thou shalt increase my greatness, and comfort me on every side." Psalm 71: 1-2, 14-21 (KJV)

Patria Francis is a prayerful woman of God. Over the years, she has loved the Lord with all her mind and soul. Patria loves to share the Gospel and what God has done in her life. She has held positions as a Sunday School teacher, and worship leader, took part in prayer meetings, and ministered to the shut-ins. It is Patria's desire to be used by God in whatever way to help the needy.

 patriamarcia1974@gmail.com

CHAPTER NINETEEN - Marcia Hall

You Can Make It on Broken Pieces

As women, we have many titles. I have been a daughter, sister, single woman, wife, mother, divorced single mother, and single mature woman. I have come full circle.

As a young girl in the church, I dreamed of growing up and finding Mr. Right, having my own family, and living happily ever after. Amos 3:3 states:

"Can two walk together unless they agree?" (NKJV)

I did not achieve my happy ever after but that is another chapter for another book.

Let me share a little about my background before I delve into my story. My parents were born in the Caribbean, moved to the United Kingdom, and got married. They had two children relatively quickly into their married life. I grew up in the church and did not know much about the outside world. This was by design. Like most young women in the church, I had this vision of growing up, marrying the man that God would provide for me, having a family, and raising them in the ways of the Lord. It took many years before I would marry. I wanted to do things God's way. I was thirty-six years old by the time the Lord provided me with a husband. We lived together for twenty years before the marriage broke down and I became a single parent raising two teenage children alone.

It was Valentine's Day, 2018, and I was looking forward to going on a double date with some friends to celebrate. That date did not happen. I laid in my bed wondering how I was going to tell the world that my marriage had failed. I had no Plan B. I knew there would be challenging times and we would weather those times together. I never envisaged a divorce. I could not have imagined being a single mother raising my children to adulthood alone.

I had recently been made redundant. I did not have any savings or anything that I could fall back on. When two salaries are coming into the household, you do not worry about having a backup plan or any real savings to speak of. With both children going to secondary school, I could go back to work full-time. We were going to start building our savings and pay off our mortgage.

I was paralyzed with fear. I turned to God and asked Him, *"How could you let this happen to me? You must have known this day was coming and you did not prepare me for it."* I started asking myself if I truly heard from God when I got married. And if I did, how could my story end this way? Well, God was silent! I did not hear anything for many weeks and months. If I did, I was not capable of interpreting, or coherently understanding what God was saying to me.

I was overcome with every emotion imaginable. How would I explain it to my family and friends? What was I going to tell my children who were going to be devastated by the breakdown of our family?

Eventually, I told my immediate family, church family, and close friends. Everyone was understanding, giving, loving, and extremely supportive. My church family was fantastic, especially my Life Group (Cell Group). They cooked for me, visited, and encouraged me at every turn. However, no matter how loving and caring others are, there comes a moment when you are alone with your thoughts, feelings, emotions, and children. There is no one to share your pain with. There used to be two of you sharing everything – the good and the bad. Now you are alone. In those moments, my life felt dark and full of despair. I felt like God had abandoned me; thrown me to the wolves! How could a "good Christian woman," as this is how I perceived myself, be in this position? The scripture that comes to mind is Matthew 5:45:

"...for He makes His sun rise on the evil and the good and sends rain on the just and on the unjust." (NKJV)

I used to believe that because I was a woman of faith, certain events should not happen to me. The truth is, what is happening to families outside the church, is being echoed inside the church and we are not immune. But neither are we equipped!

I was ashamed, embarrassed, and felt like a failure. Not only did I have to deal with my pain, but I also had to be there for my children. I needed to help them understand what was happening and why when I did not even understand it myself.

Many nights I went to sleep with Joel Osteen's audiobook *"Blessed in the Darkness"* playing all night. This audiobook saved my life. It reminded me of a sermon I heard preached years ago in my youth, entitled *"You Can Make It, Even on Broken Pieces."* It would be years later when this message from God and its true meaning would manifest in my life and become a lifeboat for me to hold on to. Both the book and the sermon were saying that whatever happens to us in life, God can make that tragic, traumatic experience work in our favor.

"And we know that all things work together for good to those who love God, to those who are the called according to His purpose." Roman 8:28 (NKJV)

I could not understand how my marriage breaking down and leaving me as a single mother was ever going to work in my favor or for my good.

After the initial shock, I had to start rebuilding my life and enable my children to grieve the loss of the family structure they once knew. Many people helped me on that journey – brothers and sisters in the faith and others who were not in the faith.

What helped me during this season:

- The practical help of others, meals, lifts, repairs, childcare, etc.
- Not being too proud to ask for help when I needed it. Watching YouTube videos when I needed to do repairs for myself.

- Recognizing God was my source. Allowing others to give to me and being able to receive. God was miraculous in this way. I would go to my letter box and find an envelope with money in it, which I desperately needed. Up to this point, I had only ever heard testimonials about God's provision in this way.

- I had to seek professional help for myself and my children (both Christian counseling as well as non-Christian counseling).

- Opening up to selected and trusted strong Christians as to what I was experiencing and feeling. Acknowledging the bitterness, letting it go, and being able to forgive. My understanding of forgiveness is quite different from the norm. Forgiveness is for the injured party! We forgive others to save ourselves. It does not mean allowing a person to occupy the space and importance they once held in your life. You can forgive and let them go.

- Writing a gratitude journal. Taking the time to write down what was good in my life and what I was thankful for. When you are in a very dark place, you must take the time to see the good in your life. Example: "I am so happy and grateful now that I am alive and living in health." Just that simple statement can help you put into perspective the adverse events taking place in your life by changing your mindset about those situations.

- Prayer and meditating on various scriptures gave me hope for my future and that of my children.

I listened to my children and allowed them to express their anger, loss, and disappointment. I could not raise my children the way my parents raised me with that "tough love attitude." This was not going to work when my children were acting out due to our broken family status. I listened to my intuition, the Holy Spirit, or inner witness, and was guided by this. What do you do when your children refuse to go to school because of the trauma they are experiencing in their lives? You cannot force them to learn. You have to love them where they are and try to see things from their point of view. Yes, boundaries still have to be set but I had to reject a lot of the so-called "traditional values" I was raised with if I wanted to save my relationship with my children. I started to listen keenly to what they were expressing and focused on what they needed instead of worrying about what others would think of the choices I was making for them, even if their education took a hit.

    The experience of becoming a divorced woman/single mother has changed and altered my life and personality forever. I have evolved into a better mother and woman. I have learned to become grateful for the experience of divorce and being a single parent. I see the world with different eyes. I realize that our lives run in seasons. When a season is over and you have learned that life lesson, that season closes and the door to a new one opens. We sometimes either refuse to or don't know how to let go of the past season and embrace the new one. Several of the people I knew during my marriage moved out of my life. New relationships have been embraced to assist me in achieving and understanding the new life lessons I need to learn.

    I encourage women who are divorced or going through divorce that there is a future and various opportunities to share with other women. God still loves them and there is purpose and meaning for their lives, after divorce. God is not finished with us yet.

I read various books that spoke about changing your mindset:

- *The Power of Your Subconscious Mind* by Joseph Murphy.
- *Living in the Now* by Eckhart Tolle.
- *Change Your Paradigm, Change Your Life* by Bob Proctor.

Reading books like these aided me in reinventing myself. I lost my job, my way of life, my home, my security – so many losses just from this one experience! The scriptures empowered me during this difficult transition. You need tools that enable you to think outside the box or begin to formulate a plan for your future. God uses our trauma and disappointments to facilitate us moving forward. Nothing is ever wasted!

I want to encourage you that *"You Can Make It Even on Broken Pieces"* and become Empowered through your Transition to evolve into a stronger person than you knew was possible. I made it through the season of divorce on broken pieces. All that was left of my life was fragments. From those fragments, my life has been transformed and re-molded into the person I am today. The suffering from my old season has formulated the new beginnings for my new season! These trials of our faith mature us in our walk with God and demonstrate his goodness and power when we overcome and make it to the other side. He receives the glory and others come to know Him through our struggle.

 Marcia Hall was a Legal Secretary and Administrator with 20 years of experience in law with Secretarial/Clerical/Administrative/PA experience, a PRINCE2® Practitioner in project management, past Chair of Governors for a primary school moving from Inadequate to Good, and is currently a Patient Co-Ordinator Customer Service Advisor. She is a mother of a son and daughter and an encourager to anyone she meets. Marcia is an ex-member of the internationally known gospel group Majestic Singers, and her interests include self-development, reading, and travel.

https://tinyurl.com/Marcia-Hall

mspraise50

www.linkedin.com/in/marcia-hall-75614055/

marciahall@gmail.com

CHAPTER TWENTY - Jasmine E. Clarke

One Step Closer to Soar

Have you ever reached a place in your life where you say to yourself, *"This can't be all there is to life?"* Well, I did! I had gotten so tired of the same mundane way of life. It felt as if I was on a roundabout and just kept going in circles, but not getting anywhere. Things weren't getting any better. As a matter of fact, they seemed to get worse.

I just couldn't see myself living this way for the rest of my life. I had a strong desire to live. I needed to smell the flowers, enjoy the sun, and live life to its fullest. I needed more of God. I craved to know what was hidden from me including the treasures that God had planted inside of me. I say hidden because the enemy had blinded my eyes to them.

You see, there was a time I had stepped away from the Lord because I was carrying such a heavy load believing that I could handle it all on my own. Eventually, it became so overwhelming that I gave up everything that I used to do at church: participating in two gospel groups, directing a church youth choir, and a mass choir, just to name a few. I made myself very busy so that I would not have to face whatever dilemmas that I was going through in my life; I was hoping they would just disappear. After allowing that to continue for so many years, I couldn't keep up with it any longer and that's when everything just came crashing down on me. I was so devastated by what had happened. I needed to figure out where I had to go from there. I was not going to church, but I still read my Bible and tried to keep a relationship with the Lord. I truly have to give God glory and praise because, during that time of isolation from the church, God continually looked out for me. He always provided a job for me, a roof over my head, and food to eat. That is why I will never turn my back on the Lord because He never left me nor forsook me.

Over the years, there were countless times I would think about what I had been through and what lessons I learned. At this point, I rededicated my life to the Lord. Unfortunately, about three days after I made that decision, I received the news that my father was in transition to be with the Lord. I did not get the chance to say goodbye and it really broke my heart.

Considering the loss of my father, I found myself spiraling down into a very dark place. My way of thinking was unfavorable. I thought the worst of myself, believing that nothing ever good would happen to me. I always got the short end of the stick. God didn't love me like He loved everybody else, yet I would still hear these words repeatedly that God was a God of love. I just wasn't feeling His love. I remember thinking about the talents I had and not being able to use them. If I even tried or attempted to start something, I would get shut down by individuals or I just wouldn't complete it. I couldn't seem to accomplish anything in life, and it just didn't make any sense. It felt as if there was a stench or a mark on me, causing people to mistreat and disrespect me.

What was it? I was very confused. I was living right. I loved the Lord like never before. I loved helping people. I was a kind person. I found pleasure in helping someone in need. This felt like a terrible storm taking place in my life; like a hurricane and a tornado happening at the same time. It seemed like something was trying to pull me under the sea so that I would drown, meaning I almost died and ended up walking with a cane. I felt so helpless. I had to ask God what kind of life I had. How could I ever accomplish anything being in so much pain? I began to feel so discouraged that I became depressed. I hated the way I was feeling. It was so dark and exhausting. I ended up not being able to sleep at nights because the pain that I was experiencing was so intense…and I needed help. I just wanted my life back, and only God could fix it.

Then the Lord showed me that the enemy had stepped in and turned my life upside down. He wanted to take me out. I can say that because it was not the first time it had happened. I needed to get out of his web. I needed God to turn everything around so that I could be the woman that He had called me to be.

After reading God's Word, I finally accepted the fact that He loved me so much that He would pave the way for me to get back into alignment with Him and His Word. I knew deep in my heart that God had covered me under His wings. He redirected me to a place of claiming back my life and my future because He had a plan for my life. I didn't want to live a life of regrets. I wanted to live a life of fulfillment.

On this new path, I experienced quite a few challenges, the first of which was going back to school and taking on the calling of the Lord as a Praise and Worship Leader. I thought that I was way too old to be going back to school at my age. I didn't even notice that God had done something marvelous in me. He had taken my ashes for beauty. In other words, I didn't even look my age. A few times, some of the students were curious about my age because of the way I spoke or how I carried myself. When I revealed my age, they wanted proof, so I showed them my driver's license, which left them with embarrassed expressions on their faces. It was hilarious to see their reactions, but then I realized that it was God's grace shining through me. If you think about it, scriptures do say that you cannot pour new wine into an old wine skin. In other words, for change to take place in your life it all has to start from the inside out.

> *"Neither do men put new wine into old bottles: else the bottles break, and the wine runneth out, and the bottles perish: but they put new wine into new bottles, and both are preserved."* Matthew 9:17

My second challenge was taking college algebra. I was never one that loved math and I wished that I didn't have to take it, but I did. During the season, I realized that God was watching my attitude. I had to learn to embrace even the challenges that I had to walk through. One of my classes was psychology and I took that course embracing how the brain works and how we can make a change in our minds related to what we want to accomplish. To make a long story short, I improved my attitude, worked away at all my courses, and achieved A's, B+, and B's in every one of my classes. I surprised myself; I was so happy and proud of myself. In the psychology class, the professor came up to me and asked me to follow her to her office, which I did. She went over to her desk to get a little package and gave it to me. When I opened it, there was a pin that said *Attitude!* I looked at her, puzzled and wondering why she would come up with such a gift like that. Then she explained to me that it was my attitude that brought me thus far. Isn't it amazing how God can connect you to individuals who will usher you to the next level? God be praised!

Let me tell you this! In the past, I did not believe that I was capable of getting outstanding marks because I used to listen to the voices, which was the enemy, telling me that I wasn't capable of being successful and that I was a failure. But I realized that it was all a lie because the Holy Spirit referred me back to the Word of God that says:

"I can do all things through Christ who strengthens me." Philippians 4:13

As each day went by, I would ask the Lord to renew my mind. **I was being transformed**. I had to have faith in God to see my way through these new changes in my life. I had a passion for life. It also brought me to the place of utilizing each lesson that I had learned in my valleys and to celebrate the new levels where they had taken me. Most of all, I was so grateful for the journey that I had traveled and for knowing that my heavenly Father was with me at all times.

"And do not be conformed to this world, but be transformed by the renewing of your mind, that you may prove what is that good and acceptable and perfect will of God." Romans 12:2 (NKJV)

There are times we will find ourselves in this comfort zone where it prevents us from moving forward and we become very stagnant. To allow change to take place in our lives, we have to humble ourselves and allow God to stretch and mold us into who He ordained us to be before we were even formed in our mothers' wombs. This began to motivate and ignite a passion within me – to change and thrive to be all that the Almighty had called me to be.

"For I know the thoughts that I think toward you, says the Lord, thoughts of peace and not of evil, to give you a future and a hope." Jeremiah 29:11 (NKJV)

Not long after, I began to experience this phenomenal transformation in my life that attracted new opportunities by opening new doors. I became excited about this new adventure and the growth that I was experiencing. It allowed me to open my mind and my heart to the entities of God. I had such an incredibly different glimpse at life with extraordinary expectations. This was so rejuvenating to my soul. It definitely was my desire to live!

I experienced a tremendous amount of stretching because I had gotten so comfortable with the former way of living – I never wanted to move from where I was because I was so afraid of the unknown. I couldn't see the gifts that the Lord had bestowed upon me because the enemy had deceived me. I had to step back, let go, and trust God where He was taking me to. This was a healing sanctuary for my mind, body, soul, and spirit. It gave me more reason to live. God had so much more for me. I had to wake up, get out of my comfort zone, and fight for what was mine. I wanted to be a better person and achieve my goals in life. This shift was to make me stronger and to take a righteous authority.

It meant for me that through many prayers and fasting, I had to repent from all known and unknown sins. Repent, cancel, renounce, and nullify all generational bloodline curses and come out of every agreement that was spoken over myself and my family that was negative from my parents' generational bloodline sins and with everyone I came into contact with. I also cast out and bound any demonic spirits that attached themselves to me during the time of my trauma, which had opened many doors. Once I had completed what was required of me, I started to see a shift take place in my thoughts and my actions.

I must tell you that life is transitional! If we want to better ourselves, we must make a sacrifice to change and grow by humbling ourselves to the Lord and allowing Him and the Holy Spirit to work within us, lead us, and direct us along this journey. My whole desire is to be able to soar so high like an eagle with no intentions of turning back to the old me.

Do you not know that your bodies are temples of the Holy Spirit, who is in you, whom you have received from God? You are not your own; you were bought at a price. Therefore honor God with your bodies.

1 Corinthians 6:19-20

In your relationships with one another, have the same mindset as Christ Jesus:

Philippians 2:5

CHAPTER TWENTY-ONE - Candace Lalor

Discerning Great Perspectives: Peace That Passes All Understanding

As a believer in God, I imagined myself having an almost perfect life. I expected to plan the events and opportunities and never have to edit the details. My idea of a happy and fulfilled life was one with the least amount of troubles or setbacks.

God was about to show me that He was the author and finisher of my whole life. He was about to carve out the path it would take for me to see Him clearly, with the necessary crossroads that only His direction could guide me through.

Growing up, going to church on Sunday was not an option. Family prayer was a regular practice and constant conversations of the faithfulness of God in my parents' lives were heard during family gatherings and birthday parties.

Even though I had many doubts, I believed that if I hung around church long enough, their faith and resilience would somehow rub off on me.

My journey as a Christian began in high school.

I grew up in a home hearing about God sending His son to earth to bring salvation to everyone who believes in Him, and constantly heard about how "Sweet it is to know Jesus."

My parents and grandparents set a great example for their children in the simplest of ways like saying grace before meals, singing hymns of praise throughout the house, praying for us before heading into traffic, and speaking about how God provided for them in their times of need.

Before having a personal relationship with the Lord, I questioned what it would look like for a young person like me to believe in Him and live according to His purpose.

In the back of my mind, I had doubts that I would be a part of anything significant in the world. Fortunately, my doubts were proven wrong.

Looking back, I noticed a pattern of thinking throughout my teenage years. I constantly doubted my purpose, importance, and what my future would look like. Reading about the hard times experienced by disciples and believers in the Bible had me always thinking that any effort to spread the good news of God would always result in being tested, rejected, or failing.

I feared the possibility of being challenged and having to experience difficulty. I feared disagreeing with people, being mocked, and most of all, being misunderstood.

I was reading the Bible, a book of inspiration, but was convinced everyone but me was meant to be important and full of great potential. Even being gifted with the ability to create art without taking any online courses was a talent I overlooked and saw as useless.

Falling into the overuse of social media, I became very insecure about my body image, especially around other people. In my mind, I was overweight and not the prettiest girl to look at. I didn't think I was very ugly, but I didn't see anything appealing when I looked in the mirror. There was always going to be a girl that was prettier or smarter than me. Socializing was awkward because I would try to avoid conversations everywhere: at the mall, at school with friends, and even at church. I would often isolate myself in high school because I hardly felt likable or relatable to anyone around me.

Having these insecurities left me very vulnerable and open to almost anything that would make me feel better about myself. I told the Lord I thought my life was boring and aimless because I was just a church-going girl with no story to tell.

I didn't have a rough history with a transformation moment, an addiction I overcame, or a lifestyle change of how God met me in my darkest moment.

How was I going to relate with people that experienced hardship? What would I tell them salvation brought me through?

In the few years I took to work a part-time job after high school, I started wondering things I thought I would never question. Having a hard time seeing how a guy would ever fall in love with me, I was curious about what a relationship with a female would look like. I knew it was wrong to even consider but I was tired of feeling lonely and unattractive.

It was the weirdest thing to have desires towards the same sex, especially as a Christian. Thankfully, I never got to the point of pursuing a relationship with a female and avoided a lifestyle that would prevent me from enjoying the intimacy God meant for me.

Fighting daily convictions and condemnation, I wanted so badly to feel God's love but never thought He would love me with these desires in my heart. I prayed for change, for these feelings to leave, but they didn't completely go away. It got difficult to read and accept God's Word, so I started reading it less often, but always kept it in view on the same spot of my bedroom dresser every night.

Despite my internal struggle, there were people who occasionally crossed my path encouraging me to pursue a career that would allow me to work with youth. I was told I looked like a person who would influence and empower young men and women to believe in their value and potential.

For a while in my 20s, I started to believe that having questions and doubts was never allowed and was a sign of not having enough faith. I was convinced that my faith was weak and hadn't gained enough strength to make dreams or ambitions a reality. I never actually thought the creator of this world would even consider using me to be a part of anything that would be noticed or meaningful. This is when God displayed himself to be bigger than my lack of faith in great things taking place in my own life.

Taking the advice of those around me, I applied for a college program in Social Service Work. I was humbled to learn how much more understanding and compassion are essential in speaking with people having different opinions and cultural backgrounds. In my Christian walk, this helped me to be better at displaying the fruits of the spirit towards others. What I didn't realize was the same love I wanted to show other people was the very same love, grace, and support I needed to show to myself. This was the time in my life when I started to realize the connection between my fear of speaking and the age gap between me and my siblings.

I was the youngest of all three kids. Every step I took towards a venture was a few steps behind my older brother and sister. They had experiences in life I had yet to learn about on my own. By the time I was applying to college, they had both graduated from their post-secondary studies, were working their dream jobs, and were becoming well-established on their own. They owned their vehicles and traveled to countries I hadn't. Their independence was a little intimidating and I felt like I was lagging behind. I often thought to myself, *"What could I accomplish that my siblings already haven't?"*

When the driven desire to make an impact in the lives of others didn't make sense, I began to become more aware of how I saw myself and how much more self-love I needed to include in my day-to-day routine. Even though I didn't completely understand how to create a roadmap for my post-secondary education, God seemed to meet me in my worry and helped me trust that life would always head in the direction of destiny.

College life was an interesting adventure. My timeline and plans took a pleasant turn for the better at the end of it all. Instead of being accepted into one placement organization, I attended two, allowing me to gain experience with middle school students, teenagers, and young men in a homeless shelter environment as well as seniors who thrived in staying active through low-impact movements and physical exercise. Even though customizing my college program meant staying an extra year, it ended up being to my benefit because it prepared me with all the experiences I was going to need in my future Social Worker career. Despite the traveling, the financial sacrifice, and sleepless nights of paperwork and studying, I successfully graduated with a diploma in Social Service Work during a challenging time when college and university students were isolated during the COVID-19 pandemic and were forced to complete their studies entirely online.

As a young woman, I believed every lie that was in my mind about myself. But when I got older, God taught me how to apply the authority He's given all his children, by taking every thought captive so it would obey Him and His standards.

I didn't believe God could meet me where I was at. I didn't think He would want to get His hands dirty in the struggles I had. But that was a misunderstanding of His character, heart, and mind. When I finally realized I was believing a lie and got tired of feeling disconnected from God, I started reading my Bible again. The words were encouraging and not judgemental. The God in my head and the Bible were very different; the complete opposite to each other.

It was easy at times to think that God loved me less than other people.

There are still moments when I am insecure about my appearance, and when I look at other women and compare my beauty to theirs. But I remind myself that God purposely made each of us wonderfully with unique features and characteristics.

I'm thirty-three now and I'm still wondering what my married life will look like.

Despite the confusion I had, I can now picture myself with a family of my own, with a devoted husband who loves me, God, and my children.

Even though most of my school days are in the past, the desire to continue learning will never go away. That artistic side of myself I neglected as a teenager is something I now enjoy as a hobby. I look forward to using it in the near future to pursue Art Therapy to help people express emotions that are repressed and difficult to articulate with words.

I now know God desires for me to include His help when I need it.

God had more faith in me than I did. He never gave up on the bigger picture He had in mind for my life. He used every challenge and doubt to show me just how deep His love was for me.

Even though my plans were changed at times, disappointment was replaced with a growing trust in my heavenly Father.

He saw me as no less of a disciple because my faith needed a long time to grow into maturity. When I trusted in lies more than truth, He would always open my eyes to realize the deceit I fell for. When I found it hard to love myself, He showed me in His word that He sees goodness when He looks at me and nothing about me was made by mistake. Looking back, I can see that He counted every step of my life as a joy to walk side-by-side with me, taking control of the direction, relationships, and lessons I needed along the way.

I still have insecurities and questions from time to time. I don't have everything figured out. The only difference is now I know who to turn to.

God transformed my idea of a happy and fulfilled life. He gave me hope for a bright future and a relationship with Him that can handle all of my imperfections. There's still more of my story to write but the grace I've been shown in my past assures me that I won't have anything to fear.

Candace Lalor is a Social Service Worker. Her college years exposed her to the hardships of others experiencing unfortunate life conditions. This motivated Candace to pursue a career that allows her to be a positive voice of hope for a brighter future. Inspired to become a visual art teacher, Candace dreams of supporting teenagers and young adults impacted with traumatic experiences by creating safe spaces for difficult emotions through therapeutic workshops and classes.

- candace.lalor@gmail.com
- www.facebook.com/candace.lalor
- candace.lalor

CHAPTER TWENTY-TWO - Lesa Rose Isaacs

He Meets Your Needs

As I look back on my life, it has changed tremendously over the past three years. I can honestly say that I am not the same person I used to be. God has taken my heart and transformed it. My faith in who God says I am and who He is has been restored. So many memories come flooding back to me of how I have seen the Lord's goodness in my life and that He has never forgotten me through it all.

I have witnessed the Lord's goodness in the many ways He has chosen to speak to me. What gets me the most is that still small voice I hear many times over. The nudging of the Holy Spirit, guiding me through His Word, and pointing me in the direction I should go. Like it says in Psalms 32:8:

"I will guide you along the best pathway for your life. I will advise you and watch over you." (NLT)

But God doesn't stop there. He also speaks to me through nature. Seeing a cardinal is just one of the ways I am reminded that God is with me. When I go for a nature walk and see the birds flying or hear the trees whistling as their branches move so softly brings me such peace. When I am by the water, I pause as I listen to the sounds the waves make. It brings a calmness over me, and I just know that everything is going to be OK. Other ways He speaks to me is through songs of worship and words of encouragement given by someone directly to me. In 2021, I attended an event and at the time, I was asking God many questions for direction. He used somebody whom I had just met to pray for me and give me words that encouraged my soul. He was speaking life into me using this person. Only God can do that, and I am so glad that He did.

My faith began to grow as I started seeing that God had not forgotten me. This is played out in knowing that God is for me no matter what is happening in, around, or to me. I now believe God will never leave me nor forsake me. It was me who would walk away from Him when I was struggling. It was me who would focus on the current problem and make it bigger than God. He waited patiently for me to turn it over to Him. But sometimes I allowed situations to bring me to my knees and then I had to cry out to the Lord. I wanted to do it on my own in my own strength. He reminded me that He was always there and needed me to rely on Him for strength. Now I know that I am secure in Him, that He keeps me, and that I am His own. When I am weak, it is God that gives me the strength. He is by my side and will never let me go. He knows me more than I know myself, so I hold onto that and know that it is going to be OK. Even when it may not feel like or look like things are going to be OK, I know that He's going to work it out for my good and so I trust that, and I have faith in Him moving in my life for His purposes in His time and His will.

I have seen my faith being increased through my finances. It was a time when we were struggling. My husband and I had not been faithfully tithing then. We knew His word, but we were more focused on our circumstances and what was happening with what we had or lack of it. But God said that we should try Him. We were to tithe with each of our earnings. It was hard in the beginning, but we didn't stop. As the months went on, we started to see a shift in our finances. Our faith in what God's word said was making more sense to us. We saw that our money was being stretched even with the same earnings. With us tithing faithfully, all our bills were being paid, and we became wiser in how we used what God had given us. Only God can take what you have and increase it. Being faithful in our tithing showed us how God was moving in our lives. Our eyes were now off the situation and on Him.

God was also moving in my life by bringing healing to my heart. I've suffered a lot of pain in my life. In the last three years, it had gotten to a point where I was in and out of the hospital a few times because I had no energy and a low mood. All I could see was the physical pain that I was in and was asking God to heal my body. I was tired of being and having pain. I wanted to be free from it even if it was just for a little while. It really didn't seem like He was listening. But I was wrong – He was listening. God was showing up in a way that I wasn't expecting. His way brought so much more healing into my life than what I was asking for. God knew just what I needed at the time, and He started to heal my heart, my spirit, my emotions, and my mental state. But first, He needed to get my attention. When that happened, I could see what He was doing by bringing people into my life to help with this healing. It was worth it. I attended different groups for healing within my Church at the Bridge, and a friend of a friend put me into a clinic where I started to receive therapy. I've seen God move through my prayers, not only for healing but for other things and people. God answered and moved in my life through my marriage, bringing us together when I thought that it would be over. He stepped in and transformed our hearts and now we are closer than we have ever been. I see God moving differently bringing people into my life, restoring friendships, and answering prayers that I didn't even imagine, or think could be answered. I am thankful for His new mercies each day.

I would say in the last three years, my faith has increased so much. I have always attended church which was something that I grew up doing. I was a believer based on how I was raised. You know…attend and serve in the church. What was lacking was that I didn't have a personal relationship with God. I was struggling to truly trust God. My struggles with my earthly father and the disappointment were bringing on this lack of trust. On the outside, everything looked good, but my heart wasn't being transformed. I believed what the Bible said but I wasn't completely living it. I knew God based on what was being spoken from the pulpit but not for myself. During one of my many visits to the hospital, I rededicated my life to Christ. This time it was different from the other times. When all you have is the Word and prayer, you start to do things differently. I was spending more quality with God, reading His Word, and talking to Him. I was having conversations, but it was no longer me talking. I started to listen to what He was saying to me which deepened our relationship. I began to see that He was different from my earthly father. I can now say that I trust Him without a shadow of a doubt. His Word has brought life to my soul. I trust what He says in His Word and what He's doing. I love how He is showing up in my life. I realize that I need the Lord. He is my everything. I want to walk with Him closely. He knows what's best for me. His plan for me exceeds any plan that I could ever have for myself. I'm just thankful that things have happened the way they have because if they didn't, I don't think I would be where I am today.

The amazing thing about this journey of faith is trusting in God and then seeing the amazing things that begin to unfold. He brings people into your life just at the right time. Him opening doors like this opportunity to write and be a part of an anthology, or even be an author. Saying yes to ministry, being a co-facilitator for Life's Healing Choices and Black Women's Health. The Holy Spirit is inspiring me to move in a way that I would normally have shied away from or not believed possible like wanting to facilitate women's groups to help those who are broken, find clarity, and move forward and walk in their purpose. I am seeing the dreams of coaching as more of a possibility now and I am walking towards it. God just took the veil off my eyes so that I could see where He wants me to go and what He wants me to do. It's going to be amazing to see some of those dreams come to pass. I have a boldness to want others to know about this God who wants to inspire me to nurture and heal the brokenness in women. To God be the glory, great things He has done and is doing. He is doing a new thing making paths out of the desert for his children to walk in.

I want you to know that life may not always be easy, and you may get knocked down, but if your hope is in Jesus, you'll be able to get back up again. You will walk again. He is with you during your storm. God is good. He is a God who moves and answers our prayers, and although it may not be the way that you want, He answers. He is our healer. Our Heavenly Father has got you no matter what you're experiencing or walking through. You may be struggling with your finances but be obedient to his Word. Give him that ten percent of your earnings and watch how He turns things around for you. You may be struggling in your marriage, but God is near. Read his word, cry out to Him, and don't be afraid to ask for help. Don't hold onto things and ask for forgiveness. He has not forsaken you.

You may also be going through some health issues. All you've got to do is trust and put your faith in God. Healing isn't always about our physical bodies. Turn your situation over to Him in faith and watch Him move. He is near. He has not forgotten about you. You are not alone; you are His precious child. God is going to restore you. He's going to revive you. He's going to come alongside you just where you are. And he's going to answer all those things you've been asking and give you the desires of your heart. Our God will meet your needs. He is patient and kind and just waiting for you to ask. Just trust and believe in Him. His Word doesn't lie. God sees you and hears. You have not been displaced and he's waiting. He'll continue to wait until you are ready to step into what He's called you to step into because that's the God we serve. He's loving and faithful. His Word says in Jeremiah 29:11:

> "I, say this because I know what I am planning for you," says the Lord. "I have good plans for you, not plans to hurt you. I will give you hope and a good future." (NCV)

Let's give God Praise!

Lesa Rose Isaacs is a woman of God, a wife, and a mother of two female young adults. In 2020, she ventured into entrepreneurship by starting her company in the beauty industry. Lesa is a Lash Lift and Pedicure Specialist. She has also helped to co-facilitate different women's groups. In the future, Lesa will be working on becoming a Christian Life Coach.

in lesarosebb

@lesaroseBB

lesarosebb

CHAPTER TWENTY-THREE - Joan Steward

I'm Much Stronger

There's been a point in my life when I felt very much alone. I had no one although there were people around me.

No mother, father, brother, or sister to turn to. Yes, I do have seven siblings and parents but not at the point of my need. I felt very empty and alone. I felt like I was enclosed in a dark place and didn't know where to go or who to turn to. I couldn't see any shining light in my path then; However today I'm in a different place.

I was a single mom with a beautiful teenage daughter I was raising on my own because of a situation I brought upon myself due to my mindset at that time. Overall, I wanted to shield my daughter from the pains of my childhood. I had previously decided to stay out of relationships due to a six-year relationship that didn't end in my favor. My decision was due to the well-being of my daughter. I didn't want her to get attached to another person who may eventually leave again. I also didn't want her to grow up thinking that it was okay to get involved with different men and unstable relationships, moving from one man to another. I wanted to be a good example to her. Today I am thankful that I made that decision because my daughter is happily married to her first love and they're raising two beautiful kids.

I was working as a project manager at an IT company, and everything was going well until I walked into the office one day and was called to a meeting where we were told that the company would be outsourcing future projects. Thus, we were all released and sent home. There I was thinking everything was going to be okay because, with my experience, I would find another job easily. However, I was wrong. In my quest to find employment, I also returned to school and completed a certificate program in web design and development, yet every open door seemed to be shutting in my face. I remained unemployed for two years and eight months, and during that period my financial situation went to zero, my stress level was at zero, and it seemed like every door was now shut. I found myself in the valley of depression, my movements contained smiles with a troubled spirit. I remember lying in my apartment with tears streaming down my face, the sleepless nights, the empty pantry, the hunger, the stomach cramps, and the burning sensations throughout my body which I later found out was due to stress. I remember taking six packages of extra-strength cold medicine to help me sleep so that I would not think about my situation. Then one faithful day, I received a phone call from someone whom I still call my guardian Angel. She prayed with me and said, "I'll be picking you up tomorrow evening for church." This became the turning point of everything for me.

I attended church with her and when I walked into that building, I felt as if I arrived at a place I could call home for the very first time in my life. On that day, I found myself at the altar where I decided to serve God with all my heart, soul, and mind. Please note that prior to that, I more-or-less grew up in church and knew God, but I didn't know Him as a father, I didn't know how to pray, and I didn't have a relationship with Him.

Once I prayed and turned my life over to God, I asked Him to take control and just draw me closer to Himself. I committed myself to spending more time in the Word of God, prayer meetings, fasting, etc. 1 Thessalonians 5:17 says *"pray without ceasing"* and this became my new norm. I also fell in love with Psalm 77:1:

"I cried unto God with my voice, even unto God with my voice; and he gave ear unto me." (KJV)

As mentioned previously, I grew up in church. I started attending as a young teenager to get away from the domestic violence in my parents' house. It was a home where I never felt loved or wanted, where I would have done anything to get a smile or hug from my dad, a home where I was living a tormented life of fear. My mom eventually left home, followed by my dad when I was fourteen years old, leaving me to care for my younger brother, sister, and myself. This experience left me with a mindset that everyone hates me, and I should never trust anyone under any circumstances amongst other things.

However, I came to realize that I was wrong in my thinking.

I knew God but did not have a relationship with Him, thus I didn't know Him as a father; neither did I know how to trust in Him. I knew what I wanted in life and had my own plans as to how I was going to achieve it.

I came to know Him as a father then – my Father, the one person who loves and cares about me. The father that I always wanted and never had. The one who was protecting me even though I wasn't aware of it. The one who loves me unconditionally.

Developing a relationship with God changed the course of my life until this very day. It made me realize that Jesus is the only one who can give peace and fulfillment within me. I learned all that was missing from my life was Jesus and as I drew closer to Him and placed my hope in Him, I felt such a great sense of peace and contentment like never before. God promises in many books of the bible that He is always with us and will never leave nor forsake us (Hebrews 13:5, Deuteronomy 31:6-8, amongst others).

I learned that the Lord will always be with me and for me. The Lord promised me that He will strengthen me and help me. He will always do what's right for me if I continue to serve and trust Him. He will always be on my side (see Isaiah 41:10 KJV).

The years from then to now have been a roller coaster. I've been to the valley and back, but I was never alone. It was in the valley that God gave me a great job that lasted fifteen years. It was in the valley God gave me keys to a brand-new home. It was in the valley that He paid off my $87,000 debt and turned my credit around. It was in the valley that He took away the spirit of depression and stress and gave me peace. It was in the same valley that He promised I would never suffer lack another day in my life.

I am a stronger and wiser woman today because of what I've been through. Through it all, I've learned that God has a great plan for my life and that's the path I had to walk to get to the place He has prepared for me – the place where I am now and also the place where He is taking me.

Life still presents me with great challenges as I travel along my pathway but because of my faith in God, I can embrace it with grace and strength. In those times, I can hold on to the fact that God's love is everlasting, and He will always be with me as I continue to put Him first and trust in Him. There will never be the fear of going through whatever He took me out of because of my strengthened faith in Him. He has also promised to meet my needs according to His riches in Glory and He will never fail to do so. He has also taken away my weaknesses and strengthened me. I now know that what I do not have is what I do not need, thus I can be at peace and content with what He has given me and where He is taking me. I will rest in Him.

Know that when next you face trials, difficulties, and various obstacles, when your face is against that dark wall, when friends and loved ones are all gone, all you need to do is enter that valley knowing that God is there and he will do whatever it takes to get you on top of that mountain with everything you need. No matter what adversity comes your way, be patient and continue to persevere for this will bring you closer to what God has in store for you. He will also ensure you're much stronger than when you entered that valley, enabling you to face the next battle.

My friend, when you are alone in the valley and Your burden is very heavy, look up at the mountain and see the shining light at the very top. This is where you need to go. It will not be easy to get to the very top with the heavy burden you're carrying, neither can you get there alone. The load is too heavy for you alone to carry. I admonish you to call on Jesus because He will empty your baggage, He will take the load off your shoulders, He will take the load off your back, and He will guide you up to the very top of the mountain. Continue to fix your eyes on Him as you go up and no matter what you see in front of you, keep your eyes fixed on Jesus. He is there holding you, guiding you, and leading you. Be patient and continue to move forward.

I know you may be thinking that Jesus is moving too slowly for you. You want to move faster but be patient. Even if you were to drop that load quickly and rush up that mountain, it would do you no good because you're alone. Be patient and wait on Him. Put your hope and faith in Him.

"The Lord is good to those whose hope is in him, to the one who seeks him." Lamentations 3:25 (NKJV)

Continue to have faith and believe that God will always show up for you when you call on his name.

In conclusion, I can truly say that according to Psalm 46:1-2:

"God is our refuge and strength, an ever-present help in times of trouble. Therefore, we will not fear, though the earth gives away and the mountains fall into the heart of the sea."

Hold onto Him – trust, hope, pray, and believe.

Pray always, in every place. There is no limit to the times, places, and different ways in which to pray. God will never fail us,

Prayer

Heavenly Father, this is your daughter _____. Father, in this season of my life, help me to remember that you're with me. Your Word says "You're my ever-present help in times of trials." Faithful God, unchanging changer, helps me to face my many trials with grace and strength. Help me to put you first in everything. Father, grant me hope when I am faced with rejection. Grant me strength when I'm weak, love me when I feel forsaken, replace my fears with courage, comfort me when I feel alone, and Father, fill me with a greater level of faith so I will remain humble and not get carried away by things that are not important.

Oh, the joy of leaving the valley with Jesus. Once you've committed your life to Him, He promises never to leave you alone.

Oh, the peace and strength that's usually flowing from within as we climb the mountain and wait for the next.

Joan Steward has a history of being locked in a room reading a romantic novel or faith-based book. Writing her own book has always been on her bucket list until she was approached by Jasmine E. Clarke and it became a reality as a co-author. Joan Steward (Spice Isle Queen) is a single mother, hair stylist, Computer Systems Programmer Analyst, IT Project Coordinator, web designer, and entrepreneur. She will be coming to you with her own anthology in 2024.

CHAPTER TWENTY-FOUR - Judy Brown

Empowered to Shine

Imagine yourself entering a beautiful, open field with radiant, green grass. The sun shines brightly. The temperature is perfect – not too hot, not too cold. A slight breeze balances the heat from the sun. You are running, jumping, skipping, enjoying the beauty, experiencing freedom and abundance. It is bliss. You see your reflection in a nearby river; everything changes. Everything around you looks withered, dark, and cold. The beauty and strength you saw in the reflection becomes something you want to hide. You were standing in your promised land and now you see yourself as weak, vulnerable, and unable to take hold of the blessings before you and move in the freedom you had before the water exposed you.

"You are the light of the world. A city that is set on a hill cannot be hidden. Nor do they light a lamp and put it under a basket, but

on a lampstand, and it gives light to all who are in the house. Let your light so shine before men, that they may see your good works and glorify your Father in heaven." Matthew 5:14-16 (NKJV)

That is one of my favorite passages of scripture and has been for a long time. It is what I desire and find challenging to live out in my life. My preference is to remain hidden, although, that is not the life God has designed for me. When I look at my life, what I see is that reflection in the water, something to be hidden. However, when I reflect on my life, despite my best efforts, God has allowed my light to shine and allowed Him to be seen in and through me.

I am the youngest of three with almost a decade between me and my older brothers. My brothers were popular, had lots of friends, and were involved in many activities that made them known. This included sports, singing, teaching, and leading. I would always tag along and be quite content to let them be in the limelight while I remained in their shadow. From what I remember, I would be there but quiet. I connected with some of their friends, but some were surprised to know my brothers had a younger sister.

Living life in their shadow allowed me to hide; to be present and not seen. It almost felt like there was a sense of peace and protection while still enjoying life. Also, when you live in someone's shadow, you can rely on their great qualities to get you where you want to be, at least it can look that way. Growing up, I lived what I would describe as in the shadows. I was present but quiet, especially if I did not know you. In most cases, I preferred to be in the background. A friend once referred to me as a closet extrovert. If I know you and am comfortable around you, you may not describe me as quiet. In a room full of people, I would gravitate to someone I knew or find a spot where I could comfortably stay and be silent. When with someone I knew, I could depend on them carrying the conversation. That way, I could do what I thought I did best: quietly listen and remain hidden. That quiet listening eventually became my superpower and made me shine.

As I mentioned before, my brothers were athletic. Sometimes my brothers would take me with them to their athletic activities or involve me in their training. I remember when my one brother would train by running up the stairs in our building, sometimes I would run with him. When going to a friend's house, riding as a passenger on the bike would get uncomfortable so I decided to run alongside my brother while he rode the bike. And yes, I do really mean run. Athleticism placed and helped me in social situations simply because I successfully played sports.

Growing up in a single-parent home, my brothers were the ones who looked out for me when my mom was working. So that meant that I tagged along with them wherever they went. Concerts, services, choir practices, and friends' houses; I was with them pretty much whenever they went out. I must say I quite enjoyed it. In a way, I was everybody's little sister, at least to their closest friends. Well, that's the way I saw it. Still, I was quiet to the point where, although I was with them all the time, as I mentioned before, there were people who didn't realize I existed. I found that I preferred to be in the shadows. I became extremely self-conscious not wanting to say the wrong thing, do the wrong things, or stand out in any way. I viewed it as a form of protection. I would not have to worry about being embarrassed, taken advantage of, or rejected. I would not have to worry about being seen the way I saw myself in that reflection in the river. That's the way I viewed it. What I did not realize was that living life that way causes you to live below all that God has for you and adds extra hurdles to achieving your destiny. A part of me hated that. Living that way meant you couldn't fully experience life, fully experience relationships, fully gain all the skills you needed to progress in life, and live out your destiny. Because you couldn't fully live out who you are, you couldn't completely be who God created you to be, you couldn't experience that feeling of freely moving in that beautiful green field that represented abundance. The result would be that you wouldn't shine for Him and experience full joy. It wasn't until university that I understood that and allowed my light to shine.

Now, I did have friends and went to their houses, and at school, I was successful academically and athletically just like my older brothers. I played football with the boys as well as British bulldog. Still, there was this desire to remain in the safety of the shadows. So, once again, if I was close to you, you may say that I was a chatterbox but, if I was with someone I didn't know, then my preference was to say nothing. I believed I was not a conversationalist so, we would experience that awkward silence unless that person was a talker. I avoided that at all costs since, to me, it was something bad.

As I grow older and look back, I don't even know if that's true. I think I am more of a listener than a talker and it was perceived as a weakness, even abnormal although it could be a strength, something good. Still, speaking felt like exposing what was revealed in the reflection in the river and that was to remain hidden. This led me back to preferring to remain in the shadows because I could be silent and, therefore safe. So, I continued with my athletic activities throughout high school, playing sports in each term, every year: basketball, volleyball, track and field. I was especially successful in volleyball and track. Now notice these are all team sports and, especially in volleyball and track, we were winning so being in the shadows, hidden, was a little harder to accomplish.

In university, the thought was to give up sports to focus on my studies. There was an expectation that one would graduate from high school and go to university then graduate university and become a professional "something." In university, I gained a more intimate relationship with God and a better understanding of who I was and who I was called to be; more of a willingness to be that light and in the light. Understanding my faith better explains this.

I grew up in the church. My mother is a strong woman of faith who was also involved in many ministries including choir, Sunday School, and even was the church's magazine editor. And as I said before, my brothers were involved in ministry as well. They sang in a group and more than one choir. One of my brothers played guitar and pretty much any instrument that was placed in his hands. He's really gifted musically. For me, I was involved in such things mostly because I was forced to. In those days, you had to be ready to sing, testify, or do whatever at a moment's notice. Imagine the anxiety I felt sitting in the pew. You never knew when you were going to be called upon and we were at every service. I remember us kids were called up to sing and, when we were done, someone had to come and give an offering so that you could go back to your seat. Now imagine how someone, who would rather remain hidden, felt having to stand in the front and just pray that somebody would come help them get down from there. Don't worry, someone always came. So that was my experience from a babe till the end of high school. I knew of God and was well versed in doing church but didn't really have a relationship with Him.

Now back to university. You walk into this big, huge building and you know no one. I didn't have anyone from church, school, or sports to help with socializing. No one's shadow was present to hide me, so I decided to try and step out. I remember, during orientation, I was sitting with a group of girls of a particular ethnicity, and they were nice. I also remember that at some point they asked, *"Why aren't you hanging out with your own people?"* So, I ended up experiencing emotions I was trying desperately to avoid; the feelings of exposure, like I saw in that reflection in the river, and rejection. The new safe space I attempted to create… epic fail. Fortunately, God was looking out for me, as He had always been. Turns out this young man that I knew in grade school attended the same university…and he was a believer as well. He was involved with the Christian ministry at the school too, and he invited me to attend. That's when everything changed. Not only did I start attending this ministry on a regular basis, but I also started moving from hiding in the shadows to being at the forefront of many things. I guess one could say the gene that was in my brothers and my mom started to express itself in my life as well. I led Bible studies and prayer meetings which included singing and playing the guitar. I even was a part of the worship team at a retreat. Not only did I lead some activities, but I also became one of the leaders in the ministry. What I gained from being in that environment also let me be a part of leadership in the church I was attending. The more the

Word of God enlightens me, the harder it is to find a shadow in which to hide and the harder it is for darkness to overwhelm me. Am I still what I consider to be quiet? Yes, I am, and I am also empowered by the Holy Spirit to stand out and be the light God has called me to be, whenever the opportunity arises.

Now I see myself running, jumping, and skipping in that beautiful field where the grass is the most radiant green I have ever seen. The sun shines brightly, and the temperature is perfect. A slight breeze balances the heat coming from the sun. I run to the river, look at my reflection, and everything looks healthy and bright. And I see beauty all around me and in me. I am standing in my promised land, and I am strong, courageous, and able to take hold of all the blessings God has for me. I am experiencing freedom and abundance and my light guides others to do the same.

Judy Brown is a university graduate with a Bachelor's Degree in Biology. Over the years, she has had various leadership positions in Christian groups at university and church. Judy's primary mission is to build, connect, and inspire people to live with purpose, passion, and freedom to show that, with God's help, one can freely and authentically be who He created them to be, living the abundant life God established for them.

 judybrown3808@gmail.com

CHAPTER TWENTY-FIVE - Lisia Malcolm-Burnett

It Will Work Out for Your Good

What is Transformation? According to the Cambridge Dictionary, *"Transformation is a complete change in the appearance or character of something or someone, especially so that thing or person is improved."*

My life has been a metamorphosis of transformational moments, and it all began with one decision – to surrender my life to Jesus.

I desire to share a glimpse of my life story with you and the journey I have been on in my development, empowered by my relationship with God.

Where It All Began

I was born in Ottawa, Ontario, Canada, to a humble Christian couple. My parents were Jamaican immigrants to the country at the time with tremendous ambitions and desires for a better life. My loving parents were some of the most dedicated Ottawa Church of God members of an evangelical, Pentecostal congregation.

My mother and aunt were the pioneers, and they began with gatherings in their apartment building. The church was later organized and flourished with the appointed Senior Pastor.

My parents were devout followers of Jesus Christ and my first examples of selflessness and hard work. They put God first in all their decision-making, and consequently, our Heavenly Father blessed them.

When I was eight years old, my parents moved the family to Aylmer, Quebec. It was a small French-speaking town across the bridge from Ottawa where they bought their first home in Canada. The reasons for the move were twofold: to give us, the children, the opportunity to learn French; and the other to plant a mission church.

Before the move, I, amongst other kids at the Ottawa Church of God, acknowledged that we were sinners needing the forgiveness of our sins. After accepting the gospel message of salvation, we repented in prayer and asked Jesus to be the Lord of our lives.

In a public demonstration of the transformation happening in our hearts and minds, we got baptized by the submersion in water.

Accepting Jesus into my heart was the catalyst for all other transformations in my life. I fell in love with Jesus at the tender age of seven and have been ever since. I fell in love with the one who loved me sacrificially, despite my mistakes, wrong decisions, and selfish pride.

You may be thinking, *"What does a seven-year-old know about sin or pride?"* The reality is that once we open our hearts to the possibility of there being a Heavenly Father who desires a relationship with his creation, the Holy Spirit then reveals the truth to us and does a work in us that only He can.

Knowing I am chosen, accepted, forgiven, protected, and defended by God is priceless.

My visceral love for people and my family was birthed from the unconditional love I have experienced in my relationship with Jesus Christ. It truly has empowered my transformation into the person I am today.

By no means does it mean that it is easy to love everyone! I have been in situations where it has taken all the "Jesus" in me to love. I have been betrayed, hurt, lied about, bullied, rejected, you name it, yet I am often reminded of the words of Jesus as he was teaching his disciples in Matthew 6:14-15 where he said:

> *"If you forgive those who sin against you, your heavenly Father will forgive you. But if you refuse to forgive others, your Father will not forgive your sins."* (NLT)

God knows that I am guilty of sinning both unconsciously and even knowingly. Needless to say, I desperately need His forgiveness.

With the same grace and mercy He has extended to us, He expects us to give freely to others.

Many have suffered severely at the hands of others, and forgiveness may seem impossible. Know this, if you are willing, God is able. I am a living example of this.

When You Feel Like Quitting

Many years ago, while working at Inside Sales, I allowed myself to be bullied at work by a particular colleague. The bullying continued for several years and resulted in me developing high blood pressure. I often escaped to the restroom to pray, cry, and seek the strength to get through each day. My faith in Jesus sustained me and empowered me to remain focused amidst the pain. Many would have rightfully quit their job and sought a "better environment" to work in elsewhere. I was confident that God placed me there for a reason and that this was going to make me stronger in the end. I chose to bloom where I was planted. God has been faithful in fighting my battles for me. The promotions I have been blessed with and the success I have experienced have been the result of my grit, relentless focus, faith, and work ethic.

In Psalm 37:5-7 God instructs us to do the following:

"Commit everything you do to the Lord. Trust Him, and he will help you. He will make your innocence radiate like the dawn, and the justice of your cause will shine like the noonday sun. Be still in the presence of the Lord, and wait patiently for him to act. Don't worry about evil people who prosper or fret about their wicked schemes." (NLT)

I trusted God to keep His word and pushed through it all. I met or exceeded my sales quota five consecutive years in a row, setting a record for Inside Sales. Moreover, those who mistreated me are no longer with the organization.

Our Heavenly Father cares for His children and He defends the weak. God empowered me to be relentless in a season when I often wanted to quit and enabled me to pass the test of faith while growing in endurance.

In hindsight, I now realize that my adverse reaction to conflict did not help the situation; I would often shut down as I lacked the confidence to face my giants and set boundaries.

I am stronger today and now understand my value and worth. I am uniquely me, just as God has made you uniquely YOU. No one in this world can do a better job at being you, but you.

Still in the Miracle-Working Business

Have you ever made plans only to see them unfold differently?

In my early singles, I had a timeline all sketched out. I would get married at twenty-five and have all my kids by the age of thirty.

As I write this, I laugh at my innocence in thinking I had any insight into the future or power to ensure that my timeline would materialize.

I got married when I was twenty-seven, not twenty-five. Moreover, once I did get married, we could not get pregnant. Simon and I had been married for two years when I suggested we go for testing. Something appeared to be amiss. Reluctantly he agreed, and we started the process of testing. The results! They could find no reason for the misfortune. I desperately wanted to be a mother. I resolved to pray. Funny how we often go to prayer as a last resort instead of our first recourse.

Sensing that my biological clock was ticking, I determined that I would ask for a miracle. Yes, you read that right, a miracle! If God could give the barren women in the Old Testament children, He could do the same for me. I prayed a simple prayer and said this:

> *"God, I know I'm getting older so I'm asking if I can please get two at once. I know that I am asking for a miracle because I don't have any twins in my family, nor does my husband. But if you could do it for Hannah, Rebecca, and Rachel of the Old Testament, you can surely do it for me."*

God took his time, as He often does. Five years into our marriage, I discovered that I was pregnant. At three months, we went for our first ultrasound. To our surprise and delight, there were two babies. God had answered! He did it! I was so overwhelmed with joy and gratitude at the mercy and love of God. Our twin girls are living proof that God is still in the miracle-working business. If He could do it for me, He can certainly do it for you.

Transforming Faith

As a child, I saw my dad's dedication to sharing the hope of the gospel with people he encountered. He often carried pamphlets with a simple message of salvation. One of those tracks was entitled *"Your Decisions Determine Your Destiny."* My dad often reminded us that the decisions we made in life would indeed dictate our future and, to choose wisely.

I chose to stay close to God and to work daily on my relationship with Jesus by reading the scriptures, praying, and following His guidelines for life as prescribed in the Bible.

I will be the first to tell you that I have made my fair share of bad decisions and have had to live through the consequences of my sins.

In 2020, amid the pandemic, I was on maternity leave from work and feeling despair with our financial situation. One thing I intensely dislike is owing money. I felt like I was suffocating with the debt we owed. It was not the amount but the fact that it was owing, with no means of the debt getting paid off quickly. I was literally living the consequences of unwise actions.

I somehow discovered a money mindset program and decided to explore the possibility. We had the discovery call, felt a flicker of hope, and believed that somehow, by doing this program, we could get our finances in order. This faith-based program would require a huge step of faith. If we were barely managing our bills, how would we be able to pay for this?

We decided to use some of our home equity to fund it. You may be reading this and thinking, *"That's quite brave!"* seeing that we had no guarantee that it would help us. I will tell you this! That decision transformed my life. The program was holistic and got to the root of our financial situation while addressing other areas of our lives.

My potential as a leader, as the owner of my career journey, and as a Trailblazer was unearthed through this process. I am now free to be everything God desires me to be. I have grown in confidence and feel empowered to serve my community in a greater capacity with love and excellence.

That decision to step out in faith saved us financially. We can now focus on building wealth and leaving a legacy for our children.

Hebrews 11:1 says:

"Faith shows the reality of what we hope for; it is the evidence of things we cannot see." (NLT)

The author of the book of Hebrews goes on to say in verse 6 that without faith, it is impossible to please God. The Holy Spirit empowers us to trust and believe in God's providence. God can redeem our situations even after we have made a mess of things on our own. God is merciful, loving, and kind. In accepting His gift of salvation through Jesus Christ, His son, you secure your eternal destiny in Heaven.

I surrendered my life to God at the tender age of seven and have never regretted that decision. Empowered by the Holy Spirit, I am being transformed daily into the best version of Lisia Malcolm-Burnett. I thank God for the individuals He has placed in my life to support, mentor, sponsor me, and affirm the calling on my life to serve in a unique way.

God has proven to be true to His word. He answers prayers, comforts us in our time of pain and sorrow, and rescues us from evil. He provides for our every need. God never fails. He walks through every season with us, and most importantly, God empowers us to love Him and to love others.

The journey continues and you are on it with me. You are part of my journey, and I thank you.

Lisia Malcolm-Burnett is an Ordained Minister with the Church of God and a second-generation pastor. She currently serves on the Diversity, Equity & Inclusion Council at Dentsply Sirona and is also the Chair for the Women's Employee Resource Group in Canada. Lisia is primarily wife to Simon Burnett, her partner in Ministry for the last sixteen years. She is a mother to her twin 11-year-old girls and her 3-year-old toddler.

- Lisia Malcolm-Burnett
- Lisia Malcolm

CHAPTER TWENTY-SIX - Rachel Colley

God's Love Healed Our Family

I stood staring at the phone in my hand, my heart stopped beating, and time stood still. The doctor just told me that my precious two-year-old baby boy had Leukemia and I needed to get to the Emergency Department immediately! My head was dancing from one thought to another because it must have been a mistake. What would I do though if it was real? I called my pastor, and he told me not to delay but go as instructed and he would meet me there.

I looked around the room at both of my children wondering what to do first. My beautiful six-year-old daughter needed someone to care for her. With the phone still in my hand, I called a friend from the church and made arrangements for her to get my daughter after school. My friend would keep her safe and was trustworthy.

With so much to think about and so much to arrange, I felt panicked. I fell to my knees and asked God to please help me. I needed the Lord now more than ever and I prayed for God to give me strength and wisdom. I had only been a Christian for two years but knew that the only way to get through this traumatizing situation was with prayer and trusting God.

I was finally able to head to the hospital, so with my son held tightly in my arms, I packed up the car with an overnight bag and prayed all the way to the hospital. Once we arrived, the emergency door looked so huge, but I entered with the Lord beside me. Little did I know my life and my children's lives were about to change dramatically in the blink of an eye.

The doctors rushed to my son's aid and started doing tests and frantically moving about. After hours of waiting, a small blonde hair doctor who was very soft and kind in speech, broke the news to me that my son would not live through the night. The tumor on his chest was so large and it was basically too late to help him. They would attempt to do whatever they could to relieve his pain but needed me to be prepared for what they said was the "inevitable."

I was in such shock and could only believe that my son had a bad virus. I literally told the doctors they were wrong and truly believed that from the bottom of my heart. In the meantime, I received comfort and prayers from the pastors and dear friends who had arrived at the hospital just shortly after I did. They provided support and encouragement as time passed and also contacted the church for continued prayer through the night. I knew that only God could do something to save my baby.

During the next several hours, the doctors did what they could to ease the baby's pain and make him comfortable. It was a waiting game, but the pastors, my friends, and I were trusting and believing that God would show up in a mighty way.

I received many messages of continued prayers and support and was advised to believe that God would do a miracle. My daughter was safe and sound and well taken care of, which brought comfort to me, and I was receiving so much love that it reached the depth of every part of my being. I prayed for the Lord to save my son and keep our family of three together.

Miraculously, my baby made it through the night and the doctors were all shocked and astounded! The doctors started having hope and spent the next number of hours discussing a treatment plan and possible new outcomes, as my little boy had shown improvement that they did not expect.

They moved him to the ICU and then advised me that he had a 30% chance of survival. There was a three-year treatment plan they could start which would consist of many months in the hospital and then daily visits and a lot of medications. They expressed that clearly "the prayers" changed my son's story so they too had become hopeful for a successful treatment that would remove the cancer from his body. They said he could be cancer-free after all the treatment, giving him a 70% chance of survival at the age of 5 ½.

I sat with my head in my hands, praying inside for God to show me how I would manage this as a single parent. I had a full-time job that I needed to keep so I could provide for my family. My son would need me full-time to care for him and my daughter needed me as well but with no family living in the same province, how would I manage this? I had my church family but there was only so much they could do as well. I spent much time asking God to give me peace that passes understanding and to help me just get through one minute at a time.

I sat on my son's bedside looking at all the tubes, his swollen body, lethargic state, and prayed again for God to please help me have the strength and courage to take on this situation that I was faced with. I noticed someone touching my shoulder and it was the blonde lady who was smiling and told me because he made it through the night and defied the doctors' words, she now believed he would be okay and said not to worry but to keep praying. We went to her office where a bunch of forms had to be filled out and many issues were discussed but there was a peace from God that filled that room and brought great comfort to me.

Even though I was feeling overwhelmed with all that was going on, like wondering how I would pay rent, have money for food, and be able to care for my six-year-old daughter on top of all that my son needed, I whispered to the Lord to provide me with perseverance and show me the way.

The woman helped me gather information about all services that I could access to assist with the necessities of life and help for my daughter. It comforted me and at that point, I just knew that God would get me through, and it would be okay. It was a journey that me and my children would be taking, and in the end, it was going to build up my faith and result in God getting all the Glory for His miracle!

Many waking hours were spent with my son giving him comfort and trying to ease the pain he was in. It was confusing for a two-year-old, but having his mother's love and familiarity was all that he needed. Many times, my church family or friends would come and sit with him so I could go spend time with my daughter or even just have a break so that I could take care of my own well-being during such a difficult time.

At one point, my mother was able to visit from another province and stay for a few weeks. She helped with my daughter's care and provided a calm home environment. It was so hard not having family live nearby as I felt like I was battling everything on my own, but I knew that my prayers would get me through, and God would take care of my children.

After almost six months in the hospital, finally being home was a relief and my son had improved so much. The prayers of a mother are powerful, and they imparted strength to me and my children in times of pain and struggle. I now had to depend on the prayers to help keep me from giving up. A couple of weeks after returning home, I just couldn't get out of bed. Depression had come upon me greatly and it was also close to Christmas. The weight of all that was going on was too heavy and I couldn't move.

I prayed and cried out to God saying that it was impossible to do this alone and would start to solely rely on His power and strength to keep me from giving up. Exhaustion seemed to envelop me, so I closed my eyes and decided to just let go. I let go of the hurt, the worry, the tears, and allowed myself to rest in the Lord's arms. I was filled with the love of God, His comfort, and felt the knowledge of His goodness. I finally knew that prayers and leaving it all in God's hands were going to get me and my children through the next years.

At 5 ½ years of age, he was declared cancer-free but I knew the miracle from God happened that night at the hospital when the doctors said he wouldn't get through. Fast forward to when he turned eighteen years old and seeing all the Lord had done through me staying steadfast in prayer was amazing. Sixteen years of watching and having faith that my son would be completely healed and grow to be strong and healthy was a journey that was overcome through prayer.

Hearing the doctors say he was free now from checkups was an indication that God's love really healed us all! He healed not only my son but also my small family of three as we depended on and trusted God through all the prayers over the years.

This is a prayer that I prayed continually during my journey:

Heavenly Father, I come before you now to place my children into your hands and leave them at the foot of the cross. You are all powerful, all-knowing, all-seeing, and sovereign God and you know what my children need more than I do. You know what the future holds for them and in Jeremiah 29:11, your word says, "For I know the plans I have for you," declares the LORD, "plans to prosper you and not to harm you, plans to give you hope and a future." So I surrender them completely to you now and trust this promise will come to pass. In Jesus Name, Amen.

This is a prayer I said after being strengthened by my many prayers as a mom:

Heavenly Father, As I hold the hands of my older children and feel their heartbeat; I praise you. You, who have shown your mercy in healing my son and keeping us together as a family; I thank you. You walked with my daughter and guided her during her young life amidst turmoil and pain and I'm so grateful Lord. You lifted me up and carried me in your hands. You opened our eyes to all of your Glory and Power, and you continue to surround us with your amazing love, so I give you all praise and thanks. In Jesus name, Amen.

Rachel Colley has two adult children whom she raised on her own and contributes their success in life to God's mercy and grace upon their lives. She is grateful to the Lord for life and for always providing for her needs as a single parent. She has a deep passion for animals, newborn babies, and has her own bookkeeping business.

 http://www.fourty8bookkeeping.com

CHAPTER TWENTY-SEVEN - Maryanna Stevanovic

Now Unto Him

Let me ask you, how do you get from here to there? How do you cross that bridge which you've longed to cross most of your life? In one lifetime, there will be many bridges to cross. Some we cross very carefully, inching ourselves along the way. Some can be very frightening, and we never look down. Some bridges might allow for others to carry us across and still some we are pushed across. Regardless, bridges take us from here to there.

I have always been fascinated by bridges especially tall, huge, majestic ones stretching across miles of water as they reach up towards the sky. However, none of them – not one – can compare to the bridge the Lord God has built to allow mankind to cross from death to life, from mortality to immortality, from bondage to freedom, from hell to heaven, and from damnation to grace.

What do we do with this bridge? Most people cross it only when they are in dire straits, are at the bottom of that deep dark pit and need a miracle to exit, or are begging for the life of a loved one.

No matter what the situation, people are encouraged to look to the Lord and see what He has done, to cross that bridge, and wholeheartedly accept the whole package of salvation. We children of God are encouraged to look up, up to the heavens where our help comes from. I have chosen Ephesians 3:20 which reads:

"Now unto Him that is able to do exceedingly above all that we ask or think, according to the power that works in us." (KJV)

This is a testimony of one of my life experiences with the Lord. For most of my life, I have struggled with poverty (which changes almost your whole identity), but now am doing quite well, even giving to others. It is true that God never gives us more than we can handle but it's a long road getting there.

A few years ago, I was at my breaking point. I was feeling helpless watching life go by, not being able to dream or see any desire come to fruition. I was tired of the endless struggles to provide, support, give, encourage, or just hold my head above water. I had to make decisions that were detrimental to me and my family's health. Most who have struggled with poverty know the shame, the guilt, the self-inflicted punishment, and the downward fall of self-esteem. Being convicted in our heart to do well for not only our children but others, and having to endure the endless punishment of not having enough. Birthday parties were the worst for me, having to apologize once again for not bringing a gift. This was very shameful and caused suspicious thoughts to arise, such as, *"Do they like me? Do I match up? Am I good enough?* Of course, the answer in Christ is, "Yes, they like you. How can they not? You are more than enough. I have given you value and worth through the cross."

The Lord gave exceedingly abundantly above all that I could ask or thought possible. I was contacted by a very reliable source, a true woman of God, who told me God spoke to her giving her specific instructions as to what I was to do in order to change my circumstances. She said I was to fast for three days (no food, just water) and repeat a particular scripture over and over again during those days. It was not so much the action that was required but the faith to do it. I did as she said believing things would change and indeed they did. A few days later, something came in the mail that changed our whole way of living. It provided my family with a step up, a way into the freedom adequate finances can support. It took the pressure off. The struggles were gone, and the worry was left behind. I couldn't help but notice how it changed me – making me feel confident, able, worthy, valid, happy, and relaxed. Money can do that, but nothing comes close to knowing who you are in Christ. We had hope for a happier future, however, our hope was as it always had been, in Christ.

Christ's superiority. Christ's Word tells me that I am a child of God led by the Spirit of God. I am saved by grace through faith, redeemed, forgiven, justified, healed, by His wounds, rescued from darkness, an heir of eternal life, transformed by the renewing of my mind, an overcomer. I am triumphant, more than a conqueror, knowing Christ has won the war. I am totally blessed not by my circumstances or what this world can offer, but by what was done on the cross.

All of my life experiences with the Lord, everything I have learned and have been a witness to others and their experiences, boils do to one thing and that is love. Love. There is no greater thing. The kind of love God has for us cannot compare nor can we even begin to understand it. However, we get a glimpse of it, a taste of it when He does go above and beyond exceedingly abundantly all that we ask or think. There are no limitations on His love for us. He put the love we have in our hearts, He put the desires we have in our hearts, and He put joy in our hearts so we can delight ourselves in Him. To true believers, nothing else matters, only He. As Charles Spurgeon said, *"You will never know the fullness of Christ until you know the emptiness of everything but Christ."*

Not only is the Lord loving and kind, but He is also faithful to us. He often tells us what we see in the physical form is nothing compared to what He is doing in the spiritual realm. He says He longs for our faith to increase so that nothing can shake us or prevent us from believing in Him. Yet, how many times do we let it slide not doing our part, not spending time with Him, not praying fervently, not studying to show ourselves approved? Still, He overlooks that and continues to love us endlessly giving of Himself, imparting to us, and giving how much He thinks we can handle. His willingness to do for His people has no limitations, therefore, they should not put Him in a box. He is the limitless God, and it is unfortunate that most people are not willing to go beyond the limits. Yet His love endures forever.

Psalm 37:4-5 reads:

> *"Delight thyself also in the Lord, and He shall give thee the desires of thine heart. Commit thy way unto the Lord; trust in Him and He shall bring it to pass."*

I look at this and take it not as a suggestion, a recommendation, or an idea but as a commandment (which I am happy to receive) of the Lord. He wants those desires to be fulfilled, to come to fruition because He put them there. He also gave us other commandments such as pray, fast, and give. In praying we draw closer to our God, in fasting we draw closer to the spiritual, and in giving we draw closer to Jesus. Giving is the way to receiving, Jesus has made that clear.

In the story of the widow's mite, she is a poor widow who gives two small coins out of her lack but is operating on the faith principle. Jesus said she gave more than anyone else and I always thought because out of her little, she gave much, not realizing He said that because she gave the most in faith. God is generous and He gives. Just like a handful of seeds will grow when we plant them in the ground, we receive the fruit thereof. People say God grows that seed but actually the seeds grow under the principle of the earth being obedient to God's previous command. The roots take in water and food, and the seeds are pliable enough to open up and grow. These are principles God set in motion before the foundation of the world. So it is with us. There are commandments, principles, statutes, and systems that we all must adhere to if we want to break the back of poverty. Yet God makes it simple because He loves us and He wants us to know exactly how much. Instead of trying to figure it out ourselves, He asks that we draw closer to Him to experience His love. Once we do that, we are amazed that the Holy Spirit's power is love, we are amazed at how it moves on our heart, and how capable we become to love others.

God loves reaches the deepest depth of our souls, heals our wounds, binds up the broken pieces, and gives us a new heart and a new heart level which allows us to change not only our hearts but our minds as well. He gives us a Christ-like mind which alters the way we think. If we have always thought of ourselves as negative, critical, unable, unworthy, or depleted,

He can change that. We must start by honoring God's word first, respecting His word, seeking His kingdom first, and then giving. If you don't know how, train yourself. Start small by giving yourself a compliment, giving yourself time, and giving yourself money. Love yourself a little more and think about how much God loves you. Most people agree that God is able, but they don't believe He is willing. They say, *"Why would He do it for me?"* The answer is, *"Why not, if HE is love and you are His child, then believe it and receive it."* The secret is believing with great expectations. The most powerful revelation we could ever get is how much God loves us.

Keep in mind that God loves the world, His children, the church, the sinner, the spiritual and carnal Christian, His Son, and the cheerful giver. His ability to do for us is connected with our capability of understanding how much He loves us. This is such a great and powerful gift, and I believe there is none like it. I read something a long time ago written by John Piper:

> *"What is sin?*
> *It is the glory of God not honored.*
> *The holiness of God not reverenced.*
> *The greatness of God not admired.*
> *The power of God not praised.*
> *The truth of God not sought.*
> *The wisdom of God not esteemed.*
> *The beauty of God not treasured.*
> *The goodness of God not savored.*
> *The faithfulness of God not trusted.*
> *The commandments of God not obeyed.*
> *The justice of God not respected.*
> *The wrath of God not feared.*
> *The grace of God not cherished.*

*The presence of God not prized.
The person of God not loved.
That is sin."*

Now I would like to add my thoughts: *"The grace of God not extended"* and *"The love of God not accepted, understood, believed, or experienced."*

Do we have to believe first so we can experience it? Or when we experience it, we can believe. I'm not sure; all I know is that they go hand in hand, and it happens individually for every person.

We look up to our God, the creator of the universe; up to Him who holds the world in His hands. The God who is omniscient, meaning all-knowing, possessing complete knowledge, universal, and intimate.

- He is omnipresent, meaning He is everywhere with His whole being all at the same time.
- He is infinite and yet finite.

We give glory to Him who has created a plan, a purpose, a destiny, a future, and an eternity.

- He who sees us beyond our limitations to our potential.
- He who sees our uniqueness and is patient until we are transformed into His marvelous image.
- He who is always available, is loyal and faithful.
- He who has undeserving mercy, compassion, and grace for us.
- He never gives up on us as He teaches us His ways.
- He straightens our paths and helps us by giving us examples of men and women who have pursued Him as they live a Godly life.

- He who thinks the best of us, helps us to succeed and even excel beyond ourselves and any vision we may have had.
- He who gives us discernment and corrects us as He admonishes us of all evil practices or beliefs.
- He who protects us and wards off our enemies giving us an opportunity to develop our own strength.
- He who is molding us into the image of His own son so that when we see Him, we will recognize not only Him but ourselves also.

I would say that is a good place to look: up to the heavenlies. Ephesians 1:3 reads:

"Blessed be the God and Father of our Lord Jesus Christ, who has blessed us with every spiritual blessing in the heavenly places in Christ." (NKJV)

The English dictionary defines heavenlies as alluring, wonderful, sublime; of or occurring in space; and divine, holy. Divine and holy, that is our God…Father, Son, and Holy Spirit working together as one. We have a Father who is able, through His Son with the help of the Holy Spirit, to do, to give, to save, to protect, to redeem, to build up in excellence to the glory of Himself. This is a God worth getting to know as He reveals Himself through His Living Word, however, a transfer of ownership is required, and a humble submission of our lives is necessary. We lift up holy hands in praise and worship as it is a sign of surrender giving ourselves over completely to Him.

Now I carry on looking forward to more bridges to cross, more truths to unfold as I walk with Him in life knowing I have a part to play in His purpose and His plan. I have a responsibility to carry out and that is to tell others what I know to be true as I help them on their journey. My testimony is that God loves us so much that He sent His only begotten Son to die for us and save us from the condemnation of sin and give us eternal life. Not only life in heaven but also here on earth, making a way where there is no way, not even a path, an edge, or ledge, but a bridge to redeem us unto Himself in the eternal glory that is He. I pray many people will come to the full saving knowledge of what Christ has done for us. As a mother hen gathers her children, so Christ would love to sweep everyone up into His arms and make us His own.

Are you willing?

See you on the other side.

Maryanna Stevanovic is enjoying her retirement years after decades of working as a Home Daycare Provider, Quality Control Inspector, and Small Business Assistant. Her passion is serving the Lord by volunteering at her local church, helping those in need, or spreading the Gospel. Maryanna loves God, children, music, writing, and has hopes of becoming a Children's Book Author. She immigrated with her parents to Canada from Serbia as a child and now lives in Stoney Creek, Ontario with her husband, two grown sons, and a wonderful daughter-in-law. For her, there is nothing greater than the will and plan of our Lord Jesus Christ.

   Mare.loves.God@gmail.com

CHAPTER TWENTY-EIGHT - Lesley C. Morgan

Darkness to Destiny

"Trust in the Lord with all your heart. Lean not on your own understanding. In all of your ways acknowledge Him and He will direct your path!" Proverbs 3:5,6 (NKJV)

My story is about how God can use ordinary people to do extraordinary things. This is a story of darkness to destiny. A story of how God can take you from living in depression to the majestic mountains of the Yukon to a life worth living.

This is how it all began.

I was raised in a good Christian home with wonderful parents and was the oldest of three children. I always felt extremely shy as a child and as I got into the teenage years, the shyness increased along with a feeling of being invisible. By my late teens,

I became severely depressed, even suicidal. I cried most of the time. I had few friends and rarely spoke to anyone because I felt that I had nothing of importance to say. I remember feeling like I was in a deep dark pit with no way out and I can remember calling out to God, asking Him to make me feel happy again. I felt like everyone had deserted me, even God.

In my early 20s, I had a major nervous breakdown and was hospitalized for two months. The doctors in the psychiatric ward did not know how to help me so they experimented with different medications and even shock treatments. Nothing helped. Little did I know this was all part of God's bigger plan.

Soon after my release from the hospital, and still on antidepressants, an amazing opportunity arose for me to go to the Yukon on a mission trip for the summer. This was the last thing I wanted to do. I was still depressed and really did not want to leave my room, let alone go to the other side of the country! God in His infinite wisdom had the right people in the right places at the right time. They saw my need to get away and refocus my priorities.

The summer of 1974 found me in the Yukon, God's country, surrounded by His beautiful, majestic mountains and crystal-clear lakes. I soon forgot my problems as I worked hard that summer rebuilding old churches throughout the Yukon all the way to Dawson City. We also spent time ministering to the North Cree Indians. We would set up craft centers for the children in each town we stayed in, teaching about the love of Jesus.

For the first time in my life, I felt a sense of purpose. As we sang praise and worship songs on the side of a mountain overlooking the Yukon River, I experienced a Peace that I had never felt before.

That summer was an interesting turning point for me. There was daylight 24/7! The days in July and August were very warm but as we hiked up the mountains the temperature would drop very quickly. God was definitely "directing my path" as I experienced for the first time the comforting warmth of the presence of the Holy Spirit.

When I returned home at the end of the summer, I no longer required medication or a psychiatrist and have never to this day been depressed! This was really the beginning of my search for Truth. I wanted to know Jesus better, and I had many questions going through my mind about what I had experienced in the Yukon that summer. My transformation was real.

The following year, I was married and two years later I was blessed with a son. From day one, he came to church with me and was a source of great joy, but I still had a lot of questions about what I had experienced in the Yukon. My neighbor would come over frequently and talk about Jesus as if He were her best friend. This was new to me. She invited me to her little attic apartment every morning to watch a new program on the air called 100 Huntley Street. It was only a half-hour program at the time but what I heard made a major impact on my life. In fact, I got cable installed so that I could watch it in my own little home. The testimonies I heard of what God was doing in people's lives amazed me! Then one day I heard a testimony from a woman who had received healing from severe depression! Now my Yukon experience started to make sense. Now I knew I needed Jesus more than ever in my life.

I remember very clearly the day when I prayed the sinner's prayer. I had heard David Mainse extend the invitation many times and this day I made up my mind to "do it." I had been vacuuming so, I turned it off, sat on my coffee table, and asked Jesus into my heart right in the middle of my living room. I will never forget the tingling sensation that flowed through my body from head to toe and the peace and joy that washed over me like a bubbling mountain brook. It was amazing how all of a sudden, the Bible came alive to me, and I couldn't get enough of it. I felt like the whole world needed to know that Jesus can be very real, and that church is not about **religion** but about **relationship**. God knew that I would need this reassuring memory to help me in the coming years.

Two years later, God blessed us with a beautiful little girl. She was another source of joy. Life seemed to be going along just fine. Like most new Christians, I asked God many times to use me for His Glory and then wondered why He wasn't taking me up on my offer.

For the next eighteen years, my faith continued to grow as I regularly attended Bible studies, women's ministries meetings, and choir practice. 100 Huntley Street continued to be a source of encouragement for me. At the same time, I endured many hardships not uncommon to most people. We had major financial problems including living on welfare for a time. We were experiencing difficulties in our marriage. One of our children struggled with a learning disability, and my husband's health began to deteriorate. He experienced a life-threatening illness as well as serious back problems resulting in surgery. Unfortunately, he did not know the peace of the Lord, and his anger became more and more evident over the years.

As with everyone, we all go through our own problems and difficult circumstances, many beyond our control, but I viewed this time as a time of spiritual growth for me. I learned that He will stretch out our difficult situations in order to increase our

Faith! I still remained quiet and reserved but, in my heart, I knew that God had a plan for me (Jeremiah 29:11).

During those eighteen years, God blessed us with another lovely daughter. She came along later in life, and I have always considered her my special gift from God.

In 1997, an incident occurred in my life that seemed to turn it upside down and caused me to seriously re-evaluate myself, where I was in my Christian walk, and where God wanted me to be. By this time, I sensed God leading me to organize community outreach concerts despite the fact that I did not have a clue how to proceed. I was still lacking self-confidence.

The next year, I was asked help to organize the music portion of the March for Jesus in Brampton. I loved the whole concept of unifying the Body of Christ to take the Gospel message into the streets through music. By the year 2000, together with the director of the MFJ, I found myself in the position of coordinating the music end of the March for Jesus as well as the concert following the march in Gage Park, Brampton. Immediately following this June event, God began to really impress on me the vision of *Inspirational Music in the Park*. The concept of bringing Christian music out of all the churches and into the public for all to be blessed was now becoming a reality.

I could clearly see how God had been preparing me over the years. I now had more confidence in myself, I had connections with many of the churches in Brampton, and I also recognized how much talent there was in every church that needed to be brought out of the four walls of the church and into a public place for all to be blessed with the message of Hope!

Gage Park in Brampton is a very beautiful established park with lofty old trees and a storybook white gazebo, making it the perfect venue for Christian Music. The vision was so clear. God was saying, *"GO"* while I was still saying, *"NOT YET, I'm not ready."* Again, He said, *"GO and simply trust Me."* So, I went! I "stepped out of the boat" and by faith alone, I followed the vision God had given me. It was then that He whispered to me, *"Remember when you asked me to **use you** many years ago? I had to allow you to experience the suffering world, and **now** you are ready."* God led me every step of the way into this new adventure. Again, He was "directing my path" as I trusted Him with all my heart!

In August of 2000, I held the first concert in Gage Park and my vision became reality.

My Dream: This is the only time where God spoke to me in a vivid dream. It was the night before the first concert. I had been worrying about the weather. In my dream, a band was playing, and it was raining – only inside the gazebo. All the performers were getting wet. The water rose to overflowing over the white railings of the gazebo and flooded the park and surrounding area. God was making it clear that He would pour His Anointing out onto all the Christian performers over the coming years. His Message of Hope would flow into the surrounding area for all to hear!

I am in awe of what God has done through this ministry that has reached many hundreds of people weekly during the summer months with the gospel message. By providing faithful people to work alongside me, encourage me, and pray for me, God gave me the boldness to break free from the bondage of depression to be able to speak out freely for His Glory.

Another interesting God moment came right after another glorious concert in July of 2001. As we were packing up, a woman approached me with a little old lady on her arm and said, *"You need to hear what she just told me."* This is what the elderly lady said. *"Fifty years ago, my bible study group would meet here in Gage Park. We prayed that God would use this park for His Glory. Tonight, I have seen our prayers of fifty years answered!"* WOW! Another confirmation that I was indeed following God's calling.

The following twenty years of *Inspirational Music in the Park* was another Faith Adventure with many unexpected twists and turns along the way, but God's Grace was amazing! My Motto has always been "There is always Hope." As I look back over the years, I am in awe of how God has empowered me by the power of His Holy Spirit to transform me into the person I was meant to be.

Who says God cannot use ordinary people to do extraordinary things?

My prayer for each one of you reading my story is that when you feel like giving up…keep on trusting and believing! He will direct your Path!

Lesley C. Morgan has been a concert organizer for 25 years. These include 20 years of *Inspirational Music in the Park*, two concerts at the Rose Theatre, plus other concerts at various venues. Lesley has been secretary to the Brampton Ministerial Association for many years and organizes monthly prayer meetings at the City Hall. Unity among churches has always been her desire. Lesley has lived in Brampton since 1962 and enjoys spending time with her children and grandchildren.

CHAPTER TWENTY-NINE - Denese Dihele

Babies Come from The Man Upstairs

In the fall of 1997, I met my husband in Toronto, the most multicultural city in the World. He spoke little English, and I speak no French. One day in a busy downtown Toronto lunchtime our eyes met, and we went for a walk. After that, he came to see me every day at lunchtime and we became inseparable. Our love grew as we figured out a way to communicate. He went to English as a Second Language (ESL) classes as those were free and I tried going to French classes. He actually lost his bilingual job the same week we met, as he did not understand or speak English, but somehow when we were together, we always found a way. We communicated in many ways that did not make words necessary. We found that in prayer, we were connected and the chemistry was real. Three months after we met, he told me he already knew he would marry me and I would have twins: Umba and Shako. We were from different continents and we knew no one in common, but we knew Jesus and that was enough. We found out later that my Pastor was acquainted with his Pastor.

We were married in the summer of 1999 with many dreams and hopes of having children (my husband wanted five altogether). However, following our marriage, it became challenging. My husband and I were in church leadership: I was leading praise and worship and he was leading the prayer ministry. Month after month, when "that time of the month" came, we would get down and hard on ourselves. How do we encourage others? How do we pray for others when the obvious thing that we desired seemed like our prayers were not being answered? We prayed together, my husband prayed, my pastor prayed, and many people from revival meetings, prayer meetings, and regular church meetings prayed…and we waited and prayed some more. During this time of waiting, we became godparents to many children. Some of our very close friends thought they would help us out by making us responsible for their own children because they believed we would be such great parents. But, every Mother's Day I cried. Actually, every month at "that time of the month," I cried.

I went to many doctors on this journey, starting with my family doctor. She told us to just relax because she did not have children at that time and she was thirty-seven years old. Some time passed and my husband suggested I should go to see his doctor who did some tests right away, which proved nothing was wrong as far as they could see, so he referred us to a Fertility Specialist. After many months of trial, there was no solution. A friend referred us to another specialist and then another friend referred us to someone else who was deemed as one of the best fertility specialists in our area. After he tried everything he thought to do and two surgeries later, he told us, *"I have done what I can. Babies come from the man upstairs."* My husband's response was, *"I work for the man upstairs. I will check in with him."* At that moment, I was dumb-struck. I did not expect the doctor to tell me what I should have already known, that babies come from God. I was just so desperate, so very desperate going from doctor to doctor relying on them to make this happen when I should really be relying on God.

I was going from doctor to doctor and as long as my credit card was approved, it did not matter to me how much they told me to pay for the visit, or how much they told me to pay for the medication. I spent thousands of dollars; some I was able to have reimbursed from insurance but a lot of the money spent was not recoverable. I was almost upset with the doctor as I expected him to write me another prescription and tell me what I should do next. When he told me babies come from God, I wanted to scream, *"I know!"* But, it gave me something to think about. I had to reassess if I was relying on the God whom I knew or if was I relying on the doctors. That day when we left the doctor's office, my husband and I in the car began to talk and refocus our decisions.

We vowed to return to God, so we confessed and repented. We said, *"God, You lead, we will follow."* A few months passed and we didn't go to any doctors, we just spent time praying and fasting and waiting on God for the next move. We began to pray deeply then God started to speak to both of us about forgiveness and forgiving everyone who had hurt us. We confessed and repented and forgave, which took us on a trip to Jamaica. God certainly moves in mysterious ways.

In that year, we spent time focusing more attention on God and asking him for His direction. During one of my annual checkups with my doctor, he recommended another doctor and other specialists to me, so we went to a fertility clinic and met with a doctor, a Christian. This man of God recommended that we start some treatments and directed us to continue our fasting and prayers. During this time, we conceived our first son. Understanding that this is ministry, we were overjoyed. Our son arrived and two years later, our twin girls were born. At our first follow-up with this doctor, he told us he was relocating to a city two hours away. It was almost like he was there just for us and then he moved away. We now believe that when God wants to do you good, he can even make someone's plan be delayed just for you. Nothing is too hard for God to do.

It was only after the twins were born that the Spirit of the Lord became so intense, we could not say no. The direction was for us to plant a Bilingual French/English church in Mississauga, which was the first of its kind in the Region of Peel. At first, I told my husband that all the years when we had no children, we had so much spare time. How was this the right time when we had three small children? The Holy Spirit reminded us that the God who brought us through the journey so far will never leave us. We trusted God to move us into ministry and tell the world of the goodness of the Lord according to Isaiah 61:1-3:

> *"The Spirit of the Sovereign Lord is on me because the Lord has anointed me to proclaim good news to the poor. He has sent me to bind up the broken-hearted, to proclaim good news to the poor. He has sent me to bind up the broken-hearted to proclaim freedom for the captives and release from darkness for the prisoners to proclaim the year of the Lord's favour and the day of vengeance of our God*

to comfort all who mourn and provide for those who grieve in Zion – to bestow on them a crown of beauty instead of ashes the oil of joy instead of mourning, a garment of praise instead of the spirit of despair. They will be called Oaks of Righteousness a planting of the Lord for the display of His splendour." (NIV)

The church is called Oaks of Righteousness; a planting of the Lord to display His glory and praise through us. The Lord was to let the Oaks of Righteousness be a place where we got the understanding that children are not only biological, or adopted, but also spiritual. Children came to us from the North, South, East, and West to become a part of our family and today, we have over 200 children calling us Mama and Papa. This is an amazing blessing that we do not take for granted.

Through this medium, I want to inspire hope in someone who might be saying, *"I have been waiting for my children for so long and they have not come."* I want to let you know today that God can give you children whichever way He chooses. God sometimes chooses biological, sometimes spiritual, and sometimes through adoption but they are all beautiful through Him. God loves each of us and gives us the capacity to love others as He declares in John 13:34:

"Love one another as I have loved you, so you must love one another." (NIV)

He gives us so much love because He loved us, and He also gives us the capacity to love each other. I offer hope today to encourage the one who says, *"I have been waiting and longing and hoping."* I say, *"Continue to trust God and ask Him to show you which way the blessing will come, and through which means the blessing will come."* Do not give up hope, but continue to ask, continue to trust, and continue to seek. Matthew 7:7 says:

"Ask and it will be given to you; seek and you will find; knock and the door will be opened to you." (NIV)

Do not give up, do not give up. Ask God and He will show you how, what to do. and where to go.

I also want to encourage someone who is just waiting on God for anything: a promotion, a business, or a decision of any kind. God has many solutions in heaven and your problem is not a surprise to Him. God wants you to ask, seek, and knock. Know that God is able. Sometimes God answers, but we were expecting Him to answer in a different way. Sometimes the person or persons whom He chooses to bless us is not who we were expecting. I did not think I needed fertility treatments. I expected God to answer in a different way, but when I did what God asked, I received what I wanted – packaged differently, but God came through and my obedience gave me the gift I asked for.

Be intentional in your prayer. Be prepared to do what God says! Be prepared to go where God says! Be prepared to be obedient to the voice of God! The Holy Spirit will confirm in your heart what you need to do, and you must say, *"Here I am Lord. Use me."*

For those who are struggling with the decision that you know God has already spoken, give it to Jesus. I am a big advocate for counseling and coaching. Sometimes, you just need to talk to someone whom you trust: a pastor, spiritual advisor, mentor, or professional. If you need a referral, feel free to connect.

Prayer

Father in heaven, giver of life, maker of the universe. You are all-sufficient, all-knowing, and wise. I acknowledge you as the one true God. You make all things beautiful in YOUR time. You are the master of time and circumstance. I ask you O Lord to make your Spirit known to every woman or man reading this book today. Give them your peace that passes all understanding. Help them to understand that your ways are higher than our ways and your thoughts higher than our thoughts.

Help us to forgive those who have wronged us so that we may receive your forgiveness. Heal all of our brokenness, broken hearts, broken spirits, and broken lives that have made us sin against you. Forgive us as we forgive those who have hurt us. You know what each person needs right now: healing, restoration, love, kindness, joy, and peace. You give as no one can. Do it again, O Lord. Do it again, now.

Grant them their desire to have children, biologically, spiritually, or adoptive. Let your will be done in their lives, I pray. In Jesus' Name. AMEN.

Denese Dihele is a 30-year banker, experienced in building and leading teams. She is a passionate pastor, humanitarian, and community leader. Denese is the co-founder of The Oaks of Righteousness Church and Global Family Community Centre with her husband, Rev. Daniel Dihele. Together, they built a Community Outreach Centre and developed outreach programs for families, youth, and seniors in the Greater Toronto Area. Denese loves spending quality time with her family and being a social media influencer!

CHAPTER THIRTY - Nerrissa Myers

I'm An Overcomer

The journey of my life has not always been easy. I have learned how to overcome disappointments, setbacks, and challenges every step of the way. There were moments when I was on the mountaintop where everything was going great, and then other moments when I just plummeted right down into the valley.

It all began as I was a young girl growing up in St. Vincent and the Grenadines. I witnessed the abuse of my mother at the hands of my father. Their separation from each other left me destitute, heartbroken, lonely, rejected, and confused. My father and I were very close. When his attitude toward my mother changed, it seemed like it had changed toward me too. When he left home, life seemed like it had ended for me. Often, there was no money to put food on the table. We begged. My mother found a job and as she got busy, I became more isolated, spending a lot of time daydreaming. I would watch for the airplanes when they flew overhead, which was seldom, and thought, one day…

As I played with dolls I made from grass, I imagined that when I grew up, I would have a great life. I didn't know how to process everything I was facing so I internalized it as my fault. Even though I had some neighborhood friends, there was something missing on the inside. There were deep feelings of loneliness and inadequacy. My mother got an opportunity to migrate to Canada for a better life while my younger sister and I stayed with an aunt. These were some tough and painful years of my life. Many nights, I cried myself to sleep. I felt very much like an orphan, having no mother or father close by. I had no one to share my feelings with. I felt alone in the world and it seemed like no one understood me. I knew I was different. I attended church regularly on Sundays and accepted the Lord Jesus Christ into my heart when the Pastor did an altar call. I was around twelve years old.

A great shock came when I migrated to Canada in the year 1990 to be with my mother, but God had a great plan. I was invited to Church where I was baptized in Jesus' name at the age of thirteen and later became filled with the Holy Spirit. Immigration Canada denied extending our visa and placed a deportation order and a warrant for my mother's arrest. For years, we lived like fugitives, moving from house to house. As a precaution for our safety, my mother encouraged me to keep our business private, which also meant that I could not let anyone too close to me. They could not know our secret that we were on a deportation order. Immigration Canada somehow found our address and sent an officer to look for us. Thankfully, we were not at home. They inquired with the other tenant to confirm if we lived there, and he denied knowing us. We were still not out of the woods. We lived looking over our shoulders daily. We were not free. As a result, I could not do a lot of things that a regular teenager would do. Looking back, it is only by God's grace they did not come to the school to get my sister and me.

I made it safely through elementary school and even though I excelled as an honor student, I had to forfeit my dream of going to university to become a lawyer. I had to settle for college, which was less expensive. And since I had no legal status in Canada, I could not afford the fees. I was an active part of my school community and demonstrated integrity. During my senior high school years, God positioned me around two amazing teachers. I got the courage to explain my challenges with going to postsecondary and they did not hesitate to help me. They went beyond the normal duties of teachers to help push me forward. They contacted several colleges on my behalf as a highly recommended student. I did not have to do anything. What a great favor from God. I was accepted into the Early Childhood Education program on the condition that I provide an updated immigration status within a specific time frame. Therefore, I did not have to pay the international student fee. God was using me during this time. I was trusting Him for everything in my life and He was drawing me closer. I was constantly seeking His face and praying that our permanent status application would be granted. Our application was approved and were given a date to sign the documents. I was able to provide this information to the college in order to complete the program. We became permanent residents of Canada in 1999 and I graduated that same year with very high honors. I became a Canadian citizen a short time later. There were no disappointments when we waited patiently on the Lord.

Another barrier was overcoming prejudice and racial stereotypes. I remember the first boy that I was interested in was Caucasian. We were walking in the mall, and he held my hand. This was noticed by a black lady, a total stranger, who made the nasty remark, *"You're letting down your race."* I was very hurt and took it personally. I broke off the relationship with this person. There were not a lot of visible interracial relationships as there are now. I realized, however, that someone else's opinion had influenced how I lived, what I did, and who I was. It influenced how I viewed myself as an independent woman. This was something I had to overcome. I had to believe in myself and accept myself for who I am. I had to learn that not everyone will accept me and that's ok. I accepted myself and most importantly, God accepted me. I am reminded by God's Word that I am made in His image and after His likeness (Genesis 1:26-28). This was difficult to do because I internalized every criticism or negative comment and projection. I often resorted to myself. As I began to read and meditate on God's word more, I began to feel inner peace. People's opinions became less important because I know that I am fearfully and wonderfully made. I know that God has made me to be unique and stand out, therefore I began to embrace my uniqueness. I no longer tried to fit in. Each day I became more confident in the woman God has created me to be.

I met my husband in the church we both attended and got married at the age of twenty-four. As our family started to increase, so did the challenges of marriage. I thank God for bringing us this far. Looking back, we didn't have the best support or network system to encourage us. We had to navigate life on our own as a young Christian couple. Trying to balance work and raising children plus being a godly wife presented some difficulties. I remember seeking out godly pastoral counsel at a crucial point in our marriage and my husband was told to leave our family. We sought the Lord in prayer and fasting, and by His grace and mercies, we are still married for over twenty-two years and are pursuing a life in Christ. Our lives and family are a daily work in progress.

Life still had its challenges and ups and downs. I was still trying to find myself. As I grew older, I noticed that I never seemed to fit in, whether in work cliques, church cliques, or friend groups. Building connections or lasting friendships was difficult. So instead, I spent more and more time to myself, reading or engaging in some type of personal activity. I declined many invitations due to the pressure and anxiousness that arose. As a result, I was often misjudged or misunderstood by others. Even though I am not a social butterfly, I saw where the enemy wanted to keep me, hostage and in isolation from everyone. I realized that this was an area that needed development. I preferred being by myself and not socializing, except for the one or two people I considered friends. This was way more comfortable and safer. In doing so, I missed out on some great opportunities even to be a witness for the Lord. I labeled myself as "shy." I began to speak God's word over my life and declared that God did not give to me the spirit of fear, but power, love, and a sound mind (2 Timothy 1:7). I also spoke, *"I can do all things through Christ who strengthened me"* (Philippians 4:13).

I knew that God had a calling upon my life, but I kept running. I spent most of my life running from something. I became ordained as an Evangelist in 2013 and began to preach the Word of God. I know that this is a gift from God, but even this brought a lot of opposition. I began to face a lot of spiritual attacks upon my life and family. One of the things I found that helped me to overcome these struggles and barriers in life is my strong faith. The God that knows my future knew the things that I would encounter in my life. He had me in the church from a very young age memorizing and reciting the Holy Scriptures. They were ingrained in me, so when the storms of life came, I had an anchor in the Lord. I am built on the true foundation. I have a relationship with Him and His Word brought comfort, peace, and knowledge.

My life's challenges have made me relentless and fierce in prayer. After encountering two near-death accidents in 2016 and 2019, I realized that my life truly has a purpose. I cried out, *"Jesus, save me!"* as a driver ran the stop sign and I was headed for a collision. I could not see a path of escape, but God already had one prepared for me. He heard my cry and He answered. It was a miracle. I did not die but lived. The vehicle was totaled, but God kept me! I came out of that accident without fractures or any life-threatening injuries. The enemy tried to take my life and failed. I was diagnosed with depression that came to steal my mind, but God healed me. He soothed me from the aches and pains that gripped my body. God preserved me. He protected me and delivered me from all my fears. I overcame! I am an overcomer in Christ Jesus. I overcame by the Blood of Jesus Christ and by the word of my testimonies. No weapon formed against me shall prosper. My life is for God's glory.

As I reflected on my life, I thank God for the mountains and the valleys. I thank Him for the many tests and trials I had to endure. I thank him for my past and humble beginnings. Many things that I did not understand then are clear now. The process was worth it. I am a stronger woman of faith today because of all those experiences. The lack of self-acceptance, racial barriers, accidents, and depression did not define who I was. They proved that with God by my side, I can overcome anything. My desire is to live the abundant life that God has intended for me and to be all that He created me to be because I'm destined for greatness. I want more.

I encourage you to keep on persevering until you overcome. Whatever is holding you back, do not give up. The same God who helped me is more than able to help you win. I encourage you to trust in the Lord and in His marvelous plans for your life. All things are possible with God. You are alive because there is more for you. You are an overcomer.

Nerrissa Myers is an evangelist who is passionate about reaching souls for the Kingdom of God. She serves and leads in the areas of praise and prayer ministry. Nerrissa has a background in Early Childhood Education and Criminal Justice Services and uses her gifts and skills to educate and empower young people. Nerrissa is married and raises four children with her husband.

CHAPTER THIRTY-ONE - Marilin Reid-Henry

Turning Lemons into Lemonade

How It All Began

My life began on the Caribbean Island of Jamaica in 1960. I grew up in a loving household with my parents and siblings, and I was the second of four children. My mother was a very strict Christian and a Bible scholar who was a graduate of the renowned Jamaica Bible College. Her lifestyle reflected the teachings from the Bible, and she would instruct us as well as model practical Christian principles. Based on my upbringing, accepting the Lord as Savior was a natural thing to do, and I made that decision at the early age of eleven. My mother contributed to my interest and love for children's ministry and singing. This caused me to embark on youth and music ministry in the church shortly after my conversion.

I was always admonished that as a Christian if I remained faithful to God, *"He will grant me the desires of my heart"* (Psalm chapter 37:4). My dream and aspiration was to find a Christian husband, be happily married, and have a family. I envisioned my marriage to be similar to that of my parents who were committed to each other as well as respected their marriage vows in every way. In September 1985, after about six months of courtship, I got married. The onset of this relationship was good. I was happy because I remained faithful to God, and I believed that it had paid off.

The Dilemma

My happiness was short-lived and was soon replaced with repeated incidences of physical, financial, emotional, and mental abuse. On the rare occasions that I attempted to call the police, I would be reminded of my immigration status along with the threat of deportation back to Jamaica. At the time I did not have permanent residency status, and my husband was aware of it. He had agreed to help by sponsoring me as a spouse, but instead, he used this to his advantage as a way to prolong his abuse. He often blamed me for the cause of his abusive actions. I was forced into giving up things that I love, especially singing in groups at concerts. There were also efforts to ostracize me from friends and family, as he embarked on a tirade of abusive and controlling behaviors.

The shame of a failed marriage made going to church an uncomfortable experience at the onset as I felt the need to pretend that all was well. I would listen to the preached word and chastise myself for not enjoying the victorious Christian life that I should be living. I felt that If I was living up to the standards of a good Christian, my marriage would result differently.

An added devastating experience for my children and I was being homeless. I purchased my first home in 1993, and due to limited finances, I became delinquent in my mortgage payments. Walking away from the home that my children and I had known for almost two years into the uncertain future of our homeless misfortune only added to my already tragic life. Again, I questioned God but continued to put my trust in Him. I pulled from Biblical examples like Daniel going through his lion's den, and Joseph in the pit as well as his prison experience. I also recall Jesus' prayer asking for the cup of the crucifixion to be removed, but then relinquishing that request and accepting God's plan instead amidst its painful process (Matthew chapter 26:39).

During the six months of homelessness and being housed at a motel, my children were unaware that we were without a home, because I ensured that I would not allow them to feel the burden of things that were not their responsibility. Their attendance and progress at school were unaffected, and my ministry and attendance at church continued. I recall leaving the motel at Kingston Road and Lawrence Avenue East in Toronto at about 8 a.m. Sunday morning in order to arrive before 10 a.m. at my home church. I was the Superintendent for the Junior department, and I had to be on time for Sunday School no matter what challenges I encountered. The journey was long and tiring, nonetheless, I dutifully repeated it every Sunday for six months. My commitment to God did not have conditions. He is to be worshipped regardless of my circumstances.

I was also the director for both the Junior choir as well as the Vacation Bible School in the summer. The Church Summer Camp continued to be an annual occurrence for my family and I.

Years after, during some reflections, I realized that my ministry involvement was very therapeutic as it provided a helpful and healthy balance to my life. Doing something that gave me purpose while maintaining a spiritual connection with God was the recipe that I needed.

The Outcome

While getting prenatal care during my first pregnancy, I inquired and received immigration information from an immigration lawyer for free. He also accompanied me to the immigration office. The lawyer included the domestic abuse and relationship breakdown as the main defense for my immigration status to be legalized. It so happened that a program (The Administrative Review Program) was initiated and all who had applied to the date of my application would be considered for landed status. During this time, there were numerous attempts at reconciliation, but the abuse continued as well.

The night prior to my immigration interview for landed status, my then-husband decided that he would come with me. His reasoning was that if the immigration decision was not favorable, he would then apply for me. Seeing it as an opportunity to be abusive, he continued an argument, and after leaving and returning a few times, he eventually left.

I went for my interview and received a positive outcome. The result would have been different had he shown up, as the immigration officer made an emphasis about the abuse that I encountered from him. I was elated. I left the immigration office to celebrate with my family. I felt free and I felt good.

Amidst the marriage counseling attempts, the abuse continued, and the numerous separations led to a divorce that was finalized in 1994.

Seeing God Through It All

At the onset of my failed marriage, I did question God because I considered myself to be faithful, and the reward should have been a "happily ever after" marriage. I felt shame now being single with three children, I felt like my life was over, and had become a total mess. I felt like God had failed me. I was hurt, bruised, felt used, and abandoned. I was a walking dead. Amidst my relationship challenges, I pushed beyond it and went back to school in 1988 to pursue Practical Nursing as my aim was to become a nurse. I recall receiving the result of my provincial nursing board exam and although the result was a positive one, I cried because it was hard to see its benefit as I was now stuck alone with three young children with all the challenges that accompany a single mother.

One day, I decided to attempt to take the Toronto Transit bus and visit my mother with all three children. I went to the bus stop with my three children secured in the double stroller and with the assistance of the bus driver, taking it became a possibility. On exiting the bus, I ran pushing the stroller, and calling out to my mother. I screamed with excitement, *"I did it! I can do it!"* My mother asked what the excitement was about, to which I explained that I was able to take the bus with all three children because I had just done so. My children at the time were three years old, two years old, and a few months old.

As time went on, and as I remained involved in church ministry, I started to feel happy again. I started to smile as the radiance returned to my heart and was expressed on my face. I recalled entering a Mother's Day pageant at my local church. I noted the other participants introduced themselves as being happily married, etc. I then decided to use my situation and introduced myself as being happily divorced. I could see the smiles on the faces of the audience and judges, who even commented that they had never heard that term before. I was now on the journey of enjoying being single, being happy, and being content. I celebrated that I was no longer experiencing abuse, and my children were no longer exposed to it.

A few years later, a minister who had firsthand knowledge of the abuse I had experienced, suggested that I pray for my now-divorced husband to return. My response was, *"If God delivered me from Egypt, why should I pray to go back into bondage?"* I asked her to explain how this would have benefitted my children and me, to which she acknowledged that it would not be good.

I continued to use my challenges as a catalyst to success and again, I returned to school, this time to complete my studies as an RN. My journey also took me from homelessness to being a homeowner for the second time in 2003. The feeling was and still is surreal at times. God does have a timing that is unmatched and incomparable.

I was committed to focusing on taking care of my children, so I shunned the idea of dating and remarriage while they were young. During my travels, I reconnected with a childhood friend from my teenage years, and after three years of reconnecting, we started dating. Three years later we were married, resulting in a blended family. We are currently approaching our eight-year anniversary on December 11, 2023. I am happy to know that I am married to a man who loves and adores me, and my adult children enjoy a good relationship with him and call him Dad.

I am able to see now that God did not forsake me but was with me all through this journey. Although my first marriage failed, God did not. God had a plan for me, and even though I could not see it then, I can see it now. He wanted to use my life as a message and testimony for His glory. I have been able to help others who experienced domestic abuse, abandonment, and single-parent challenges as I can identify with them. I have helped them to see themselves as victors instead of victims. I remember helping a domestic violence survivor to overcome suicidal as well as homicidal attempts. She expressed on numerous occasions that her being alive is because of my support and non-judgmental approach. Many others have been helped to increase their self-esteem and self-confidence.

My journey was a blessing in disguise. It may seem strange to say, but my resilience is a result of my life's journey. I am convinced that it is the blueprint of the direction that God had for me. My testing resulted in powerful testimonies. It is a good feeling to know that I am an overcomer. Being unable to see my way during my many dark moments, I was forced to rely on God as my help and deliverer. I learned to cast my cares upon Him because He is the one who cares for my well-being (First Peter 5:7). I had to literally put faith into action by adding the works, as the scripture informs us that *"Faith without work is dead,"* (James 2:26). I have used all my lemons of life to make tasty and refreshing lemonade, and I continue to enjoy its taste and aroma.

Marilin Reid-Henry has been faithfully serving the Lord for over fifty years. She is currently a praise and worship leader, Benevolence ministry coordinator, involved with the Upper Room Prayer Line Ministry, and facilitates the Nurse Education / Health and Wellness Ministry by providing health information to her local church Covenant of Promise Ministry. Marilin's nursing profession spans over thirty years and has taken her to Northern Ontario and First Nations Communities in Manitoba, Alberta, Nunavut and Northwest Territories.

CHAPTER THIRTY-TWO - Dr. Rev. Inez R. Brown

My Encounter with the Man, Jesus – Where Real Life Begins

I attended the First Baptist Church for thirteen years, singing in the choir at which time we received a new minister. I noticed he received his package of envelopes for yearly contributions. I was so surprised that I went to him and asked him how he got his envelopes so fast. I'd been there thirteen years and never got mine. Every January, I would look to see if there were envelopes for me, but there were none. He asked me a question, *"Are you baptized?"* I said, *"No. Do I need to be baptized to get my envelopes?"* He said, *"Yes."* Once again, he asked me if I wanted to be baptized, and then he said, *"There is a baptism class coming up. Would you like to be in it?"* I was so happy, I said, *"Yes."* It was about three or so classes after that conversation that we were dressed in our white gowns and white socks and got baptized. About a year later, I received my envelope package. I felt like I was on cloud nine.

Approximately two months after the baptism, I received a visitation sometime during the night while I was asleep. I felt as though someone was in my room watching me. My sleep was being disturbed by their presence. I twisted and turned for a while, then I jumped out of my sleep only to see the figure of a man. So, I turned my face to the window and covered my head with the sheet, and became afraid and very restless. I turned my face back to the door again and saw a man sitting on a stool with his legs crossed. His elbow was resting on his thighs and his hand at his chin. His clothes were super white, and it appeared as though the breeze was blowing on them. His hair was past his neck and was more like gold. As I looked down at his feet, he was wearing slippers. His face was like a slow flashing light with a glow over it. I knew I was in trouble because my desire was to turn and run to one of the children's rooms, but he was blocking my path. I knew if I tried, he would grab me. The next thought was to scream but that would scare the children, so I decided to play dead because there was no way out. I covered my head; my heart was beating so fast.

Suddenly, I heard this thunderous voice as though it was coming from the end of the earth saying, *"Repent, repent, repent I say, repent."* I was so scared from my previous encounter, and now, there were no words to describe how frightened I was. This went on for a while before I started arguing with him. I asked him who he thought he was, but he just kept on saying repent three times. He never answered my question. He just kept repeating the same thing.

I went on to ask him where he was when I got baptized at First Baptist Church. He still did not answer me. Then I asked him if he wanted to see my baptism certificate. He did not answer me.

Instead, his voice became so loud and much more frightening, and my eardrums felt as though they would burst. I was crying, sweating, scared out of my wits, and I literally felt as though I was about to die. As scared as I was, the after-effect of his voice was wearing off and I calmed down long enough to let him know that I didn't know how to repent. I must have repeated this sentence more than three times when his voice went into a high pitch mode. After a little while, I said to him, *"Of a truth, I don't know how to repent."* There was silence for a short while. Then he said, *"Get down off the bed. Get on your knees and repent."* How could I do that when my back would be to his face? I had the fear that he could grab me because I did not obey his command. His voice sounded like my father's voice when he was very serious. It went through my heart. This time I repeated that I did not know how to repent but he held his ground. No more talking. I got off the bed, knelt at my bedside, and told him again that I didn't know how to repent.

There was a pause, a stillness. Then he said, *"Repeat these words after me."* So, I did. I was so messed up that even to this day I cannot remember any of the words he told me to repeat. After that, a great calm came over me, my fighting was over, and I did not hear him again. My fear was gone. I wept for a good while, kneeling at my bedside.

Somehow, I got back in my bed (don't know how) because when I woke up, I was on my bed and everything was soaking wet from my pillow to my night clothes (I mean everything), but I knew something happened to me. I felt like I was in a different world so much so that when I got out of my room and carried all the wet things to hang them outside, my neighbor was making fun of me saying, *"She slept so hard she wet her bed. She even wet the pillow."* When I looked at my neighbors, they looked so strange. They tried their best to make me laugh or get angry with them, but it did not work because as far as I could see, they were not real. They were all aliens. So, I walked away telling them, *"Don't touch me."* I went back to my house to my room. From that night, my entire life and world changed.

After that dramatic night, lots of strange events started to happen that had never occurred before. It was so frightening to me and caused my siblings to be concerned. They went as far as to take me to the doctor who could not find anything medically wrong with me. After so many tests and X-rays, they couldn't find anything wrong with me. At the consultation, I spoke up and told the doctor that I knew what was going on with me. After listening to me, she thanked me for clearing the mystery up. She told them I was not crazy. She knew what she was saying. Thank God, they left me alone for a while to express that to her.

What I'm about to say is not a dream or a vision. These are real experiences that happened when I was awake.

I would be given names, phone numbers, and the condition of the person. Before I could digest it, I dialed the number and asked to speak to the lady whose name was given to me. When she answered the phone, I told her what the man told me about her son and the instructions she should follow. The reality hit me in a way I can't explain and her screams as she responded to the message. Then for a while, she dropped the phone, but I could hear her as she ran backwards and forwards in her house. This went on for a while. I was so scared. I had no idea what to do so I sat there dying with fright. She came back, picked up the phone, and asked, *"Who are you? How did you know my son was sick?"* I told her about the man who came, gave me her name, her son's name, and her phone number. Then she started screaming again, but much louder than before. She dropped the phone again and I could hear her until the screaming faded away. There were a few minutes of silence, and then she came back on the phone with her son who was sick. Now I heard his crying and her shouting. This woman and son were real. I've been going to the Baptist Church for years and nothing like this ever happened.

I called the second number I was given, and a lady answered. I gave her the boy's name and his condition. She started weeping and crying out, *"Oh Lord! Oh Lord!"* repeatedly. The name of this boy was Michael, who was about twelve years old. Something was troubling him and left him with a massive headache. Without hesitation, I told her what I was given by the man. I said, *"Go and lay your hand on his head and he will be delivered."* She went and did what I told her to do, and the boy was delivered.

I was so frightened by these occurrences that I cried and shut myself in from everyone. I'm alone, my children are off to school, and my family thinks I'm going mad. Who can I talk to or where can I go? I'm so scared; the drama was too much for me. All I could do was sing.

Everything was so confusing and overwhelming that I started to believe my family was right, and that I was going mad. I thought this was a one-time thing, but I was so wrong – it was a new life and experience for me.

After seventeen years at the Baptist church, I now found myself traveling on buses and trains throughout Canada and other parts of the world. At this time, the importance of my envelopes faded.

My church started to search for me by putting three ads in the newspaper. This is what I call love but although I love being there in every sense of the word, I had a new assignment. I had to go!

The phone calls, people being saved, healed, delivered, immigration documents cleared, babies being born to barren wombs, the crippled healed, blind, deaf, and dumb receiving their healing and deliverance, and being led to be a Pastor's Pastor when they suffer from burnout.

I traveled to many countries such as Canada, the U.S., and The islands (i.e., Jamaica, Guyana, St. Vincent, and Grenada). I was preaching under the big tents, parks, house prayer meetings, revivals and crusades, conferences, prison ministry, hospitals, and nursing homes. I was sharing the blessings the man had blessed me with on radio, TV, and social media platforms.

These are just a sampling of how God revolutionized my life.

Now I will speak about the results of my obedience to the man and the endless benefits of knowing this man, Christ Jesus.

He teaches me about His great love and how to love others (John 3:16).

He teaches me wisdom, knowledge, and understanding (Proverbs 9:10).

He gives me true joy, peace, and comfort (Galatians 5:29).

He caused me to experience His miraculous deliverance and healing touch (I Peter 2:24).

Delivered me from blindness for three days (Mark 10:50-52).

I've experienced His resurrection power. He brought me back from death and gave me a new lease on life (John 11:38-44).

This would be one of the most powerful experiences I could ever imagine. Throughout this ordeal, I am not even conscious of the magnitude of what I'm caught up in. From just a puny and fearful person to a brave and strong one, I know now of all these things that He used me to do. It was not in my power, but it was the power and working of the Holy Spirit through me. All this time, I thought I had outgrown the man, but I learned He had no intention of letting me go. The special man took over my life. I have no regrets in obedience to this call for so many lives have been changed and are still being changed.

Rev. Dr. Inez R. Brown is a licensed ordained minister and a world traveler, preaching and promoting the Gospel for more than fifty years. She is a mother, grandmother, great-grandmother, a pastor to pastors, and miraculously restored from death to life. Dr. Brown has earned many recognitions in biblical leadership studies and an honorary Decorate Degree for her humanitarian services. She speaks at conferences, crusades, and revivals.

- DrInezBrown?mibextid=ZbWKwL
- inez.brown.5011?mibextid=ZbWKwL
- inez.brown.5011?igshid=MzRIODBiNWFIZA==
- revirbrown@gmail.com

CHAPTER THIRTY-THREE - Lisa Harewood

Expressions of God's Love and Faith

In 1998, I got married. Like every bride, I thought this would be the happiest time of my life. I had many dreams and goals and thought it would all work out. It wasn't a good marriage, after all. I experienced verbal, emotional, mental, physical, and financial abuse in my marriage. I went through a few miscarriages, including an ectopic pregnancy that cost me a fallopian tube. But in my pain and loneliness being in a marriage and not loved by my husband, God still extended His love to me. He kept me from losing my mind and still provided for my needs. The hurt and the inner pain were too much to bear, and God knew it had to end before it got worse. I prayed that God would help me as I suffered silently, pretending everything was good.

Because my husband held essential roles in the church and community, we displayed a marriage of love and happiness when that was furthest from the truth. After seven years of marriage and after an ectopic pregnancy, the babies started popping out. After each child, my thoughts were like Leah in the bible, thinking my husband would finally love me. Each time I conceived, I thought he would love me the way a husband should love a wife, but the contrary would be exhibited. This was devastating for me because I felt bound in a prison. My house was not a home of love but a home of confusion, pain, loneliness, control, and manipulation. The counseling topic came up many times, but he would shut it down, saying he didn't need it – but I did.

In 2010 after four babies, my husband of twelve years at the time chose to walk out on me and our children. My daughter was eighteen months old, and my oldest son was 4 ½. I remember when he took his last belongings and went out the door. My babies were sleeping upstairs, and I recall having a glass of wine and listening to a song entitled "Who's Lovin' You." The lease was up that month, and I had to move anyway.

My faith grew as I took steps into the unknown and watched God open doors for me. With each step I took, He parted the Red Sea and guided and protected me. I was afraid because I was now a single mom raising four babies alone. I was unemployed then, but God started opening doors for me. When my husband left, I had to move, so I went to stay with my parents for two months while I looked for a place for me and my children. As I was searching, I was led to a women's shelter (being on OW, I was provided with services that helped me) to look at some market-rent homes and subsidized homes. The subsidy was a ten-year waiting list, but as I talked to the shelter supervisor, the topic of abuse came up, and I told her I was in an abusive relationship. This information allowed me to be put at the top of the list, so instead of waiting for ten years, I was now waiting for two years. God truly made a way; He used my horrible experiences and made them a blessing.

During my waiting period for a subsidy, God opened up an opportunity to move into a semi-detached home (the owner was a Christian). It was a four-bedroom end-unit house with a living room and family room. The backyard was huge, and I had access to the garage inside the house, making it easy with the kids in the winter. The rent was reasonable, and I had money to live; it was not a strain. I lived comfortably in peace. However, the utilities and food became too much for me as the two years came up. It started to become overwhelming for me. Although I took my husband to court for child support, the payments were sporadic, which made it even more challenging to provide. I prayed and asked the Lord for another place to live.

I remember driving one day looking for co-op homes and was told about a place. As I drove along the area, I remember telling myself that this was where I wanted to live. It was kept clean, the homes didn't look run down, and they maintained the property carefully. *"I can see my kids growing up here,"* I told myself. I saw the school in front of the co-op, which would make going to school much easier for them. I drove around the area and started to pray and declare that I would live there. This is where I want to be. I asked God to open up the opportunity. I also had to move because the landlord needed to sell the house, so time was against me.

Not long after seeing the co-op (maybe a month or two), my OW case worker called me and told me that my name was next on the list and that a vacancy came up at the co-op and asked me if I was interested in looking at it. I was elated; that was God. He answered my prayer. I gladly accepted the offer and said I would look at the unit. Of course, it wasn't as big as I was accustomed to, but it had everything I needed for me and the kids. I had three bedrooms, two washrooms, a garage, a walk-out backyard, a basement where the kids could play, and a school within walking distance. I couldn't ask for more. I said yes, I would take it, and because I was subsidized, I only paid $150.00 for the whole house. I was also blessed to have subsidized daycare, which I was approved for years before. This was God, for sure. My faith catapulted to another level. Trusting God became easier, and my relationship with Christ became more intimate.

Fast forward two years and my youngest daughter was finally four years of age. I dropped her off at JK as it was her first day of school. When I came home from doing that, I sat down at the top of my stairs and asked the Lord, *"What now? I don't want to live under the system and be comfortable living off the government. I needed to do something with my life."* God said, *"Go now and apply for massage school."* I didn't hesitate and immediately went to college to apply. There were some hiccups along the way, but how many of you know that when you are on the right pathway, there may be stumbling blocks that the enemy will put in your way to slow you down or stop you from achieving your goals?

My hurdles came from having to clean up my bankruptcy issues. I was discharged, but the banks needed proof. I had student loan debt because I didn't complete my nursing program in 1998. There were some things I needed to clear up with the banks. Once those were cleared up, it was smooth sailing from then on. I was approved for OSAP again which covered all my expenses and gave me grants (which I didn't have to pay back) that allowed me to come off OW indefinitely. God also helped me get out of my debt and help me rebuild my credit. I started to spend wisely and pay off bills. I was no longer under the system.

Doors of opportunity flew open. School schedules worked out for me and around daycare schedules. Going to school full-time, raising four small children, and maintaining a home was challenging, but God gave me grace. He gave me strength. I didn't think I had the mental capacity to go to school because I doubted my ability to process the info. But as I studied, I realized I was retaining and understanding the info, and it was exciting to learn. I had to go to school all year round and make sacrifices. Having childcare and help from family and friends were blessings. When it came to OSCE and MCQ prep, I started to get nervous about testing. I graduated with an 87%. The OSCE and MCQ exams were challenging; I needed to pass them all to be licensed. When I did my OSCE, I came out of there not convinced I did it. But a few days later, I got an email stating I passed. I was ecstatic and relieved.

I think the MCQ was the worst. I know God was with me from the beginning and was showing me in small ways. The night I went to do my test, I got to the parking meter and found a ticket sitting in the meter, all paid for. I knew God was with me and loved me so much. When I began doing the exam, I asked the Lord to help me with the answers. Although I studied a lot, I felt I didn't know anything, but it was all in my memory. There were 150 questions, and I had 90 minutes to complete them. I felt like leaving in the middle of my exam. As I was about to give up, pack my bags, and walk out, the Holy Spirit stopped me and said to sit down and finish it. I heard the urgency in His voice. I listened to Him and finished it.

I was overcome with emotion and cried and called my friend, telling her I thought I had failed it. My parents and others were praying for me. I was not looking forward to the email. Several days went by, and I finally got a message from CMTO. I saw the notification on my phone and my heart was pounding because this would determine whether I was licensed. I opened my email and the first thing I saw was "Congratulations." I didn't even read the rest of the email. I fell to my knees, was overcome with joy, wept, and thanked the Lord for helping me. I could not put a price tag on that moment. His love overwhelmed me, and I was so delighted I listened to him and finished the exam. I was finally a Registered Massage Therapist. Wow!

The studies and raising the children were heavy, but God saw me through. I celebrated and had a party with my close friends and family. I landed a position at Massage Addict immediately to earn income and grow my experience. Seeing that I was subcontracted, I could finally make some good money and be flexible with my hours; it worked for me. This experience grew my faith. A few years passed, and I opened my Practice in my home. In 2020, I owned my own home with the help of my mom. I thank God for her because I wasn't always an easy daughter, but I appreciate all she has done for me. I couldn't ask for a better mom. She is a blessing to me, and I love her dearly. My dad, at the time, was suffering from Alzheimer's disease and was slowly slipping away from us, which was heartbreaking. So, my mother and I bought a house together, and my dad was able to get the care he needed. Looking back, I see the hand of God steering my wheel. This is His movie, and I am the cast member. He produced my story, and it is still being written. There are a lot of ups and downs, failures and successes that I need to write about, and I will do so in my own book. God has shown me that my purpose is to help people through my Practice and life experiences. I've had the opportunity to speak and empower women who have been through abuse and divorce with children. I give God the glory. My kids are growing up all in their teens, and God is still providing and extending His unconditional love. My eldest son ended up with a full soccer scholarship. My dad, unfortunately, passed away in October 2022, and a part of me died with him as well. But I know I will see him again. SIP, my Daddy.

God is still preparing me for my suitable partner and he will come in God's time. When I let go and let God have His way, so much beauty unfolds, which can be breathtaking. His splendor and beauty that he wishes to flow through us are captivating. I couldn't be here without God knowing I did all this as a single mom. He connected me with a great ministry called Open Arms for several years, which helped me grow. I thank the Lord for my close friends; you know who you are, and my family, who support and believe in me. Thank you, Mom, for your prayers. This is the beginning of God's love and provision for me and the children. My story is still being written, so stay tuned.

Lisa Harewood is a Registered Massage Therapist who owns her practice and is working on finishing her Bachelors in Christian Counseling. She is a single mom of four beautiful children. Lisa plays the piano, sings, and also performs with her sisters and brother-in-law in Heart Of Worship. She has been called to empower others to develop and reach their destinies. Lisa's mandate in life is to affect and change lives.

- ljlorray@gmail.com
- ljharewood@gmail.com
- www.rmtinmotion.com

CHAPTER THIRTY-FOUR - Janice Prescott

Never Alone

"Wherefore comfort yourselves together, and edify one another, even as also ye do." 1 Thessalonians 5:11 (KJV)

As single individuals who still hope, no matter how many times our relationships fail, it seems that we just won't give up on trying to find what we're looking for. Love is sometimes a painful situation, yet we still hold fast and believe in the happily-ever-after and long for true intimacy with someone. It doesn't matter how many frogs we have to kiss or rocks we attempt to turn into diamonds, we continue to look for that person who meets at least some of the criteria on our list.

We all have beliefs about the way we think our lives should be, particularly when it comes to becoming a couple, falling in love, and living happily ever after. Society, the media, and even the church help to frame these beliefs, and sometimes, hold us captive under the stigma of being single. Those of us who are still looking have unwillingly tempered our list of must-haves to a list of nice-to-haves when faced with the reality of a long waiting game. Sometimes as we wait, we hold our potential mates up to the high standards that we ourselves cannot meet, paving the way for relationships in trouble. Have we done the work that being single gives us the time to do?

God created a recipe for a successful relationship in the garden with two individuals who were complete on their own. However, because of sin, we've stepped far away from the model. As singles, are we whole, fulfilled, and content? Only when we allow God to lead us will we truly be fulfilled. Only by the grace of God can we really set the standards that He would want us to live by, whether individually or as a couple.

I have always enjoyed my own company. To me, there is no better time spent than with myself. I actually use my alone time to rejuvenate my spirit. I remember the day when I discovered that I was an introvert after completing a personality-type exercise in school. It was quite liberating because I had always wondered why I was just fine all by myself. I have always had great friends and family, but more often than not when I was growing up, I enjoyed the solace of my bedroom rather than the activity of the family room. Because of this, I sometimes wonder if I translated my penchant for my own company into a lifestyle choice. I still hoped and yearned and felt the pressure to fulfill the societal norm that others have achieved. Yet, ultimately, I also wanted to live the life God gave me to live and refused to let my status define me or frustrate my dreams.

Consequently, I refuse to wear my singleness as a badge or an identifying factor. Despite the high divorce rate or that millennials are choosing to remain single longer, the world is focused on families and couples. In some situations, we are made to feel that we are nothing without a spouse. Have you ever tried to take your car into the dealership as a single woman? I truly believe that only women and men who are connected to God can properly navigate the landscape of life's uncertainties as a single individual.

I would admit that I struggle with the frustration of the whole thing at times. I really don't believe I chose this life. It just found me…and time slipped away. The die-hard single people in my circle believe I, like them, am fine with my status. More power to us. I remember my single aunt saying to me at a family function, *"Look at us, single and living successfully. See, it can be done."* I have thought of that moment several times over the years. Was I really on the bandwagon? Do I really believe it's true? Some of my married friends believe I am single by choice or because my independent attitude does not lean toward "submission" or being coupled up. That's not the truth either. There are times I wonder if I uttered some self-fulfilling prophecy somewhere in the past. In fact, when I was younger, I did not want to get married or experience the kinds of marriages I witnessed. Now as I look back, I realize I was trying to protect myself. Because of the trauma of my past, I didn't think I would find a place to belong or that someone I wanted would choose me.

It is both very difficult and very easy to be single at the same time. That is the dichotomy of the life of a single person who actually has a life – blessed and led by God. We want and yearn, but, by the grace of God, we are not suffocated by it. It would be nice to not have to search for a plus 1 for events. Yet, there is so much richness to experience and so much life to live. Why get lost in the deficits? As a single woman, I have found that there are some who behave as if I am not enough or not a whole person because l am unmarried and have no children. And the pity. I don't pity myself so please do not pity me. The Lord has shown us how to go through life rejoicing despite grief, reproach, and even shame.

There are so many factors that contribute to being successfully single. Yet instead of striving for completeness and a full life as a single person, many of us give up on our dreams and settle into a mediocre existence tinged with fear and desperation – fear that it will always be like this and desperation because we don't see how it can change in our present reality. Granted, we're continually bombarded with images of romance and intimacy in media and music. That does not help our peace of mind. Judging from the number of second marriages, no one wants to be alone for long. However, we can have a great life whether we're married or not. The secret to being successfully anything is to live a life that is connected to Christ.

Yes, we have prayed, fasted, and made lists. Yes, we have listened to wise spiritual council, joined singles groups, or even led Singles Ministry as in my case. Yet, for some, the situation does not change, and the frustrating stigma remains. We've asked married friends, aunties, uncles, and colleagues for referrals. We have gone on the App, went to the lounge, or smiled at the good-looking stranger. There is no guarantee that any of that will have lasting effects. However, there is no greater attraction than someone who appears happy with their life. Because we know we are never really alone, those of us who have decided to forge on have learned to be content with the status quo while keeping our hearts open to the possibilities. We are active participants in our own lives. We are transformed and remain content despite the constant questions and innuendos that stir up yearnings. God has established a life for us that we can simply rest and rejoice in.

Some old married folks may be uncomfortable with our brand of happy. If we do not appear to be actively looking, they assume that our patience is akin to laziness or the fear of getting out there. Faith and works go together, after all. In some cases, they may have a point. Cordoning yourself off or hiding in your own home is not the way for anyone to live, especially someone who is so blessed. It may be hard to find social outlets and places of interest that you can attend without feeling that everyone can tell you are alone. However, if we let it, life will pass us by. We must connect ourselves to fun and fruitful pursuits, and to those individuals who will be our rocks of strength and encouragement when it feels like nothing is happening.

At times, I still wonder if I am doing enough to change my situation. There seems to always be somebody who will remind me that I am not. On the other hand, some assume I am content with the status quo. However, who is ever really fully content in this fallen world? We all want better. There is always a striving, a yearning to increase, improve, and maintain hope. That is human. If God is sovereign, then He must know how annoying this situation and the burden of appearing unaffected by it all can be. Thankfully, when I call on Him in frustration or despair, God shows up, reminds me of His goodness, and lightens the darkness. He sends the spirit to soothe my soul and help me focus on the blessings in front of me. Eventually, I come full circle and realize that whatever the circumstances, I am never alone.

As the sum total of my experiences, I am not who other people say l am. Having the faith to believe that l am enough is not easy, but it is possible. Yes, people may behave as if l am not relevant because I do not have a family of my own. However, because I am part of God's family, I do not see myself as incomplete.

I am glad that God has given me the time and opportunity to develop my self-awareness and work on myself without becoming self-absorbed. He has also given me the freedom to pursue my dreams and encourage others. He created me and helped me to accept myself, even though His timelines may be frustrating. I strive daily to live a great and full life. There is no lack here. God is good, no matter the circumstances or my marital status. His favor is constant. I am never alone, even on the days I have to take out my own garbage or mow the lawn.

When I was younger, I struggled to find that place for me, but the Lord showed me that I wasn't broken or unwanted. Apart from Him, everyone is living far from their full potential. He brought great people into my life and showed me that I could sustain loving relationships. I did not have to be angry or upset all the time. He helped to bring out parts of me that were long hidden. As I surrendered more and more to Him, He increased my confidence and told me I was enough. It has been a lifelong journey to self-awareness, self-love, and appreciation.

There are gifts and benefits in each of us that we should not ever diminish or take for granted. God is our refuge, our hiding place, and where we can rest from societal expectations and feeling like our dreams will never come true. Loneliness is an unfortunate reality. Yet, there is a richness and joy in the community that we introverts must never avoid. The evil one wants us to feel like we are alone, as if no one understands or cares. We are not alone. We must ask God to fill our empty spaces so that we don't go looking for fulfillment in the wrong places.

Our past hurts don't have to shape who we become. We do not have to hide from the person in the mirror when the yearning gets the better of us and we make an unwise choice for companionship. The Lord meets our needs, and He answers our prayers. He is an awesome God, even when we are confronted by the frustration of His silence. God will restore all that the enemy has taken away from us. Stand your ground, believe, and strive for peace and confidence. Single men and women alike are daily robbed of their joy because they feel they do not fit into what society and the media say they should be.

Remember that surrendering your life to God does not mean that you must give up your dreams. He will make your paths straight. Whether

He finds you the person of your dreams or not, commit your way unto Him and trust in Him, for He will bring it to pass. Let His Spirit fill your empty places and take away any loneliness. It will be hard at times, but there's sunshine over the horizon. We don't have to go it alone. The Lord knows and He cares. Brighten your corner, whether you are single or married. There is work for us all to do. You have Jesus, your Savior, and you are never alone.

Janice Prescott has a career in the Information Technology Industry by day and is also an English tutor and the founder of Faith Factor Editing. She is the author of *Real Devotion: Live Life with Resonance* and a co-author in the *Confident is She* anthology. Janice discovered a love for writing in grade school and her hope is that you will read these stories, be encouraged, and draw nearer to God while positively affecting those around you.

- Presco_jl
- Janice L. Prescott
- realdevotional.com
- http://faithfactorediting.com

CHAPTER THIRTY-FIVE - Sharon Riley

A Second Chance

I am a living, walking, talking testimony! I can truly say that God is real! There is no God like our great Jehovah! Throughout my childhood, I often heard *"Taste and See that the Lord is good!"* Surely, I had encountered a crucible that I thought I would never get through, and the Lord responded in His Word by saying, *"Fear not, for I am with you; Be not dismayed, for I am your God. Yes, I will help you, I will uphold you with my righteous hand."*

How could I have been ejected from the back of a car while it was tumbling over and still be alive to tell the story? It could only be through those miraculous twins, "Grace and Mercy."

It was October 13, 1990. One late Friday night, I remember driving in a car with my friend. I recall us singing, laughing, and talking. Then the next thing I remember hearing was a loud noise and seeing a flash of light. I remember being on the side of the road in the grass. I was in and out of consciousness. A man would come running to ask if I was ok. I would later learn that it was a paramedic who was off that day and just happened to witness the accident. They were never able to find the man who called the ambulance. My mom says that it very well could have been an angel.

I would be flown from Ingersol, Ontario to Sunnybrook Hospital in downtown Toronto. All that surrounded me now was the sounds of the machines hooked up to my body and the constant movements of doctors and nurses coming in and out of my room. I was in the ICU, and I knew somehow that my life was never going to be the same again.

I was now coherent enough to understand the extent of my injuries. Both legs were badly damaged. My left hip was crushed in pieces and my lower right leg was broken. There were now conversations about extensive surgeries and the idea that they possibly may have to amputate my right leg.

While all of this was taking place, the University I was attending, my church family, and my family and friends were bombarding Heaven on my behalf.

They began to pray for healing and restorative power in the name of JESUS! We all knew that this was serious! Each day, a team of doctors would come in to discuss the order in which surgeries would occur. The first surgery/procedure they did was to put hardware in my lower right leg and a skin graph to cover the hardware placed in my lower right leg (the Tibia and Fibula bones). They also put in place an external fixator. The first time they did the skin graph, it failed.

My family and I were disheartened by the news! I was in such excruciating pain! Even taking simple breaths in and out caused so much pain. Again, my village continued to pray for me. The doctors would try again to place a skin graph on my lower right leg and this time it worked! Hallelujah! God was moving! This meant that they were able to save my right leg. Despite how horrific the situation was at the time; the Holy Spirit was moving throughout my hospital room.

The next surgery was to stabilize my hip joint. Both my Acetabulum and Femur were crushed. The doctors had to put in more hardware to mimic a hip joint. The pain in my body increasingly worsened by the minute. All the morphine in the world could not suppress the pain that I was feeling. I had to solely depend on the God my parents had told me about since I was a child. I would ask the nurse to place my bible on my chest. I was never strong enough to even read. However, I knew by having God's holy Word on my chest and desperately believing in God's healing power, He would reduce my pain. I knew that He was still on the throne protecting me and covering me and would in time heal me.

They would go on to do roughly about seven surgeries. When would this end? After staying at the hospital four months, I was transferred to a rehabilitation facility. I still had the external fixator on my leg. I was curious and nervous not knowing what the next couple of months were going to be like while staying at this new facility. Even though my faith was wavering at times, I continued to put all my faith and trust in God. Within the next few days of arriving at the new facility, I got the chance to meet my physiotherapist. She walked in with a cute dress and a smile. I couldn't help but notice that her right leg looked like mine. How could that be? Her right leg was disfigured just like mine. I felt bad looking at her leg, but she chuckled, noticed that I was staring, and said, *"I'll tell you what happened to me if you'd like. I don't mind sharing."* She began telling me that when she was a child, she had leukemia and unfortunately, she had an accident in her hospital room which caused her right leg to be deformed. Only God would have connected me with someone whose leg looked just like mine. What were the odds? When I saw her walk into the room, I knew that if she could make it, so would I.

It would be a while before I could start my rehabilitation. The fixator was still in my right leg and would not be removed until the skin on my lower right leg was completely healed. Several weeks went by and finally, the fixator was removed. To say I was excited was an understatement! For the first time, they would transfer me from my bed to a wheelchair. I was elated to finally get the chance to be somewhat independent. Even though it hurt to be transferred from wheelchair to bed and bed to wheelchair, I knew that it was the first step to rehabilitation. The day finally came when I would start my rehab. The first thing that I ever did was to learn how to stand. I would stand on and off for ten minutes, hold on to the bars, and then sit down in the wheelchair. I would do this for one or two weeks and then eventually progress to learning how to take baby steps. It was not at all easy as the pain was excruciating!

Each time I was brought down to the gym, I had a glimpse of hope! You see, every time I saw my physiotherapist, it reminded me that I could do this! Each step and pain that I would endure reminded me that it was necessary to suffer or work hard in order to succeed or make progress. I don't even have to mention all the prayers that were going up for me. I wouldn't give up, not now at least.

Each day, it got harder because I was challenged to slowly start weight-bearing. The pain was so atrocious that I would begin to sweat. I would beg my physiotherapist for us to stop. I would begin to cry because I would lose faith. I was blessed to have the therapist that I had. She would encourage me and say, *"Sharon, you've got to keep going! Don't give up!"* I was reminded of the scripture that simply said, *"Be strong and courageous do not be frightened and do not be dismayed for the Lord your God is with you wherever you go."* After each breakdown, I would get back up and keep going. She was right, I couldn't give up!

Now a few months had gone by, and I was slowly learning and comprehending how to walk a little. I even had an opportunity to go home for the first time in five months for a couple of hours. These were signs that very soon I would eventually be discharged from the Rehabilitation facility. Many people take it for granted, but you literally must conceptualize how to stand and conceptualize how to walk. It had been so long since I had done either and now my brain was finally learning how to do all of that again. The sun was starting to shine both outside of my room and inside my heart, and the weather was slowly warming up. I knew if I wanted to go home, I had to work harder. I was improving and was now graduating from a wheelchair to crutches.

Once I had mastered using the crutches, I would have more frequent home visits. God was truly moving! The prayers that were lifted on my behalf were working! So many people that came to visit me were a source of encouragement and strength. I do not know what I would do without the prayers and the love of my parents and my sister. Their love and sacrifices meant everything to me!

During the painful days and nights at the facility, I was one day presented with an unconventional proposal. I was asked to be the choir director for a new choir. I thought the idea was crazy.

But somehow, I was crazy enough to accept. My dad would pick me up from the facility and take me to church, where I would teach music and conduct the choir from my wheelchair. This would go on for a while.

God works in mysterious ways! Without really paying attention to what was happening, I was somehow being healed by not only being at the facility but also being healed by the feeling of a sense of belonging and accomplishment being the director of this new choir family. I was also humbled by the fact that this choir respected and loved me enough even with my disability. I was elated because I was now becoming stronger and stronger! I would eventually be discharged from the rehabilitation facility seven months after the accident. I was now an outpatient!

Oh, how awesome God truly is! I was finally home! I would go on to use crutches for three more years and then would graduate to using two canes to one cane. While all of this was taking place, my choir was growing and blessing people across the country. And now I had a testimony of how extraordinary this God I served was. I could sing and shout from the mountaintop as to how God healed me! Through my fears, I believe that God truly heard my cries!

> *"Confess your trespasses to one another, and pray for one another, that you may be healed. The effective, fervent prayer of a righteous man avails much."* James 5:16 (NKJV)

My choir and I would go on to minister to many and be blessed with numerous awards. God knew what my future would be that day when that off-duty paramedic came and found me on the side of the road on October 13, 1990. Many times, we question God when we are experiencing a crucible. However, He is always there even when we cannot trace Him. Thirty-two years have gone by, and I am still giving God praise. Even though my body will never be the same, I'm still giving God praise! Even though as I grow older and my body aches and pains have increased, I'm still giving God praise! We should learn to praise God in the good and bad times. I believe that God allows our battle scars to be a reminder of where He has brought us from.

Dear Heavenly Father, I thank you for the trials because they come to make us stronger. Help us to remember to pray when we face the struggles of life. And that we should always continue to put you first. Lord, I thank you for my second chance.

Sharon Riley has established herself as a premier vocalist in the genre of Canadian Gospel Music. After a life-changing incident in 1990, she continues to stay strong. Sharon's religious faith and her determination to not be limited by her physical disability have aided in her achieving legendary status. Sharon is best known for being the choir director for the Juno Award-winning Toronto-based Gospel Ensemble known as "Sharon Riley and Faith Chorale" established in 1992.

- Sharon Riley
- Sharon Riley & Faith Chorale
- RileyJuno

CHAPTER THIRTY-SIX - Jean Lawrence-Scotland

Restoration

It was a beautiful summer day in 2006, and I was socializing with some of my sister/friends when I experienced the worst abdominal pain I ever felt in my life. My friends immediately rushed me to the hospital. I found myself in the emergency room going through hours of tests and assessments to get to the root cause of my health crisis which resulted in me having life-saving surgery, two weeks later. After five hours of risky surgery and major blood loss, the result was still deemed unsuccessful.

The following couple of months required total rest and recovery, to strengthen my body for a second surgery which eventually resulted in a total hysterectomy and changed the trajectory of my life.

Learning that I had a large cyst that was causing me excruciating pain and required life-saving surgery was alarming and scary. I went into preparation mode. I was praying, asking God for healing, and seeking support from my family and friends. I believed that despite what was going on with my health, I was going to have the surgery, get through it, and get back to my family, friends, job, and life.

Little did I know it would not play out the way I envisioned! In my career as a Social Worker, I encourage clients to identify the issue and determine ways to problem-solve the situation, to move forward in their life. I couldn't apply the same process to myself. It was all occurring so quickly, and I had no control over the process or the outcome.

After the first unsuccessful surgery, hearing the doctor explain what happened was an out-of-body experience. His words hung in the air, *"I am sorry. The Cyst was attached to all your organs. You almost bled to death. We had to stop the surgery to save your life. Another team of doctors at another hospital will need to perform the second surgery."* It was surreal! What did all that mean for my job and my life? I prayed, I cried, and I prayed!

When you have a traumatic experience that you can't explain or you don't expect, you experience a myriad of emotions! That was no different for me. I live my life seeing the glass half full and I am a woman of faith, a strong believer who *"…can do all things through Christ that strengthens me"* (Philippians 4:13). This time, I had to have a conversation with God. I didn't ask, *"Why me?"* because why not me? But I cried to God to help me understand what was going on. I just didn't get what was occurring in my body and why the doctors failed to fix my body on the first attempt. I asked God to give me strength, mentally and psychologically, because the time between surgeries with no real answers was anxiety-provoking. I have always seen myself as a strong person able to deal with whatever life brought my way, but this was a bit different because I did not have answers, and nothing was in my control. I needed to leave it in God's hands. To be honest, even though I was thinking and praying that I was leaving the situation in God's hands, I was not fully feeling and believing that way.

Laying in the hospital bed, my parents, brother, family, best friends, and friends all were visiting me during the week I remained in that hospital. Having to tell the tale repeatedly was draining and a constant reminder of what was to come.

My parents are people of extraordinary faith. My mother said after she and my dad came to visit me after the first surgery, she was shocked at how terrible I looked. She knew without knowing, that the operation did not go well. She did not want me to know her true reaction, so she kept it inside. My mother was scared but encouraging, and positive. She prayed for me; both my parents prayed with me. My dad is an inspiration to me. I am the only girl between two brothers, and I am my daddy's girl! My dad's unwavering faith was always an example to me in his daily life. My dad prays and leaves it to God because he believes and trusts that God is listening. I leaned on my earthy father's faith during that time because he was uplifting to me as I was questioning my own faith. I was still figuring it out and learning how to depend on God and to trust in His promise to keep me and never forsake me.

I recall one night, looking at the scar on my stomach, I cried and said, *"Why did he do this to me?"* I had an ugly crooked scar, a reminder that another surgery awaited. What would my body look like?

At that time in my life, I was a single professional woman. I had a very active social life with hopes of getting married and having children, one day. I was not in a committed relationship, but I remained hopeful. I still believed it would happen but with the scar and another surgery to come, was I being realistic to think I could find someone to love me unconditionally with all my flaws? Doubts started to seep in!

I was released from the hospital to recover and recuperate before the second surgery. I was not returning to work as I initially planned.

Another two months to ponder what was going to happen to me.

As I was healing and waiting for the second surgery, I was going on with life. I am a member and President of the Juno award-winning gospel music group, Sharon Riley & Faith Chorale. One Friday evening as I was driving to a rehearsal, the driver of another car pulled in front of me, and I hit his car. I hit my stomach, where I had surgery, on the steering wheel. My car was totaled, and I went back to the hospital. Not what I wanted. Again, I questioned God's plan for me.

I was a woman on the other side of forty, not married, no children, and all of this was happening to me. I had a health crisis, a failed surgery, and then an almost fatal car accident. I was asking God what was going on. Why was I going through all of this? Did I not have enough faith and belief in God?

The meeting with the second doctor at another hospital stood out in my mind. After seeing all the X-rays and other tests, the doctor said the surgery was going to be difficult. The first surgeon "messed up!" Not what I wanted to hear. What did that even mean? I kept praying for healing and restoration of my body.

On the day of the second surgery, my parents were with me! I wasn't sure how I was supposed to feel. I know I wanted the surgery to be over. I wanted to live and wanted a better outcome for this surgery than the first. I asked God to give the doctors the skills and tools to perform the surgery successfully this time around. This is where I felt I had no other option but to lean on God and leave everything in His hands. Finally, I believed in God's promise to never leave me nor forsake me! I prayed for peace of mind and for God to hear and answer my prayer.

Post-surgery, I opened my eyes in the recovery room! The sense of relief, peace, and pure joy I felt was unexplainable. I knew my body was healed before the doctor came to see me. I prayed and cried out to

God, *"Thank you, Jesus. Your promises are true. God, you heard my prayers. God, you fought for me and gave me another chance to worship you. Thank you, God!"*

The doctor explained the surgery took four hours, which was longer than expected. He stated he had to do major repair work inside of me but the news that hit the hardest was he was left with no choice but to do a full hysterectomy. The realization of not being able to biologically have children was painful. I don't think at that moment I realized the magnitude of what that meant. Maybe because I was single and on the other side of forty, I told myself it was God's will for me to not have children.

After two months of recovery, I saw the doctor for a post-surgery update. He informed me I was healing well and there were no signs of cancer. That comment took me off guard because I didn't know that was a possibility. I prayed and just felt very thankful to God for sparing my life, for repairing my body, and for building my faith in Him. I was thankful for the stronger faith and the empowerment that brought.

I know God performed a miracle in my life. I have a testimony. I had a real experience that demonstrated there is a God! He is real in my life, and He is real in yours.

You may be asking how my life has changed this then. In 2007, a year later, I met a wonderful, amazing Christian man. He is intelligent, compassionate, and a humble man with extraordinary faith. Born with Spina Bifida and Hydrocephalus, he has his own testimony of survival, perseverance, and how he trusts God. How we met could have only been orchestrated by God! We have been married for over 10 years and we have no children. We truly believe it is God's will for our lives. God demonstrates that he puts people together to fulfill our needs, not our wants. Maybe there will be a fur baby in our future!

How was I transformed by that experience? What I do know is that tough times will always come, and I trust God through the process. I know for myself that I am confident in sharing with the world that God is a miracle-working God. He performed a miracle in my life and in my younger brother's life. He collapsed while playing basketball over twelve years ago. His heart stopped beating. He had no pulse and did not breathe for over thirty minutes. God brought my brother back to life. How can I not be transformed by God's work in my life and my family's life? I know what God has done for me and what He can do for you. I know and accept that God is real. I know life is not filled with all good things and I expect to have ups and downs. It's important to create wonderful joy-filled moments. Enjoy, be engaged and be present when you are living your best life with loved ones.

In retrospect, what lessons did I learn from my life-altering experience? God's promises are true, I leaned on him, and he answered by prayer. He has a plan for my life that I do not see or understand. He picked the day and the hour I was born. He knows the journey of my entire life and as my life continues to play itself out, I fully leave it in His hands. I learned I don't have and truly don't need to have control over everything.

I was raised in church from the age of eight, and in my teens, I chose to follow Christ. As an adult, I am learning that the journey I am on is determined by God. He supplies all my needs. I trust that God has my life in His hands. He hears my prayers. I live in thankfulness and gratefulness to God!

I give God thanks every morning for waking me, my husband, family, and friends up. I say, Lord, lead me through this day. Only you see and know what lies ahead. Tomorrow is not promised, I am committed to living in the moment and enjoying all the positive and good times God grants us each day.

Jean Lawrence-Scotland earned a Bachelor of Social Worker degree and a Master of Arts degree from Andrews University. Currently employed in a management position at the Children's Aid Society of Toronto, she ensures that Black families' identities and cultures are honored. Since 1992, Jean has been the president and a singer in the Juno award-winning gospel music group Sharon Riley & Faith Chorale. She loves God, sports, cooking, and baking.

- Jean Lawrence-Scotland
- Jean Lawrence-Scotland
- jeanl_777@yahoo.ca
- Jean Lawrence-Scotland

CHAPTER THIRTY-SEVEN - Nasha Alexis

Troubles with Low Self-Esteem

In the dictionary, self-esteem is described as confidence in one's own worth or abilities and self-respect. On the other hand, when these qualities are not present, it's then referred to as having low self-esteem. As in the case of a person, he/she would lack confidence about what they can do but, more importantly, about who they are.

That was me, who came with more baggage than anyone should have. I felt incompetent, inadequate, and unloved. This led me to be fearful of being myself and of making mistakes, which sometimes led to more mistakes, some with dire consequences. I was also afraid of letting people down, so I settled and followed whoever and whatever others said. How does a person get to such a place where others are making decisions for you and having you believe that's what you want? Sometimes it's through major traumatic situations; while in other cases, it only takes the right or wrong person saying the right or wrong things based on your life's experiences. In other words, the right soil to plant the wrong seeds into.

There were many small, some may say insignificant situations that took place as I was growing up. Somewhere along the way, I stopped trying to convince people otherwise of who I was. I wasn't interested in trying to prove myself or convince anyone to see me or think of me differently. Whatever they thought of me, I let them. Nothing good was expected of me so I lived my life as such. Even as a young adult, I didn't question – I just followed along. During those years, I thought of myself as being stupid and did not know what was good for me, but there was always someone in my life who seemed to know me better than I knew myself. I don't remember when or at what age, but I finally gave up. During those years I got into relationships I knew I shouldn't have or didn't want, but I continued anyway. Not to give the enemy any credit here, but I can see now that my negative life experiences were used to take away the confidence I had in myself, become complacent, and doubt myself but, more importantly, doubt God.

After a couple of failed relationships and with a broken heart, I found myself in yet another one I shouldn't have been in. Looking back, I can see that I attracted the same type of men – those who picked up on my neediness to please, my vulnerability, and my low self-esteem. This time, it was a person who was stronger than me in so many ways. He made me feel like I was responsible for every bad thing that happened to him and was the worst person, while at the same time, he was the only one who ever loved me or will ever love me. By then, I had little to no confidence in myself and honestly speaking, I believed something was really wrong with me. From the start of our relationship, he was controlling and would often tell me what I liked or disliked, and what was good for me. I went along with it each time so as not to cause an argument. At first, it was subtle and what he said made sense, most of the time, with a mixture of truth and manipulation that left me questioning myself. There were times when he would say something and that little bell in my head would ring and the red flags would go up, but I ignored all the warning signs. I often made excuses that he didn't mean what he said or that I misunderstood what I heard.

Eventually, I became pregnant, and being my first time, I was scared. I was also about to go into my final year of college and that didn't help. Added to that, I was facing homelessness with a young child. So, imagine being twenty-three, not working, the home situation on thin ice, and being pregnant. With a heavy heart, I broke the news to my then-partner. I was hoping for excitement but instead, I was met with, *"How can you be so stupid to let that happen? What were you thinking?"* And worse yet, *"You must get rid of it."* I was so devastated that I went numb. I couldn't believe what I was hearing. So, without much consideration, I spoke to my family doctor, who then made the appointment for me to get it done. I didn't know how to get there but the date was set. I had asked two people to go with me, but they refused because they didn't want me to go through with the procedure.

Then came the morning of my appointment, I woke up and proceeded to get ready but as I went to the washroom, I passed by a mirror on the small wall unit. I only glanced at myself, but I found that I couldn't move or look away from my image. Right there as I stared in the mirror, I heard, *"You are not alone."* Then I realized that my hands were on my small round tummy and with tears running down my face, I didn't know what was happening, I apologized to my baby for considering aborting her. I also told her that I loved her and couldn't wait to hold her. It was a brief, strange, and peaceful moment. After washing my face, I went back to bed and had the best sleep ever. That was the first time I can remember hearing from the Holy Spirit, but I didn't realize it then.

That was a major decision I had to make for me and my daughter. I also realized that it wasn't going to be easy raising a child on my own, but I had no regrets then about my choice and still have no regrets, twenty-four years later. I believe that because of my low self-esteem, I attracted the wrong people in my life, which led me to compromising situations and to doubt myself. I thank God for His grace and mercy for being with me in all that I have been through. At the time I may not have recognized His hands of protection or faithfulness, but now I know He was with me – His Spirit was and is still with me today.

When a person has low self-esteem and no confidence in themself, it's much easier for that person to make decisions that they would not have otherwise or get into compromising situations. I now know that this can lead you away from your God-given destiny permanently or take you off track for some time. In the sight of God, there are no accidents. Each person to be born was already spoken of by Him. Each of us is here for a purpose – to do the will of the Father. Overcoming struggles or battles of any kind is nothing to scoff at or to think that it's easy to do on your own. I am still a work in progress, but with each passing day, I am getting louder and louder as I find my voice. In all of this, what I have come to know full well is that I am not on my own. In the past, I was made to feel and believe that my voice meant nothing, but God is changing that. I have the Holy Spirit to guide, teach, and counsel me.

"Do you not know that your bodies are the temples of the Holy Spirit, who is in you, whom you have received from God? You are not your own." 1 Corinthians 6:19 (NIV)

When we are filled with the Holy Spirit, there's no room for anything else to come in and take up space. We are to only listen to one voice – the One who already knows to whom we belong and who will lead us to life everlasting. Remember, the meaning of low self-esteem is the lack of confidence in your abilities or in who you are. The only person who has the authority to define our identity is the One who made us in the first place and that is God, Himself. We can't allow others to tell us who we are, what's best for us, or to dictate what we want especially when we know they are wrong, and they don't have our best interests at heart. We must come to the realization that our identity is found in Christ Jesus, which means we don't have to live our lives according to what others may say or think about us.

With that in mind, I have come to look at my past without anger or contempt but as the building blocks to who I am now and will eventually become. As mentioned before, I am still a work in progress. There are more areas of work to be done but I am not doing them on my own anymore. I have the Holy Spirit to lead and guide me. The time I spent in what I used to call the "shadows" will be what is used to help me move forward and break free. Think of Psalm 23 and verse 4:

"Even though I walk through the darkest valley, I will fear no evil, for You are with me; your rod and your staff, they comfort me."

The rod of correction to protect me and the staff will be used to guide me along the right paths for my good and His glory.

The Holy Spirit is called the Counselor for a good reason. God already knows all the trouble and trials we will go through, so

He gave us His Holy Spirit to guide us. Jesus has already made the way for us. John 16:33 NIV, tells us plainly:

"I have told you these things, so that in me you may have peace. In this world, you will have troubles. But take heart I have overcome the world."

The provision for us to have peace was there before the beginning of time. One thing I had to do to move forward was surrender it all to Jesus, to lay everything at the foot of the cross. Trust me when I say it wasn't easy because I had the tendency to pick things up again to fix them myself but would fail. There will come a point when you realize that you can't do this thing called life on your own. You must surrender and ask Jesus to take over.

Sometimes, the pain and disappointment we go through are the same things that God will use to propel us forward. It's those things that will help to transform your life for the better. It may be your shyness, doubts in your abilities, disappointments in life or people, illness/sickness, or just everyday struggles that you face. Remember, He's God and He can turn your messes into messages and your tests into testimonies. All that's required of you and me is to give Him what we have.

"Just like clay in the hands of a potter, so God can transform us." Jeremiah 18:6 (NIV)

He created us in His image. "Let us make mankind in our image" Genesis 1:26 (NIV), so He knows us. When we take what we have and are willing to give it to Him, He now has something to work with. So just stand still then and allow Him to work. It may be painful at times, but it's part of the process that we must go through if we want to see changes in our lives.

Trials and troubles **will** come, but we can go through them with strength and confidence, knowing that Jesus has already **overcome** the world. We're overcomers through Him.

Nasha Alexis was born in Grenada, aka, Spice Island. She immigrated to Canada when she was sixteen years old and has made Brampton, Ontario her new home. Nasha is the proud parent of two wonderful and beautiful daughters and is a Registered Early childhood educator with a special interest and focus on children with special abilities. Nasha loves music and is privileged to use the gift of dance and flagging to minister and lead others in worship before the King of Kings. She believes that each person must honor God with the gift he/she is blessed with.

nasha.alexis@gmail.com

Empress4love

Nasha Alexis

CHAPTER THIRTY-EIGHT - Ruth Odia

Equipped to Serve

One of the earliest memories of my childhood years was waking up when it was still dark to the sound of the hushed voices of my parents praying. Both were solid and committed believers in God. They made sure we, as their children, stayed connected to God and fellowship. Sunday School was a priority. I remember how my mother would press an offering into each of our little palms before we set off. We had an energetic Sunday school teacher who loved the Lord Jesus with a passion. I remember him teaching us about Jesus, and telling of His great love for us. He would demonstrate the Bible stories with illustrations of the way of life that Jesus taught that left us wide-eyed with amazement.

My parents had a very respectful and dignified marriage and they still do. My three brothers turned out to be perfect gentlemen in their own married lives as adults as they followed the example set by my father. My parents did have their share of disagreements, but my mother always told me that it was between them to settle privately, so for a long time I did not know that my parents sometimes disagreed!

So that is the naivety with which I looked at the marriage institution as I grew into adulthood. It was also against the picture of a Christian marriage as depicted in the Word of God and that was preached from the pulpits that I developed my own views and expectations of what it should entail.

I had been working for some time after graduating, and all through my young adult years, I was serving in the church, singing in the choir, and was a part of the peer group fellowships. But somehow, I felt there was a great disconnect between the church and the picture of the early church. Where was the fire, the passion in the Book of Acts? I would say at that time it seemed to me that the church was in a happy lukewarm state, and I was naturally a part of it, but deep inside, I knew I had to find a way out of it. One day, an elderly prophetess from Canada visited our church and painted that exact picture of the state of the church. She prophesied concerning things the Lord was not pleased with, and mainly spoke from 2 Timothy 3:5, concerning having a form of godliness but denying the power thereof, which describes people who act religious but reject the power that could make them godly. From then on, I desired that godliness, and one day I told the Lord that though I had already given my life to Him, I had not laid it down for Him one hundred percent. I went on to make a covenant with God and signed a blank piece of paper, asking the Lord Jesus to fill in the blank space representing my whole life that I was totally surrendering to Him. I had great peace after doing that, but had I known what that action was going to entail, I would have most likely backtracked on my promise to God.

I finally got married, rightfully within the church, to a brother who at the time was very focused on serving God. His zeal fit the bill for what a servant of God should look like. Just after the proposal for marriage, the Lord gave me the following scripture as a rhema word. At that time, I had no idea what it was all about. It was as though I could literally hear the Lord speak these words directly into my spirit in what sounded like a decree from Psalms 66:10-12:

"For You have put us to the test, O God; You have refined us as silver is refined. You trapped us with a snare; You have laid upon our backs a heavy burden. You allowed us to be conquered and let our enemies run over us. We journeyed through dangers, through fire and flood, But You led us finally to a safe place, a land rich and abundant." (The Voice)

And that was the part of the Word of God that filled the blank space I had left for Him to fill not very long before that. Little did I know that God was going to take me at my word when I told Him to do whatever it took to make my life pleasing to Him. It was in this setting that my dreams of a godly marriage blew up in smoke. I did not know how I was going to navigate this new terrain that fell so short of what I had imagined it would be.

That is where I began the journey of being refined as silver, with all the pressure and heat that comes in the refining process. I had indeed walked into what seemed like a snare, full of heavy burdens. How many times during those years did I feel like God had abandoned me to my enemies! My life seemed to be a literal journey through dangers, fire, and flood. Sometimes it seemed to me that I went through all the perilous entrapments possible, and felt like I was never going to come out to a place of rest. God had blessed me with five wonderful children, and I had to walk in a way that they would see Christ lifted up and obeyed, no matter what!

Satan continuously whispered words of discouragement in my ears, yet the Lord constantly reminded me to dwell on His promise of HOPE He had given me at the end of the passage, and it is this hope that gave me the power to endure because God is faithful to keep His Word:

"But You led us finally to a safe place, a land rich and abundant." (The Voice)

It was in this wilderness season that God prepared and empowered me to be who am I today. It was a treacherous slope through swamp, bog, and mire, through great difficulty, often encountering the giant of despair. But in all this the Lord was working, dislodging me from the driving seat of my life to take full control. That is what God does with all believers who take the step of faith to let God transform them by the regenerating power of the Holy Spirit.

During this dark season as the Lord walked with me, He was reshaping me, scouring, and polishing me into His image. His desire is to work in us until He can see a reflection of Himself in us. He was changing me one day at a time, to become more than a conqueror. I learned the reality and practicality of many of His teachings; to forgive seventy times seven times on a daily basis, to love my enemies, to fight the evil darts of the enemy, to come to Him when I was battle weary and receive His rest to name a few. At the same time, I experienced all of God's love, as well as the support and backing of His heavenly and earthly resources.

There were many instances where God sent me helpers along the way and gave me precious times of respite. From time to time, I would come upon an oasis where I could stop, rest, and regain my strength before the journey continued. I remember often slipping into deep and dark despair and not even fully recognizing what was happening to me. One day I went to church with my children – based on my childhood Sunday school experience, I wanted to make sure my own children were also supplementally taught within a strong Bible-based fellowship setting, and it was also a good reason to be out of the house for an occasional break. On this day, a certain woman who was new to the church sat next to me. She introduced herself and said she was visiting relatives in Canada. This friendly woman was filled with the Spirit of God and I believe God sent her to help me and pray with me for a season. She quickly discerned that I had slipped into depression and told me so. Every morning at 7 a.m. while she was in Canada, she called to pray with me. Once in a while, she came to the house and cooked a nutritious meal for us, as at that time, my children were very young and my hands were full with no family or help. I fondly remember her as the "angel" God sent to minister to me.

Then there was a time I was driving out of the house during a winter storm and my car got stuck in the snow as I backed out of the driveway and onto the road. I had just my little toddlers and a newborn baby with me in the car at that time. It was obvious I would never be able to move the car on my own, but there was no one in sight. Eventually, the only way out it seemed was to leave the car on the road and take the children back into the house until I could get some help to move it. We lived in a quiet neighborhood where most of the neighbors were retired folk. Everything was white and still – no one was out that early morning in the bad weather and I breathed a prayer for God to help me. Suddenly from nowhere it seems, I saw a very slender man, about six feet tall walking directly toward me. What was odd was that he was not dressed for this kind of winter weather. I will never forget how he looked because he had a short spring jacket and a spring cap on his head. I could see the grey hair peeping out from under the cap. As he walked towards me, he made a sweeping motion with his hand as he looked beyond my car, as though he was giving instructions to someone else behind us. I turned to look because at first, I thought there may have been another car behind me. I could not register my shock when I saw a young-looking woman with long brown hair, also with no winter hat on, standing at the back of the car. By this time, the tall gentleman had joined her, and they pushed and eased my car into the tracks that were already there so I could drive away.

Thanking God, I looked into the rear-view mirror to send a big "thank you" wave to the strange couple, but there was no one there! There was no way they could have disappeared into thin air in those few seconds. The driveways to the houses were long, so I would have seen them walk away. Were they angels? To this day I believe so. And I believe God wanted me to know that, so He had them dressed in spring clothes on that stormy winter day. And there were so many other supernatural occurrences in my life at that time that confirmed God's presence.

"God is our shelter and strength, always ready to help in times of trouble." Psalms 46:1 (GNB)

Everyone's journey will be different, depending on God's will and purpose for your life. God does not leave us desolate, and He will not let us be tempted beyond what we can endure. That is a promise though at the time of trouble, it may feel like it is more than we can bear.

So, child of God, the road to transformation and empowerment comes through what seems to be tough times of trial in our lives but it is in the place of testing where God works out our transformation as is so aptly described in 1 Peter 4:12-13:

"Beloved, think it not strange concerning the fiery trial which is to try you, as though some strange thing happened unto you: But rejoice, inasmuch as ye are partakers of Christ's sufferings; that, when his glory shall be revealed, ye may be glad also with exceeding joy." (KJV)

So let us keep looking to Jesus. So long as we are on earth, God is constantly working in our lives and this is our portion until the day He comes.

> *"So after you have suffered a little while, he will restore, support, and strengthen you, and he will place you on a firm foundation."* 1 Peter 5:10b (NLT)

Ruth Odia was born in Kenya and is currently living in Ontario, Canada. Ruth is a mother of five children with an entrepreneurial spirit who also loves writing, storytelling, and the great outdoors. Ruth has a passion for discipling and mentoring children and has been a leader in children's and youth church programs. She is an author and has published *The Kingdom of God: A Children's First Daily Devotional*.

- Ruth Odia
- The Glorious Kingdom
- The Glorious Kingdom
- Thegloriouskingdom.com

CHAPTER THIRTY-NINE - Lisa Arthey

My New Season of Transformation

As we walk through this year, we see the seasons change from winter to spring to summer and into fall. With each change, there's a transformation that happens to all of God's creation. I am one of God's creations and this is my new season of transformation. I'm excited to share God's grace through my chapter whether it's relationships, experiences, or spiritual. All of life is full of changes and growth and I will share some of the things I identify that God has walked me through and helped me to grow.

Upon reflecting on my past, I see so many places and seasons where things were unstable from family challenges, which happens in a family of nine children like mine to small families. I struggled with identity issues and a lack of self-confidence. I was very shy and kept to myself. I tried to be as invisible as I possibly could be because I didn't believe that I had anything important to offer the world. There were so many things going on throughout my life that I found it very hard to see God's presence. Not only did I walk through a difficult childhood with identity issues, but I also struggled as a teenager. I didn't have very many friends and my self-worth was not strong in any way, shape, or form. I went through many difficult periods where I was not seen as a person who was valuable by many of the males in the community. So, if I wasn't already grappling with identity issues, I was struggling with violation issues as well and the little light that God birthed with me was being hidden in quiet places. It was concealed in unattractive clothing and a lack of self-care. I couldn't wait for those seasons of my life to be finished.

One season seemed to flow into another, and I would say the only thing that was constant for me was being able to pour into other people to bring them the joy in their lives that I didn't have in my own. I was the last on the list. Being the oldest in a large family demanded a lot of responsibilities that flowed into caring for others outside of my family by building them up and supporting them. Bringing joy to other people made me feel really good to see their ecstatic faces, but I was living a life that wasn't honoring God. I didn't take care of myself the way God intended for me when He created me in my mother's womb. He knew the plans that he had for me and still has for me. God knows His children so intimately and wants all of His promises for me.

When I reflect on my life so far, I see one that was very troubled and traumatized. There were a lot of relationships that didn't work out with people who called themselves my friends but did not support and respect me in return. I was often seen and used for what I could do and not who I was. A good part of my past truly left me feeling sad, lonely, ugly, and emotionally and spiritually bankrupt. I went through two failed marriages which left me asking God where He was. How could so much happen to one person in a short lifetime? How is it that when God said He would never give me more than I could handle, I felt overwhelmed, invisible, and bankrupt so much of the time?

Why didn't I give up? I asked myself that question many times. So much had happened. Why didn't I give up even with everything that I had walked through? I knew God was with me always. He gave me hope that strengthened me and helped me draw closer to my relationship with Him. God says in Deuteronomy 31:8:

"The LORD himself goes before you and will be with you; he will never leave you nor forsake you. Do not be afraid; do not be discouraged." (NIV)

Hebrews 13:5 says:

"…because God has said, "Never will I leave you; never will I forsake you." (NIV)

If God put in His Word that He will never leave or forsake me, then I need to relax in His arms, trust Him, and loosen the grip I have on all the things that have been happening in my life. He is telling me that He's got me and that He's holding me in the palm of His hand. For all the things that I walked through and struggled with, my life could have been so much worse if not for God's love and protection. Thank you, Father.

As I am sitting here writing by the river, the sun is shining – the warmth of the sunshine, the reflections on the water, and

God's love surrounding me. I've come to understand that even with all that I've been through, I'm still here and I am still alive. Praise God! The reflection I see on the water is beautiful and I am part of the beauty that God has created on this earth. I am so thankful that when I look back on the things that were hard and tough, God was always there, and it was like a training ground for me. Even as I walk through each day in my vulnerability, I am now learning to identify the enemy and some of the patterns he has tried to create throughout my life. I know for sure what the enemy tried to do to destroy me and attempted to take me out but failed in Jesus' name. I didn't know how to identify the enemy and I got caught in his traps, but God carried me through. God has been training me and has been teaching me. He has brought amazing people into my life whom I can trust, whom I can pray with, and whom I can mentor with. I can grow in Christ. For the battle is not mine but belongs to the Lord.

Leading up to this new season, I'm learning to better look after myself. I have been walking through many health issues, but I don't name them, I don't claim them, and I declare that I am healed in Jesus' name. I continue to educate myself not only as a coach but in other areas, and I just drink in the Word of God so my understanding of His Word grows so He can use me where He needs me and there I will follow. In this new season, I am becoming more defined because God has said that I have walked through so much and helped, supported, cared for, and poured into so many others that now is my time of transformation to heal, grow, and follow where He can use me. Part of this is learning to repent for things that I may have said or done knowingly or unknowingly. I must forgive for my freedom but also pray for those who come against me and have tried to harm me in the past. God wants me to walk in freedom from guilt and unforgiveness. God wants me to walk in healing. God wants me to walk in forgiveness. And God wants me to walk in His love.

I spent many years pouring myself into others and defining myself according to how others saw me, blamed me, or accused me of failing. The enemy kept me very busy wrongly believing I was a failure and defining myself through others' eyes and words and not God's eyes and His Word! So, in every battle and fight, it was hard to hear God's voice telling me how much He loved me and that He had always been holding me close, waiting for me to release the baggage that He never asked me to carry, and to receive the Holy Spirit for healing and growth because of His love, His nurturing, and His forgiveness. How could I be caring for other people if I was not allowing myself to do that with God? My mom used to always say when we were growing up that God doesn't make any junk and she's right. It just took me many years to realize that and to be able to call out the devil a liar.

I'm so happy to be in this new season of growth and change defining who I am in Christ. I'm excited to be releasing all the things that I've been carrying for so many years and sit in that quiet place wherever it may be. I love the seasons that God made and how each season flows into the next – building on the previous seasons. I am so blessed to have many joyful moments in my new freedom in Christ. I am not carrying the burdens that I used to carry. I've learned to let go of the guilt and lay it all at the feet of Jesus. For everyone I poured into and lifted up in prayer, I had to forgive myself for making myself the last on the list. I was and am special to God, but I wasn't special to me.

I am so thankful that in this new season, my load is much lighter as I walk with Jesus every day. I am an empty nester watching my children grow on their own. This is a very different concept for me than what I've lived up until now, but they are prepared for their independence. God wants to be the first thought in the morning as I praise and worship Him and give Him thanksgiving until I lay my head to sleep at night. God wants me to overflow with joy and His blessings.

I have learned to forgive. I've learned to release. I've learned to reflect on things that are mine and those things that I need to deflect and return to the sender. I've learned to sever ungodly soul ties and I have learned to bind and send to the everlasting chains as in Jude 1:6. I have learned to deflect and send back to the sender the things that are not mine to own. I have learned how to love unconditionally. All these things have strengthened my walk with the Lord, accelerated my faith, and opened new doors that I never thought would ever be possible.

I want to encourage other people walking through trials that God can do all of this for you. Yes, there is hope even in the storms. This is my truth. God wants me so full of His love, grace, and joy that I carry the beautiful fragrance that is only His! And that the Holy Spirit fills all vacant spaces in me with the fruits of the Spirit and the Holy Spirit.

I want to encourage you that there is hope, forgiveness, and freedom in Christ and there is nothing that you cannot come to the Lord with. God will never leave you or forsake you and He will transform you into something most beautiful. Be encouraged. Every person will have their transformation and season. This one is mine. I am so excited to be walking into it and sharing it with you. Thank you, Father God, for transforming me and using me for Your glory. Amen.

Lisa Arthey is a Certified Life Purpose Coach, certified in Mental Health Awareness and Anxiety Awareness, and an Early Childhood Educator. She is a 6x Best-Selling co-author in the following publications: *Stronger Resilience*, *Soul Sister Letters* (revised edition), and *Rise Up!* Lisa has worked as Co-Founder of Redemption (a non-profit organization) serving those in Brampton with homelessness, mental health, and addictions. Her interests include gardening, painting, singing, crafting, and encouraging people.

CHAPTER FORTY - Karleen Juanita Poyser

Faith Over Fear

First, I want to give God thanks for His grace and mercy in my life.

I am grateful for the precious legal blood of Jesus Christ covering me and my family. I am grateful for the Word of God, for His patience, loving-kindness, and favor towards me.

Because of those blessings, I can give you a glimpse into some of the ways my life has transformed through my faith in and dependence on God's Word.

Through the years, I can truly see the goodness of God displayed in my life and how it's changed my life for His glory. Having experienced many empowering life transformations, today I wish to share two stories from my journey focused on moving from Fear to Faith.

In Romans 12:2, the Word of God says:

"And do not be conformed to this world [any longer with its superficial values and customs], but be transformed and progressively changed [as you mature spiritually] by the renewing of your mind [focusing on godly values and ethical attitudes], so that you may prove [for yourselves] what the will of God is, that which is good and acceptable and perfect [in His plan and purpose for you]." (AMP)

As I recall these stories, I understand just how important it is for parents and grandparents to instill godly principles in the minds of the children and young friends they are around as a foundation for life. Then as adults growing in our faith, how integral it is to develop an understanding of God's Word, strengthening our relationship with God through daily prayer.

I understand that it was because of my upbringing in a faith-filled family, that I too developed a love for God and faith in God's Word from a young age. And it's because of that foundation that my mind was continuously transformed, and also the reason why I was able to believe in God's ability to help me in times of great need.

Trust Through the Fog

My first account of turning from fear to faith took place on a foggy New Year's morning. After attending New Year's Eve service at my church, a friend told me that a local young people's group was having an all-night New Year's celebration. Being in my first year of high school and wanting to connect with other Christian young adults, after talking with my friends, I excitedly asked my parents for their permission. Reluctantly I got their approval, despite my mother telling me she felt it was not the best idea. It might be true that most times parents know best.

The youth service at the second church was amazing because the music and the message were on point. We had a wonderful time. As the morning hours moved on, some of the young people got restless and asked what we could do next. That's when we were told we could either go home or go with some of the leaders and youth to Mount Trashmore, a local area where people walked in the summer and went tobogganing in the winter. So, my friends and I decided to go for the adventure. When we arrived, there seemed to be a lot of us because it felt like it took ages for everyone to find their partners. At the side of the hill, people waited anxiously for their turn. Everything felt fun and wonderful although I was growing more and more nervous about this adventure. As my two friends and I were getting ready for our turn, we started walking up the hill and all the people around us appeared to be happy and excited. By the time we got to the top, it was extremely foggy, so much so that you couldn't see anything at all. We were being urged to get into the huge inner tube quickly because there were only a couple more teams to go down the hill as the leaders wanted to wrap things up. Being the tallest, they told me I had to get on the inner tube first, and then my two friends would join me. Some of the youth gathered around us to help push us towards the drop-off point but just before we took off, a bunch of people jumped on top of us, and due to the weight of everyone piling on, I got wedged deeper into the tube!

Racing down the hill, we could see people waving and yelling at us. I didn't know what was going on but the others that were on top started to jump off the tube.

I found out later that they were yelling at us to get off because people had been injured at the bottom of the hill and there were classroom portables that no one could see because of the thick fog.

As I recall this story, I just need to pause and give thanks to God for His amazing mercy towards me. Mighty God, I praise you and thank you Heavenly Father!

So, as we were spinning down the hill, everyone jumped off and I was left alone, crying out to God as fear took hold of me. Approaching the bottom of the hill, I could see the portables and all I could do was pray.

I knew God was real and I knew the angels of the Lord were real as I had seen mighty miracles in my life, but I was alone and afraid. I could hear the screams of the people on the side of the hill telling me to jump off, yet there was nothing I could do to get out. I was wedged in deeply.

I had to choose faith over fear. I was empowered at that moment by the Spirit of God to trust that He would hear me.

Today, I understand that it was the precious legal blood of Jesus Christ covering me, the angels of the Lord that were there with me, and the prayers of my god-fearing mother that prevented me from going into eternity. I found out later that God had heavily impressed upon Mom's heart to pray at that time.

As I saw the building coming towards me, all I could think of doing was put my leg out and cover my face with my arms, somehow believing that would brace me from the impact! I don't remember all the details, but I know that I ended up on the snow with a lot of people standing around me. Unable to get up and overcome by the trauma, someone helped me up. Staggering and hazy, I didn't see or feel the damage to my leg. All I know is that I was upset and I saw a huge rip in my jeans. I remember saying angrily, *"I'm going home. I going to walk home!"* It was obvious that the adrenaline rush had taken over. Stepping forward to leave,

I collapsed into the snow dazed by the trauma and the severity of the injuries I had just experienced.

The next thing I knew, we (myself and the others who had experienced minor injuries) were rushed to the hospital.

Even now, I see how gracious God was throughout all of this.

After a couple of hours in the hospital, my father arrived alone as he was told not to bring my mother with him because of the severity of my leg injury. I later found out that the surgeon on staff was in awe because he had never seen an injury like that before. After a while, they slowly recounted everything to me. I was told that the inner tube was submerged beneath the building and that before they pulled me out, it was right up to my neck.

Holy Spirit, I worship you and adore you. Thank you, Jesus, thank you Father for your mercies.

As I'm recounting this story, I'm in awe because I realize even more how much God's mercy was poured out for me. Yes, I give God thanks for the obvious miracle of saving my life, but now in writing this, I see that He also prevented me from having massive injuries and I am simply in awe.

Thank you, Lord. My God, there's no one like you. I bless your name, Jehovah Shalom, my peace.

Sky's The Limit

As a young adult, I attended a Bible college program that enabled me to experience many life-transforming events. During our first week of orientation, we went to a conservation area where the organizers of the Bible college program took us through a series of challenges and obstacle courses preparing us for leadership lessons at the end of the experience. One particular event that transformed my life was the climb up The Heavenly Street Lamp! Well, to be honest, I don't remember if that was the actual name of the activity, but it involved climbing up a never-ending lamp pole. The interesting thing was that everyone in the class had to do this exercise, but only up to a certain point. They only went as far as their faith would let them go.

So, imagine the tallest lamp pole you can find in your city. From the base, up to the midpoint, this pole appears to be super wide, with nice comfortable foot pads to use as you climb and nicely spaced-out rungs to hold onto. Then the higher you get, the rungs are spaced out making it more difficult. As I made my way up this pole, I kept praying and looking down at the group of leaders and students cheering me on while I was asking God for faith to keep going. Literally.

I climbed until I reached the top of the light pole (thanking God) in awe at the heights I had attained. But next came the real test. Two ropes were stretched to the far right attached to a similar lamp pole. At this point, you could decide to climb back down or continue to the next part of this activity – the tightrope. I decided to move on, stepping onto the small platform at the top of this pole. I placed my feet on the bottom rope, grabbed onto a rope at chest height, balanced myself, and moved slowly from the left toward the marker in the middle of this rope area just as the instructor had shown us. I remember hearing the cheers and encouraging shouts down below, but I clearly remember telling God that if He allowed me to successfully get to the center of this obstacle course, I would believe that He could do absolutely anything!

Teetering back and forth, inching across the rope, I almost slipped a couple of times, but I kept on praying. My faith grew stronger, and I arrived at the marker in the middle. I released the chain that brought me down to earth again surrounded by excited cheers from the thirty-nine people who had just witnessed the whole thing.

This experience changed my perception of God's ability to answer prayer. Throughout my life, many times when things become challenging, I replayed the events of that day to remind myself that with God, nothing's impossible.

I WAS EMPOWERED TO WIN and moved from fear to faith. My desire today is to trust God with everything, knowing His Word is true and He cannot fail. He always has our best interests in mind.

So, let me encourage you to rely on God's Word as the final authority in your life. God's Word will stand forever, and it will never fail.

In Romans 15:13, it says:

"May the God of hope fill you with all joy and peace as you trust in him, so that you may overflow with hope by the power of the Holy Spirit." (NIV)

I pray that you too will be encouraged to develop a deeper faith in God, and as you put your hope and trust in Him every day, your life will be empowered and transformed for His glory.

Shalom

Karleen Juanita Poyser is an author, gospel recording artist, worship leader, inspiring speaker for both women's & youth groups, a Certified Life Coach, a Licensed Financial Educator, and a PPLSI LegalShield advocate. She loves supporting organizations, ministries, and individuals who help young people, women, seniors, and families in need. Using her knowledge of financial literacy & LegalShield expertise, Karleen empowers people to make better financial decisions and desires to own a wellness center providing guidance, mentorship, and skill development.

- www.facebook.com/karleenjuanitapoyser
- karleenjpoyser
- karleenpoyser@gmail.com
- www.karleenjuanita.com

Conclusion

You may have felt that God has forgotten about you, or that no one knows or has experienced what you are going through. I am sure, after reading all these chapters, you may now realize there are real individuals who have faced the same kind of struggles and sufferings as you. This is a part of life that we all most likely will encounter at some point in our lives. Our experiences may not be the same, but we all have been through something and felt as if we would never make it.

If we were to sort everything out for ourselves, we probably would cause a complete disaster. This is where God comes in to help us. We will need to put our complete trust in Him and allow Him to work things out the best way so that He will get the glory out of it. God will not allow anything that we've been through to be wasted. He ensures that whatever we've been through allows us to become stronger and closer to Him and uses it to fulfill His purpose in our lives so that we can help others around us.

> *"Trust in the LORD with all thine heart; and lean not unto thine own understanding. In all thy ways acknowledge him, and he shall direct thy paths."* Proverbs 3:5-6 (KJV)

Sometimes in life, you might have to hit rock bottom to realize that there is room for transformation, which leaves room for growth and empowerment. Despite your sufferings, you're now able to expand your horizon to your new destiny. I am admonishing you not to give up on life, whenever you're going through trials because God is able to see you through it.

> *"Be strong and courageous. Do not be afraid or terrified because of them, for the LORD your God goes with you; he will never leave you or forsake you."* Deuteronomy 31:6

> *"For I know the plans I have for you, declares the Lord, plans to prosper you and not to harm you, plans to give you a hope and a future."* Jeremiah 29:11

I would like to invite you to say this prayer with me If you don't know the Lord as your personal Savior.

> *Dear Holy Father. I am a sinner who wants to be saved by your grace. I ask that You forgive me of my sins. I am so sorry for all the sins that I have committed. I need my life to be changed because I cannot live my life without You. I thank You for Your love that is beyond any other love in this world. I want to experience your peace and joy because there is no other peace like Yours. I need You to plan out my life because Your ways are better than my ways. I just want to thank You Lord for saving me. Amen.*

Do you have a story to share? Ask God to give you the COURAGE to INSPIRE someone within your lifetime. Begin to DREAM again! Why don't you join me in my next Anthology? I am looking for individuals who are mature believers, season believers, and baby believers. We all have been on a journey, and I believe your story will uplift someone out there who needs to hear that they are not the only ones walking down the same path that you have walked.

You will suit this upcoming anthology because everybody's spiritual walk is different. Having a variety of different writers who have already experienced different things in life allows the readers to realize that they're not alone and that everybody has a story or a testimony to tell.

Now, Is the Time to Challenge Yourself!

> *"In All Things, We Are More Than Conquerors Through Him Who Loved Us."* Romans 8:37

What good will it be for someone to gain the whole world, yet forfeit their soul? Or what can anyone give in exchange for their soul?

Matthew 16:26

Sinner's Prayer

Dear Heavenly Father. I acknowledge that Jesus died on the Cross for me and is your only Son. I now invite Jesus into my heart. Please forgive me of all my sins and transform my life so that I can become the loving person You need me to be as a light in this dark world. Thank you for restoring my mind, body and spirit so that I can feel Your perfect peace forevermore and receive the gift of Your salvation. Amen.

John 3:16

A Special Invitation

Dear Sir/Madam:

Thank you for supporting the authors of *Empowered Transformations* and LWL PUBLISHING HOUSE by purchasing this book.

We trust that you have enjoyed reading all of these incredible stories from individuals just like yourself.

If you have never heard our of company and have considered becoming published, here is a brief summary of who we are.

Since 2013, Anita Sechesky has coached and published over 650 men and women of all ages, backgrounds, and nationalities to establish confidence and creativity in the articulation of personal expression through writing. A majority of our clients are novice writers who benefit from our professional coaching, support, and guidance in their writing process to become Best-Selling authors.

We specialize in helping to bring out the strength in each vision while permitting the author to understand their own emotional limitations in order to release the most powerful and authentic writing. By releasing deep trauma and emotional baggage, our clients who work closely with our Publisher, Anita Sechesky, have surpassed their own expectations through their publishing journey.

Our goal is to produce books that inspire the human spirit to never give up, but instead find renewed purpose, hope, and courage.

Every person has a story. What's your vision? Let's bring it out!

- Are you ready to become published by sharing your short story? Then become a co-author in one of our active anthologies.

- Are you ready to enhance your portfolio and step up to become a leader? Then compile your own visionary anthology with our professional coaching and support from Anita Sechesky.

- Are you ready to write your book? Then contact us to schedule your personalized coaching to Best-Seller success with Anita Sechesky.

Please visit our website for more information:

  https://lwlpublishinghouse.com

  Contact Anita Sechesky: lwlclienthelp@gmail.com

www.ingramcontent.com/pod-product-compliance
Lightning Source LLC
Chambersburg PA
CBHW061426300426
44114CB00014B/1557